CLASS AND SOCIAL STRATIFICATION
IN POST-REVOLUTION CHINA

The conference upon which this volume is based
was sponsored jointly by
The Contemporary China Institute and
The Joint Committee on Contemporary China
of the Social Science Research Council (USA)
and the American Council of Learned Societies,
with funds provided by the National
Endowment for the Humanities and
the Ford Foundation

It is also included in the series
STUDIES ON CHINA NO. 3
Sponsored by the Joint Committee on Chinese Studies of the
American Council of Learned Societies and the
Social Science Research Council

CLASS AND SOCIAL STRATIFICATION IN POST-REVOLUTION CHINA

Edited by
JAMES L. WATSON

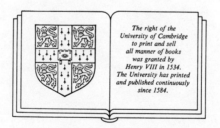

The right of the
University of Cambridge
to print and sell
all manner of books
was granted by
Henry VIII in 1534.
The University has printed
and published continuously
since 1584.

CAMBRIDGE UNIVERSITY PRESS
Cambridge
London   *New York*   *New Rochelle*
Melbourne   *Sydney*

Published by the Press Syndicate of the University of Cambridge
The Pitt Building, Trumpington Street, Cambridge CB2 1RP
32 East 57th Street, New York, NY 10022, USA
296 Beaconsfield Parade, Middle Park, Melbourne 3206, Australia

First published 1984

Printed in Great Britain at
the University Press, Cambridge

Library of Congress catalogue card number: 83–14432

British Library Cataloguing in Publication Data

Class and social stratification in post-revolution
China. – (Contemporary China Institute Publications)
1. Social classes – China – History – 20th century
I. Watson, James L.   II. Contemporary
China Institute   III. Joint Committee on
Contemporary China   IV. Series
305.5'0951   HN740.S6

ISBN 0 521 26062 0

TM

CONTENTS

PREFACE

This volume has its origins in a conference sponsored jointly by the Contemporary China Institute (School of Oriental and African Studies, University of London) and the Joint Committee on Contemporary China of the Social Science Research Council (USA) and the American Council of Learned Societies. The conference was held at Cumberland Lodge, in Windsor Park, England, from 30 June to 4 July 1980. The essays which follow, save one, were first presented at this gathering. (Professor Schram was unable to attend as he was engaged in research in China at the time.) The papers have been revised and updated in the light of conference discussions and political developments in China.

In addition to those listed in the contributors section, a number of other people participated in the conference: William S. Atwell (SOAS, London), Anita Chan (Kansas), Mark Elvin (Oxford), David Goodman (Newcastle), Brian Hook (Leeds and *The China Quarterly*), Graham Johnson (British Columbia), Don Rimmington (Leeds), Stuart Thompson (SOAS, London), R. G. Tiedemann (SOAS, London), Rubie S. Watson (LSE, London), and Gordon White (IDS, Sussex). Professors Ronald Dore (Sussex) and G. William Skinner (Stanford) served as discussants; many of their comments and suggestions have been incorporated into the final papers. On behalf of the Contemporary China Institute, I would like to thank all of these people for playing an active role in the conference. We are also indebted to Larraine Brannan (CCI Secretary) and Mike Strange (SOAS Assistant Secretary) for their expert handling of administrative details.

SOAS, London   J. L. WATSON

1

INTRODUCTION: CLASS AND CLASS FORMATION IN CHINESE SOCIETY

James L. Watson

The general theme of this book – class and social stratification – was chosen because it cuts across the disciplinary boundaries of the China field and incorporates those whose interests might be broadly defined as 'sociological', irrespective of academic title. Contributors include two anthropologists, three sociologists, three political scientists, and an historian. The project began as a conference sponsored jointly by the Contemporary China Institute and the American SSRC and ACLS. During our discussions it became apparent that we did not all share the same approach to the study of 'social class' in contemporary Chinese society. This is not surprising given that the Chinese terms for classes and status groups are very difficult to pin down. The Marxian notion of class as a set of relationships based ultimately on the ownership of the means of production is no longer applicable in China and, yet, this mode of analysis still plays an important role in society. In effect, Chinese authorities operated for thirty years (1949–79) with a vocabulary and a conceptual apparatus more suited to the needs of land reform in a traditional peasant society than to the organization of production in a modern socialist state. The problems arising are discussed at length in this book.

The study of contemporary Chinese society is made all the more difficult by the fact that little is actually known about the *pre-revolutionary* class system. Among historians, the issue has been clouded by a preoccupation with the tiny elite of scholar-bureaucrats who served the imperial state. There have been several attempts (misguided in my opinion) to treat this elite stratum as a dominant 'class'.[1] This approach has been criticized on the grounds that scholar-bureaucrats represented only the 'tip of the iceberg' and did not constitute a class in and of themselves.[2] On the whole, Western historians have not made a concerted effort to analyse the class system in late-imperial Chinese society. The situation for Western anthropologists and sociologists is even more discouraging. Anthropologists in particular have treated social class as a peripheral issue,[3] overshadowed by kinship groups (lineages, clans, etc.) and voluntary associations which cut across divisions based on class. Chinese scholars (based in the People's Republic) have, of course, contributed a great deal to our understanding of the pre-revolutionary class structure.[4] The difficulty with many of these studies is that the authors build on Mao Zedong's 1926 survey of rural classes and, as such, they tend to accept a preconceived model of society. Class is not treated as a *problem* to be analysed; it is taken for granted.

DESTRATIFICATION AND THE LIMITS OF SOCIAL ENGINEERING

It can be argued that this is a particularly opportune time to examine the Chinese class system. Party officials have reversed many of the earlier policies which were designed to transform society over-night. The post-Cultural Revolution era has been marked by a return to pragmatism and an acceptance of the fact that utopian socialism cannot be achieved in a single generation. This reversal is paralleled by a shift from radical programmes based on an ideology of destratification to the promotion of new guidelines which may lead to the restratification of Chinese society.[5]

Discussions of destratification relate to another subject of general interest: the limits of 'social engineering'. How far can a society, especially one with a strong peasant heritage, be pushed by state authorities who are determined to destroy old social institutions and introduce new ones? The process begins, according to William Parish, by redistributing key resources. He finds (Chapter 5) that, after thirty years of destratification campaigns, China is 'slightly more equal [with respect to income] than the average socialist state'. Parish acknowledges that this is indeed an important achievement, given the baseline from which the campaigns began in the 1950s. In addition to income, he considers education, housing, and

2

the distribution of consumer items – all of which are in short supply. In China the best schools are often reserved for exceptional students, most of whom tend to be the children of government officials, technocrats, and intellectuals. Housing has always been limited in China, particularly in the larger cities. As Parish notes, certain social groups (notably cadres, industrial workers, technicians) are protected from the intense competition for living space. The distribution of consumer durables and food items is another source of contention in China. Government officials and Party cadres often enjoy special access to these goods, much to the annoyance of ordinary Chinese citizens. Parish concludes, therefore, that there has indeed been a levelling of incomes since the revolution but this does not mean that all vestiges of economic and social privilege have been eliminated.

Another aspect of social engineering in China which has gained widespread publicity in the West is the women's liberation movement. It is widely assumed that the Chinese government has succeeded in its campaign to abolish traditional, androcentric attitudes and practices. There have, of course, been notable advances for women, particularly in the legal domain (see Elisabeth Croll's essay on marriage reforms, Chapter 8). But there is considerable evidence to suggest that Chinese women are far from attaining parity with their male cohorts in respect to income, employment, and education. Martin Whyte's paper (Chapter 9) examines the question of sexual equality in detail.

In order to assess the progress of women's liberation campaigns in China, Whyte compares his Chinese sample with similar samples gathered in other societies. His conclusions may come as a surprise to some: 'There does not seem to be much difference in the degree of sexual equality ... between China and the other countries surveyed.' Whyte does acknowledge that the comparison may not be entirely fair given that the Chinese began with a lower level of economic development but, nonetheless, the results of his study are not encouraging. He found that, despite determined efforts at social engineering, women still carry the 'double burden' of outside employment combined with household chores. The circumstances of life in Chinese cities (Whyte's sample is exclusively urban) makes this burden even more difficult to bear. Routine chores such as shopping for food or washing clothes consume vast amounts of time and energy. Whyte's interview data confirm Croll's view, derived from mass media sources, that Chinese wives are expected to sacrifice their own careers to provide secure home environments for their husbands (see Chapter 8). A high proportion of Chinese women (in comparison to women in other societies) are now engaged full time in the labour force, but Whyte demonstrates that they tend to cluster in segregated job sectors. In cities, women are employed disproportionately by low-status, collective enterprises (managed at the local level) while men predominate in state-run units. The latter have higher salaries, better security, and superior benefits.

THE CONCEPT OF CLASS IN CHINESE SOCIETY

The study of class in contemporary China is complicated by a number of issues, many of which – as noted earlier – relate to the question of definition. Pre-revolutionary class divisions, based on the ownership of the means of production, no longer play a role in the organization of society, but the notion of traditional classes (e.g., landlord, middle peasant, landless labourer) has survived in the conceptual system. People are still categorized and ranked by a set of class labels which they have inherited (in the patriline) from their fathers and grandfathers.* These labels were originally assigned during the first years of the revolution and, hence, they no longer bear any direct relationship to the occupational or management structures of the 1980s.

The complications of the system are such that the Chinese themselves are not always clear about the use of class terminology.[6] As Gordon White has argued ' "class" is not merely an abstract category but a term of living political significance, the definition of which has changed in response to the dynamics of modern Chinese politics'.[7] People are classified, first, in terms of their source of economic support during the three years immediately preceding 1949. The resulting categories, called *chengfen*, are rather specific, defining people as 'poor peasant', 'middle peasant', 'landless labourer', and so forth.[8] Thus, when people are given a *chengfen* label they are identified with a specific stratum which reflects their (pre-revolu-

* Class labels have been officially deemphasized since January 1979, but this does not mean that they have disappeared altogether. See Jonathan Unger's discussion in Chapter 6.

4

tionary) position as exploiters or exploited.[9] The Chinese Academy of Social Sciences defines *chengfen* as 'social role', relating to 'a person's most important background or occupational status before entering revolutionary work' (see discussion by Philip Kuhn in Chapter 2). The term is often used in conjunction with *jieji*, commonly translated as 'class' and perhaps closest to the Marxian conception of social class. *Jieji* is used to identify broader categories such as 'worker' or 'capitalist'. It thereby subsumes *chengfen* categories.[10] In Chinese the two terms are often used together, *jieji chengfen*. Gordon White refers to this combination as 'class *chengfen*';[11] it might also be translated as 'class subsection' or 'subdivision'.

To complicate matters further, another key term (*chushen*) is used to denote one's class of origin. Philip Kuhn (Chapter 2) translates *chushen* as 'social origin' and, drawing on the official dictionary of the Chinese Academy of Social Sciences, he defines it as 'a person's status as determined by his early experience or his family's economic circumstances'. This, Kuhn argues, is close to the Western concept of 'class background', in that it does not change as one's activities or consciousness change. *Chengfen* labels, on the other hand, are subject to alteration – at least in theory. More will be said about this problem below.

In Chapter 2, Philip Kuhn explores the historical dimension of *jieji*, 'social class'. His conclusions should be of interest to all scholars who work on post-revolutionary Chinese society. *Jieji*, he argues, is a very old ideographic compound. It was taken over by the Japanese in the early twentieth century to represent the Marxian concept of social class and subsequently reintroduced (in this new guise) back into Chinese. In its original form, however, *jie* referred to steps in a scale or rungs on a ladder. *Ji* was taken to be the order of threads in a fabric. Thus, according to Kuhn, this classical compound 'connotes hierarchical degrees on a continuum, rather than groups of people'. It was used to designate 'ranks on a scale' in late antiquity. Even in the 1920s and 1930s, Kuhn argues, many Chinese thinkers (including Mao Zedong) still used *jieji* in this traditional sense. Given the conceptual apparatus available, this may help explain why the Chinese have had difficulty adapting the Western concept of social class to their own society.

Kuhn supports his argument by drawing on Qing sources which show that the Chinese imperial court did not draw social boundaries on the basis of relative wealth or poverty. Differences between rich and poor, landlord and labourer, were not perceived as being part of the eternal order of society. Quoting from a Qing text, he maintains that the oscillation of family fortunes was accepted as a 'principle of heaven and earth' and, therefore, not subject to social engineering.

If Kuhn is correct, and there is considerable evidence to suggest that he is,[12] the concept of class (*jieji*) as fostered by Party cadres in the 1950s was based on an alien mode of thought. This does not mean that classes, in the Marxian sense, did not exist in China (clearly they did); nor does the absence of class consciousness on the part of peasants (see n. 12) necessarily invalidate Marxian analyses of Chinese society. But Kuhn's findings do raise some interesting questions concerning the adoption of Western Marxist categories by Chinese leaders during the 1920s, 1930s, and 1940s. As Stuart Schram shows in Chapter 3, Mao Zedong changed his views about the nature of social class several times during his long career. Following Kuhn's and Schram's lead, more research needs to be done on the 'mental history' of the Chinese revolution.[13] We might then be in a better position to understand why certain ideological constructs were adopted and others rejected.

THE NATURE OF CLASS IN MODERN CHINA

Even though it is apparent that the vocabulary of class analysis was little understood in many parts of the country, nearly everyone in China was assigned a class label during the early years of the revolution. In rural areas this was accomplished in the course of land reform campaigns. Based on Mao's 1926 analysis of rural classes,[14] the following five categories were used: landlords, rich peasants, middle peasants, poor peasants, and landless labourers. City dwellers were more difficult to categorize and a rather *ad hoc* system of class designations arose: bureaucratic bourgeoisie (exploiting capitalists and merchants), national bourgeoisie (capitalists and merchants willing to work for socialism), petit bourgeoisie (teachers, shopkeepers, low-level employees, doctors), workers, and idlers (the lumpenproletariat, some of whom were defined as 'class enemies').[15] The ambiguities of the urban class system were such that certain professionals, officials, and intellectuals were given the neutral label of 'staff'; higher-level bureaucrats who had served the Kuomintang were categorized as 'false staff'.[16] The majority of class labels were ascribed but a handful could be earned. If, for instance, the son of a landlord had distinguished himself during the revolutionary struggles against the Japanese and the Kuomintang, he might receive the label 'revolutionary cadre'. However, as Jonathan Unger notes in Chapter 6, such cases were rare. The vast majority of people had to live with ascribed labels.

The fact that certain class designations could be earned indicates that there was some flexibility in the system. Mao Zedong stressed in his early writings that people could indeed change their class nature by adhering to Party discipline and by accepting a new world view. Yet, as Stuart Schram demonstrates in Chapter 3, Mao's thought on this issue is characterized by an internal contradiction. On one hand, Mao believed that human nature was subject to change but, on the other hand, he did not trust the remnants of China's former exploiting classes. Mao undoubtedly realized that the revolution could not succeed without assistance from skilled technicians and managers. Thus, a distinction was drawn between the exploiting bourgeoisie and the national bourgeoisie – the latter consisting of scientists, technicians, managers, and intellectuals who were willing to help 'build socialism' under Party leadership. Given the circumstances it was necessary to uphold the view that these experts, who had been trained under the old regime, were capable of transforming their attitudes and, by definition, their class natures. By 1956, a mere seven years after Liberation, Deng Xiaoping justified this policy change in a remarkable statement: the old system of class designations, he argued, 'has lost or is losing its original significance'.[17] In May 1957, an editorial in the *People's Daily* went even further and stated that '[following the victory of socialist transformation] the previous several thousand years of history of a system of class exploitation has been basically concluded' (quoted in Chapter 3). As Schram notes in Chapter 3 (see his n. 13), this editorial reflects Mao's own views at that time.

This editorial was published at the end of the Hundred Flowers campaign. In the course of this movement, many Chinese intellectuals attacked the leadership and the politics of the Communist Party. Schram argues (Chapter 3) that Mao hardened his views regarding the malleability of human nature in the aftermath of this disastrous campaign. In 1962 Mao electrified China with a new slogan which became the basis for a new political era: 'Never forget the class struggle!' He called for the training of a 'vast new army of working-class intellectuals' who would not be tainted by questionable class origins. At the same time, Mao warned that the bourgeoisie could easily be 'born anew' in China, just as it had in the Soviet Union (quoted in Chapter 3). In subsequent years, social investigations were carried out to probe the class origins of people in all walks of life (see chapters by Jonathan Unger and Lynn White). The pendulum had swung back to the view that human nature is not easily changed.

During the Cultural Revolution, however, Mao gave implicit support to young radicals who believed that subjective factors, such as correct attitudes and loyalty to the Great Helmsman, should be the main criteria used when selecting Party leaders of the future. The most radical factions of the Red Guards, notably those whose class origins were questionable (i.e., children of the former bourgeoisie), maintained that revolutionary virtue was not an inherited characteristic. The idea of virtue as a key element in Chinese ideology is the theme of Susan Shirk's paper (Chapter 4).

According to Shirk, the movement to promote 'virtuocracy' had as its goal the radical reordering of society by distributing opportunities and rewards to those deemed to be morally virtuous – irrespective of class origin. Political movements based on the arbitrary assessment of virtue are, by definition, unstable; and, as Shirk demonstrates, this is exactly what happened in China. The collapse of virtuocratic policies in the aftermath of the Cultural Revolution sparked a serious crisis of belief among radical youth. Many people who reached political maturity during the mid-1960s and early 1970s are now extremely cynical. It is unlikely that they will respond to virtuocratic campaigns in the future.

CLASS AS AN INHERITED CHARACTERISTIC

The Cultural Revolution, of course, was not dominated entirely by radicals who advocated virtuocratic policies. There were others, notably the descendants of 'good class' workers, peasants, and cadres, who argued that revolutionary virtue was an inherited characteristic which could only be acquired by a 'blood transfusion of status'.[18] The doctrine of 'natural redness',[19] as it became known, is a two-edged sword. This is demonstrated by Lynn White's analysis of class struggles in Shanghai (Chapter 7). During the early years of the revolution there was considerable flexibility in the determination of class labels for urban peoples.[20] This was due primarily to the complexity of urban society (in comparison to the relative simplicity of drawing class lines in the countryside). Thus, many descendants of the former bourgeoisie rose to positions of great responsibility and power in the cities. Shanghai was a particularly complicated case. In the wake of Mao's 1962 call for a reordering of society, a 'cleansing of the class ranks' campaign was carried out. High-level managers and bureaucrats suddenly found themselves under suspicion as their family histories were investigated in minute detail. Those caught misrepresenting themselves were driven from office and many were sent to the countryside for reeducation. As White shows, the irony was that in Shanghai the purges were led by Party cadres who were themselves of bourgeois origin. White suggests that these leaders 'apparently resented their own origins but hoped to save themselves through communist faith, through a radical will to acquire a new identity' (see Chapter 7). During the Cultural Revolution it was Zhang Chunqiao (a member of the notorious Gang of Four), of bourgeois origin himself, who led the Shanghai movements to suppress those who adhered to the 'blood-line theory' (*xuetong lun*) of revolutionary succession.

There were fewer opportunities for rural leaders to disguise their class origins and, hence, the 'blood-line theory' was used with somewhat less finesse in the countryside. Hereditary notions of virtue were frequently called upon to justify the marginal advantages enjoyed by the so-called 'good class' peasants. In Chapter 6, Jonathan Unger shows how the poor and lower-middle peasants of Guangdong were quick to seize upon the doctrine of 'natural redness' when it suited their needs in the 1950s and 1960s. As circumstances changed in the 1970s, however, the doctrine was abandoned with equal rapidity. In January 1979, the central government announced that class labels were no longer to be emphasized when considering people for appointments or promotions. Based on recent interviews with emigres in Hong Kong, Unger found that the 'structure of discrimination' based on pre-revolutionary class criteria had disappeared from many Guangdong villages by 1982. He argues (Chapter 6) that this dramatic change is due primarily to economic causes: the doctrine of natural redness helped 'good class' peasants maintain a slight edge over 'bad class' elements when resources were scarce but, with the recent economic liberalization in the countryside and the push toward privatization, the state no longer holds the only key to economic security. Nearly everyone in the villages surveyed by Unger is now able to earn a reasonable living – irrespective of class background.

Philip Kuhn (Chapter 2) offers another explanation for the demise of the class label system in 1979, one that complements Unger's. According to Kuhn, there has been a shift in emphasis from social origin to social role, as Party leaders move toward a 'less conflictual view' of society. He acknowledges that there are good policy reasons for shelving class labels, but 'a more profound reason may perhaps be sought in layers of Chinese consciousness about social classification which lie far back in history' (see Chapter 2). The concept of social class, as an inherited characteristic, may have had a very brief reign in the context of Chinese history.

THE PROCESS OF CLASS FORMATION

In terms of comparative sociology, what makes the Chinese case particularly interesting is that it presents us with a unique opportunity to observe the *process* of class formation.[21] There is evidence that a new set of classes is emerging, notably in the cities. In Chapter 7, Lynn White argues that old class distinctions (based on ownership of the means of production) were obliterated soon after the revolution in Shanghai. Nonetheless, the need for technical and managerial skills remained unchanged. Engineers, technicians, high-level mechanics, and managers were essential for the smooth operation of Shanghai factories.[22] White (Chapter 7) sums up the position of technocrats in the socialist system: 'Their relation to capital was not expressed in legalistic property terms – but in fact, they controlled it exactly as if they owned it'. As Stuart Schram notes in Chapter 3, one of Mao's greatest fears was the creation of a 'new class' of privileged bureaucrats and technicians along the lines outlined by Djilas.[23]

The children of the pre-revolutionary bourgeoisie formed the core of this 'new class' of technocrats, along with selected representatives of the old proletariat. Their privileged position in the occu-

10

pational structure was reproduced primarily through access to the best urban schools – an arrangement that was subjected to severe criticism during the Cultural Revolution. These schools were characterized as 'little treasure pagodas' by certain Red Guard factions (see Chapter 5 on education as a scarce resource). However, following Mao's death and the demise of the Gang of Four a system of elite schools was reestablished.[24] It seems possible, therefore, that a 'new class' of Chinese technocrats may yet emerge.

Lynn White also shows in Chapter 7 that there is an important distinction between contract labour and unionized labour in China's cities. Workers who depend on contracts have no claim to reside permanently in Shanghai and, as a consequence, structural tensions have already emerged among the urban working classes. Susan Shirk presents some intriguing data on the process of class formation in Chinese cities. She notes in Chapter 4 that central authorities have introduced recruitment practices which encourage industrial units to hire the children of employees. The new practice ensures that retirees are replaced by their own sons or daughters. There has been a shift from what Shirk calls 'virtuocratic' considerations to 'ascriptive favouritism' in the urban employment sector. The nepotistic recruitment system has turned many work units into 'guild-like institutions in which membership [can] only be inherited' (see Chapter 4). It is, of course, difficult to predict whether these employment policies will last into the next century but, if they do, we may indeed be witnessing the formation of a new class of privileged workers.

In considering the process of class formation the question of reproduction arises: what, exactly, has to be reproduced from one generation to the next before a new class can take shape? Access to specialized training is essential for the reproduction of a bureaucratic-technocratic class (in Djilas's terms). But, in China, educational policies have not been consistent and the school system is easily disrupted. Nonetheless, it became obvious in the late 1970s that many intellectuals and technicians had managed to educate their own children during the Cultural Revolution era. In doing so they helped to reproduce social distinctions which the radicals had hoped to eradicate by closing elite schools. Among the emerging class of industrial (unionized) workers it is the ability to monopolize jobs that matters most. The reproduction of class privilege in this case depends entirely on the direction of state policies toward industrial employment.

Elisabeth Croll's paper (Chapter 8) deals with another aspect of social reproduction, namely marriage. Classes, Croll notes, tend to be endogamous. It follows, therefore, that changes in marriage strategies reflect changes in the class structure. This is particularly true in China where the league table of desirable marriage partners was dramatically altered following Liberation in 1949. Sons of the old exploiting classes found it very difficult to contract marriages while those who could claim 'good class' backgrounds had fewer problems. Croll discovered that the most desirable mates were members of the Youth League or the Communist Party; people in these elite organizations (particularly younger men) were literally showered with marriage proposals.[25] Not surprisingly, there was a tendency toward Party endogamy during the first two decades of communist rule, as activists sought to protect themselves from accusations of disloyalty (an indiscrete marriage could be very damaging to one's career). It would appear that the pressures to marry within the Party have subsided somewhat since the late-1960s and 1970s. Ironically, this may be due to the difficulties of maintaining a stable home life when both partners are expected to be full-time, dedicated professionals (see Chapters 8 and 9). Thus, there has been a rise in the divorce rate among professionals and a deemphasis on Party endogamy.

At the opposite end of the new social hierarchy are the pariah groups created by state intervention in the 1950s, the so-called 'bad class' elements composed of former exploiters and their (patrilineal) descendants. Jonathan Unger presents a rare glimpse of these pariahs in Chapter 6. Until recently the sons and grandsons of former landlords were among the least desirable marriage partners in China. Unger's village informants explained that 'bad class' males could only acquire brides through a system of sister exchange, whereby marriageable women were transferred between families who lived far apart (ensuring that the bride's origin would remain obscure). This type of marriage was referred to disparagingly as 'potato skin-taro root exchange'. The general pattern of endogamy among 'bad class' descendants was thus a direct consequence of government-sponsored discrimination; people in this category were endogamous not from choice but by necessity. Unger argues that sister exchange became less frequent in the 1970s. The 'bad class' peasants of rural Guangdong no longer find it so difficult to compete in the marriage arena and the patterns of endogamy are breaking down.

CONCLUSIONS AND PROBLEMS FOR THE FUTURE

The evidence presented in this book suggests that there have been two distinct processes of class formation in China since 1949. During the 1950s and 1960s a rigid class hierarchy, based on pre-revolutionary conceptions of society, prevailed in the rural areas. Associated with this hierarchical system was a notion of 'good' and 'bad' class labels inherited in the patriline. In effect, the state had created a new underclass in the countryside as living reminders of past exploitation.[26]

In the urban sector a very different process of class formation prevailed, one based on the principles of accommodation. During the 1950s the Party needed the technical skills and managerial expertise of the former bourgeoisie; there was no alternative short of the virtual abandonment of many industries and enterprises. In the cities, therefore, the main priority was to build a new class of technocrats who supported the goals of the Communist Party. Mao Zedong himself went to great lengths to accommodate the urban bourgeoisie and their descendants. When these efforts failed (in the wake of the Hundred Flowers campaign), the policies of accommodation were suspended and Chinese cities were racked by class struggles. Confrontation became the guiding principle of urban politics until the late-1970s. Since the fall of the Gang of Four, however, central authorities appear to have abandoned the rhetoric of confrontation in both urban and rural areas.

Given the nature of politics in China it is impossible to predict whether the emerging class system will continue to develop according to the nonconflictual principles of accommodation. Social scientists who study Chinese society must be keenly aware of policy changes over time.[27] The ability of central authorities to intercede and take control of local affairs is the single most salient feature of life in China. What appears to have been a clear pattern of class formation in the late 1950s, for instance, was suddenly and dramatically altered by Mao's 1962 pronouncement on the need for class struggle. The

Cultural Revolution also brought sudden, and sometimes catastrophic, changes for bureaucrats and technocrats who had been unaffected by earlier campaigns. It would be foolhardy in the extreme, therefore, to comment on the processes of class formation in China without reference to the intrusive power of the state.

In looking to the future of sociological research in China, the essays in this book point to one problem in particular which bears special attention: the rural–urban dichotomy. The economic and social gap between those who live in China's premier cities and those who are destined to stay in the countryside has, if anything, grown wider in the past thirty years. Susan Shirk argues (Chapter 4) that the Chinese people are themselves acutely aware of the widening gap: 'There is . . . a social consensus that status divides along the rural–urban line'. The 'winners' in the competition for social advancement tend to work in major cities while the 'losers', in Shirk's terms, usually end up in the countryside. Although official ideology has consistently held that 'good class' peasants rank relatively high on the social scale, in reality they have always had low status compared to urbanites.[28] Lynn White's paper (Chapter 7) shows how the privileged life style of Shanghai residents sets them apart from their rural counterparts. Urbanites will do almost anything to avoid the tedium and harshness of life in the countryside. Croll's research on marriage choice reveals this as well. The main strategy of social mobility for young peasant women is to marry urbanites who will take them out of the villages. Marriage to a peasant male is seen as the prelude to a life with 'no future' (see Chapter 8).

The problems arising from China's rural–urban dichotomy were discussed at length during the conference which preceded this volume. It was agreed that restrictions on rural-to-urban migration had had profound consequences for China's economic and social development. During the century immediately preceding the revolution, members of China's commercial and political elite were noted for their close links to people in rural areas. Furthermore, it was common for local systems to compete among themselves in the export of labour and talent.[29] The relative fluidity of the social hierarchy in late-imperial Chinese society[30] was due, in part, to the absence of restrictions on migration. Social mobility was inextricably tied to geographical mobility.

During the past thirty years, however, it has become more and more difficult for rural peoples to leave their native places and pursue careers in the cities. Area-specific ration cards, residence registers, and police check points at key road junctions have been introduced to stem the tide of rural-to-urban migration.[31] These changes have had an important effect on the emerging patterns of social stratification in China. Prior to the revolution the educated elite did not reside exclusively in the cities. This is no longer the case. State policies have ensured that future class divisions will correspond closely to residential patterns.

It is obvious that a great deal of basic research remains to be done in China. We know more about the formal structure of social institutions than we do about the lives of ordinary Chinese people. Furthermore, as the essays in this volume demonstrate, there is often a discrepancy between the expressed goals of political campaigns and the practical consequences of social engineering. In this China is by no means unique. However, until field research (by Chinese as well as foreign social scientists) becomes more acceptable, international understanding of the Chinese revolution will continue to be rudimentary at best.

2

CHINESE VIEWS OF SOCIAL CLASSIFICATION

Philip A. Kuhn

What is the cultural background of contemporary Chinese ideas about social classification? As China modernizes, new social groups will emerge along with new relationships among existing groups. Such reorganization will not, however, constitute an 'objective' system of social differences which need only be perceived in order to be appropriately codified. Factors such as hierarchy, division of labour, and social mobility will be mental constructions even while becoming social realities: they will (as a system) constitute one among many possible patterns of perceiving the Chinese social world. Although we can readily concede that patterns of perception do not emerge in any simple one-to-one manner from earlier patterns, we can assume as a working principle that earlier patterns do *limit* the range of mental instruments by which people classify the elements of their social environment. So it is reasonable, in any study of class and stratification in contemporary China, to pay careful attention to the values and meanings that Chinese were carrying with them as their nation entered the modern age.

What I am seeking here is a complex of views, current in late imperial times, but often inherited from earlier periods, which will illuminate some of the special features of Chinese ideas about social class since 1949. It will be important to examine not only the range of attitudes, but also the mechanisms by which those attitudes conditioned acceptance of Western social theory.

For these purposes, I shall be particularly interested in how Chinese dealt theoretically with social hierarchy: how the *causes* of human inequality were understood. We should know, for example, whether they are of cosmological origin, fitting some kind of supra-

16

social, supra-historical pattern. Or may they originate in some societal process, such as the division of labour? Perhaps they are man-made; perhaps related to inherent qualities of persons; or perhaps purely random? We should also inquire how Chinese viewed the *justness* of the inequality: did it accord with people's deserts? Was there inevitably to be social inequality and therefore no desire to change the system (as distinct from bettering the status of oneself or one's social group)? In addition to the general problem of hierarchy, our concern with the background of twentieth-century notions of social class prompts me to examine Chinese ideas about social *groups* which stand in hierarchical status relationship. Whether or not social groups were seen as constituting 'classes' (in the sense that Marx saw them), defined by their relations in a system of production, it will be important to define the total system in which such groups were seen to operate.

First, however, consider how the term 'class' in its modern sense entered the Chinese world. The word *jieji*, which is now used routinely to translate 'social class', is a very old ideographic compound. Like many other social terms, it was taken over and given new meaning by the Japanese around the turn of the twentieth century and then reintroduced into China.

Originally, the ideograph *jie* seems to mean steps, like rungs on a ladder; and *ji* is the order of threads in a fabric. The term thus connotes hierarchical degrees on a continuum, rather than groups of people. In late antiquity it seems to have meant a system of social ranks in a fixed order of aristocratic distinction, which was linked to a routinized system of political preferment. In the Wu Kingdom (third c AD), the Prince of Lu, named Ba, was accorded such favour by the monarch that his status became virtually equal to that of the heir apparent. As the story goes, the minister Gu Tan protested that rulers must make clear distinctions 'between the sons of principal and secondary wives', and must 'differentiate between the ceremonies accorded the noble and the mean, cause the statuses of high and low to be distinguished, and the degrees of rank (*jieji*) to be distantly separated'.[1] The point here is that *jieji* does not refer to groups of persons, but to ranks on a scale. Gu meant that a clear distinction among the privileges pertaining to the various degrees of rank would make relations among aristocrats harmonious by giving fewer occasions for envy. Here are reflected the norms of an aristocratic society, in which *jieji* referred to social and political rank within an accepted hierarchy of status distinctions.

The image of *jieji* as fixed degrees on a continuum is reinforced by a sixth-century usage, in which an aristocratic family is described as gaining 'a single step or a half-grade' (*ijie banji*) in its political rank over several generations.[2] By late imperial times, the meaning of *ji* had shifted entirely away from inherited aristocratic status and was associated with the eighteen-rank system of bureaucratic distinctions (*dengji*, in which *deng* was the major division and *ji* the minor). *Ji* was thus linked to the highly formalized status ladder of official rank.

The idea of *jieji* as 'rungs on a ladder' was still current when Liang Qichao first used the term in 1899, shortly after he fled to Japan and was exposed to Japanese interpretations of European social thought. Liang was gamely trying to work his mentor's theory of the 'three ages' into his new information as he laboured to deal with the distribution of social and economic power (*qiangquan*). Each age, he proposed, displayed a characteristic set of power relations among social groups. In the first age (chaos), power is very limited, because the differences in power between ruler and ruled, and between men and women, is very slight. In the second stage (approaching peace), the power of ruler over ruled increases. At the same time, the ruled begin to resist. By the third stage (great peace), everyone has power: and hence there is equality. (This equality is different from that of the primitive first age, when *nobody* had much power.) Is Europe now in the final stage of power development? Not yet, thought Liang, because the differentials (*jieji*) between capitalists and workers, and between men and women, have not yet been eliminated. Such differentials are seen by Liang as an obstacle to the full development of a society's power. Here *jieji* certainly does not refer to classes (although Liang presumably had access to such usage in Japanese writings), but rather the gradient that separated social groups: still social distance, not social groups.[3]

In this connection, Raymond Williams points out that in England, through the early nineteenth century, 'rank', 'order', and 'degree' were more commonly used than 'class' to describe hierarchically ordered social groups. 'All the older words with their essential metaphors of standing, stepping, and arranging in rows belong to a society in which position was determined by birth.'[4] In the Chinese case, these 'step' and 'arrangement' metaphors grew out of a society in which social position, while linked by distant association to feudal and aristocratic antecedents, was heavily laden with concepts of bureaucratic status.

In Japan, the use of *jieji* (Japanese: *kaikyū*) to mean 'class' as a social group was current by the first decade of the twentieth century. For example, Tazoe Tetsuji's *History of Modern Socialism* (*Kinsei shakaishugi shi*, 1907) uses the term in the Marxist manner, a social group defined by a system of production relations. 'The organization of production in certain periods' gives rise to 'two totally opposed social classes' (*shakaiteki kaikyū*). Although this is seen as a worldwide phenomenon, applicable to East Asia as well as to the West, the foreign and exotic character of the terminology is emphasized by the use of syllabic *furigana* next to the ideographs: instead of *shakaiteki kaikyū*, the author instructs us to read *sōshiaru kurasu*.[5]

In view of the wide accessibility of Marxist literature by the 1920s, it is astonishing how much trouble the young Mao Zedong had in deciding how to apply the term *jieji* to the Chinese scene. His early work 'The Great Union of the Popular Masses' (1919) uses the term not at all. Instead we have an unsystematic array of social elites (aristocrats, capitalists, and 'powerful figures') mixed with occupational and special interest groups (farmers, students, policemen, primary-school teachers). These groups are arranged according to no general theory of social order.[6]

Probably Mao's first use of the term *jieji* in print occurs in his 1921 piece, 'Founding Proclamation of the Human Self-Study University'. Here we find that *jieji* are indeed social groups arranged hierarchically: the 'intellectual class' (*zhishi jieji*) and the 'commoner class' (*pingmin jieji*). Here is a systematic analysis, which at least covers the entire social ground. The categories, however, are wholly traditional, and in fact correspond to the old Confucian dichotomy between those who labour with their minds and those who labour with their hands.[7]

So by the third decade of this century, Chinese thinkers were still having trouble relating the Western concept of class to their own sense of social organization. What that sense comprised, I suggest, appears in pre-modern sources along four axes of social differentiation.

19

(1) Occupational status

The division of Chinese society into four large occupational status groups dates from the earliest period of Chinese thought. It occurs in the *Book of Documents* and other classical texts in the expression *simin*, or the four occupational groups among the people (scholars, agriculturalists, artisans, merchants). Only a few remarks need be made here about this well-known system of social differentiation. First, it comes closest of any Chinese idea to the 'estates' idea of the West. The system says nothing about economic gradations within each group. Agriculturalists (*nong*), for example, would include both rich landowners and poor tenants. And there is a strong feeling of naturalness and universality about the system: it is thought to cover the entirety of the natural and necessary human occupations. Thus it forms a complete and interrelated system. It is generally assumed to imply hierarchy, though the actual principles on which that hierarchy is constructed are worth careful examination. By what rationale, for example, are agriculturalists thought superior to merchants? The superiority lies not in gradations of purity or virtue, but is founded on economic priorities, in which agriculture is considered a 'root' occupation (*benye*) from the standpoint of the state's fiscal interests; while trade is considered the subsidiary 'branch' (*moye*).

Unquestionably there existed a hierarchy of value among these four estates. Just how strong such a sense was, however, or how firm the conceptual separation, is not so obvious. In late imperial times it did not involve prohibitions against intermarriage. Nor was it the basis for prohibitions against commensality (as in the case of Indian castes). In fact, a curious and striking fact about this system is that, from very early times, it was used of 'subjects' in the aggregate: of all people except the ruling strata. This meaning of *simin* persisted through late imperial times, when it was used simply to mean 'ordinary subjects', as distinct from pariah groups.[8]

In short, it seems likely that, although the conception of four estates did involve a sense of hierarchy, its aggregate sense of 'ordinary subjects' was the dominant one in late imperial times. And this fits closely with an equally pervasive scheme of classification, namely that between the ruling stratum and nearly everyone else.

(2) Rulers and ruled

In 1974 a young scientist in Manchuria told me, with a perfectly straight face, that a 'cadre' was 'one who works with his brain as distinct from one who works with his hands'. Though this man was not particularly old-fashioned in other respects, he was certainly hewing to an old and respected conceptual division of society, which goes back at least to the *Mencius*. Now, when this axis of differentiation is placed next to the 'four estates' axis just discussed, the anomaly is that the estate of 'scholars' (*shi*) overlaps with the stratum of rulers: those who do brainwork. Whether the *shi* are to be considered 'ordinary subjects' or part of the ruling elite is central to the debate over the nature of the lowest stratum of the late imperial gentry, and was probably an ambiguity in Mencius' day as well. The implication that *simin* means *all* subjects (i.e., those who were neither officials nor candidate-officials), including the scholars or top-most estate, lends support to Ho Ping-ti's assertion that scholars who lacked qualification to serve in the state bureaucracy were considered the top rank of the commoners.

For our purposes, the importance of the rulers–ruled axis is the levelling effect it has on social distinctions within the scheme of estates. The equation of *simin* with 'ruled stratum' minimizes status distinctions among them by comparison with the overriding importance of the rulers–ruled axis. The rulers–ruled division, like that of the four estates, is systematic and universal in its application, covering the entire symbolic ground and leaving nobody out. Thus it takes on the appearance of a natural system, one built into the very nature of human society, neither to be legislated into existence, nor out of it.

(3) Free and unfree

Unlike the two systems just discussed, this one was by no means considered universal, nor built into the natural order. It consisted of two subcategories: hereditary service groups and pariah groups (including slaves). Although these groups have very different historical origins, the *rationale* for their existence was similar, in that they were both considered man-made. By hereditary service groups I refer to the special categories of families liable for certain types of service to the state: for example, those recorded in the vast military registers (*junji*) of Ming and Qing times, which were designed to ensure the maintenance of a self-supporting and self-perpetuating standing army. This system was reinforced in Qing times by ethnicity, with the various 'banner' garrisons registered separately from the Han population. In the economic system of the late empires, hereditary service tended to lose its efficiency and to be replaced by hired service (nowhere was this more obvious than in the military sector).

Slave and pariah groups, like the hereditary service groups, were considered to have been essentially 'man-made' rather than naturally occurring. Though the more familiar phenomenon in other societies is to see such invidious social distinctions as part of the natural order, Chinese seemed inclined to establish and maintain a causal nexus between a person's unfree status and some past circumstance which could reasonably account for it.

The work of Niida Noboru has indicated a great variety of unfree conditions in China, from ancient times onward. There were outright slaves (*nuli*), who were considered half-men and half-things, and who could be bought and sold; their status was traced to human actions, including capture in warfare or penal servitude. There were indentured retainers, who were called *buqu* in medieval times but took many institutional forms thereafter. This was an intermediate status of servitude traceable to a procedure of commendation like that connected with early Western feudalism. Such semi-servile status extended also to tenants who, by virtue of some act of renunciation of freedom, owed certain hereditary services to landlords. Certain pariah groups, descended from people who had suffered some sort of state punishment (as criminals or war captives), were attached as specialized practitioners of socially despised occupations (e.g., entertainers) and not allowed to intermarry with other strata. Here was a wide range of servility and dependency, all traceable to man-made causes, and not to the order of nature (not, for example, to be compared with an axis organized around purity and impurity).[9]

Certain attitudes toward free and unfree status can be illustrated by an edict from the Yongzheng emperor dated 1727.[10]

Edict to the Grand Secretariat: We take the improvement of customs and

22

mores as a central concern. Those who have [bad] customs and mores which are long transmitted, and have not been able to shake them off, ought all be given a route toward self-renewal (*zixin*). Such was the case with the 'entertainer households' (*yuehu*) of Shanxi and the 'lazy people' (*dohu*) of Zhejiang, all of whom have had their mean status expunged and been reclassified as 'good subjects'. This was in order to encourage honesty and a sense of shame, and to extend the transformation of values.

Now we have learned that in Huizhou prefecture, Anhui, there are 'servitors' (*bandang*) and in Ningquo prefecture there are 'hereditary servants' (*shipu*). These are called, locally, 'mean people' (*ximin*). Their status is even worse than that of the 'entertainer households' and 'lazy people'. For example, there may be two surname groups whose tax classifications are equivalent, but one surname group may be the servitors and hereditary servants of the other. When those of the first surname have weddings or funerals, those of the second must present themselves for service. If they do not comply in any small particular, they may be flogged. Inquiring as to when these servile obligations began, the matter is obscure and impossible to determine. It is not that there is really any division between superior and inferior. It is absolutely nothing more than an evil custom being long perpetuated. This matter came to our attention by hearsay. Now if there really is such a situation, we considered that they ought to be emancipated to be good subjects (*liangmin*). Thereby may they energetically raise themselves up and avoid having this vile status for their whole lives and passing it on to their descendants.

The emperor then approved a recommendation by the Anhui governor which distinguished among servile dependents bound by a written contract, and those who were not. The latter were to be freed unconditionally.[11]

What mattered to the emperor was the status of the people in question from the standpoint of the state fisc. True, servile status was correlated in some way with moral taint. Nevertheless, this was not taint in the bone and marrow, but could be expunged once the objective conditions of social inferiority were removed by law. In other words, the juridical context, which was man-made, was what made self-renewal possible. This was certainly distinguishable from any concept of caste hierarchy, in that the social impurity was a secondary characteristic. Notice the importance of contracts of indenture – whether voluntary or not – as reasonable causes to which one could ascribe social inferiority. What man could make, man could unmake as well.

(4) Rich and poor

Of our four axes of social differentiation, this is the most difficult to deal with in the Chinese case. That is because it is not entirely clear whether it really represents an axis in the Chinese scheme of classification. Is there a 'culture of poverty' in Chinese thinking? There seems to be considerable evidence to the contrary. Some questions may clarify the point. (1) What do wealth and poverty mean in terms of other systems of status differentiation? (2) What do they mean in terms of innate human qualities? (3) What are the causes of wealth and poverty with respect to particular families or groups? Here I should like to adduce some rather conventional material from stories and informal writings in which wealth and poverty play a part. Although some of these date from medieval times, all were available to readers of the late empires, and were read and reprinted.

The twelfth-century writer Hong Mai observed:[12]

When I was young, I read a passage by someone of an earlier generation as follows: 'when a rich person has a son, she does not nurse him herself but has someone put aside her own son and nurse him. When a poor person has a son, she may not nurse him herself but must put him aside in order to nurse someone else's son. A rich person travels leisurely and has people carry him by sedan chair. A poor person not only may not travel on his own but must even carry someone else.' These things exist because they have persisted customarily for a long time without being looked into. These examples may be extended to many things in the world which have so persisted, and which nobody thinks of as unusual. How tragic!

Several important attitudes toward the wealth–poverty axis are embedded here: poverty and wealth in themselves are not indicia of injustice. Differences in wealth are not wrong in themselves; rather, it is the way people treat one another in such a situation. Furthermore, the way the rich treat the poor is one cultural trait among many possible ones. Rather than a natural outgrowth of the disparity in wealth, wet-nursing and palanquins are practices which might be 'looked into', and perhaps ameliorated. As to the nature of the exploitation in this passage, it obviously has nothing to do with the system of economic production, but rather concerns basic human desiderata: nursing babies and moving about. The attitude about the universality of human needs suggests a society in which wealth and poverty are exchanged comparatively freely. Certainly there is no natural difference among men which can be said to result from their economic position.

Qian Yong, a Qing writer, likened economic fortune to seasonal changes:[13]

Wealth and high status are like flowers. They wither in less than a day. Poverty and low status are like grass: they remain green through winter and summer. But when frost and snow ensue, flowers and grass all wither, and when spring breezes suddenly arrive, flowers and grass flourish. Wealth, high status; poverty, low status; being born and being extinguished; rising and declining: this is a principle of heaven and earth.

Here the alternation of wealth and poverty is metaphorically linked to time, rather than some other universal phenomenon, such as *karma*, division of labour, virtue, or human effort. They are changeable, but not changeable arbitrarily. Rather, they replace one another with the regularity of the seasons. The natural condition of man seems to be poverty (persisting, like grass, over a long period), whereas wealth is a more exotic quality and hence more fragile. Extremely hostile conditions, however, will victimize both the rich and the poor household, and good conditions will permit both to revive and continue their modes of life. Here is a society with a broad, poor base and a very narrow elite at the top – with the elite far more vulnerable to the winds of the season. Finally, differences between wealth and poverty have nothing to do with inherent human characteristics, and there is no natural disparity in virtue between rich and poor. In another passage, Qian deals with the relationship between wealth and social roles:[14]

Merchants regard wealth as proper; for with wealth, profits and interest will be increasingly generated. Buddhist and Taoist clerics regard poverty as proper; for with poverty, desires and evil conduct will seldom come. The scholar regards as proper a condition of neither wealth nor poverty. Without wealth, there is nothing to agitate the spirit. Without poverty, he can concentrate his mind on study.

Here, wealth and poverty take on a free-floating quality not inherent to social role, but somehow furthering its appropriate vocation. Economic status has an instrumental benefit: instead of being determined by social role, it is desired in order more effectively to fill a social role.

Indeed, social role may be virtually without any necessary connection to particular economic status, as Qian goes on to relate:[15]

In the *Hongfan* chapter of the *Book of Documents*, among the five blessings, wealth is listed as number two [in descending rank order]. I, however, believe wealth to be an extremely miserable matter and a source of ill feeling. There are those who are wealthy and of high status. There are those who are wealthy and of mean status; those who work the fields and are wealthy, those who work as merchants and are wealthy. Their kinds of wealth are dissimilar, and their sufferings are of multifarious kinds. How can wealth simply be termed a blessing?

Here the connection between wealth and status is so loose as to be virtually nonexistent. Anyone can get rich, whatever his social role, so that wealth is neither a determinant nor a necessary result of one's place in the world. The wealth–poverty axis is poorly correlated with other social divisions.

Finally, an amusing Song story offers some revealing views about the relation between wealth and social position:[16]

In the *Collected Song Ephemera* (*Songbai leichao*) there is a story called 'The eight cyclical characters[17] of Duke Wenlu'. In Loyang lived an old man who shared the eight characters with Duke Wenlu. But their attainments in life were different. Once a fortune-teller was asked to predict the old man's fate. He said that, indeed, although the gulf between him and the Duke was like the division between North and South or between water and land, yet in a certain month in the following year he would rest and rise with the Duke, eat and drink with him, and share equally with him; but that this situation would not last beyond the ninth month. The next year, the Duke entered Loyang and desired to meet with an old-timer to chat about past events. Someone recommended the old man to him. As soon as the Duke met him, he was delighted. He caused the old man to accompany him wherever he went. Whenever there was an official banquet, or a visit to relations or friends, he took him along. When the Duke sat on the right, he would seat the oldster on his left, and vice versa. After the ninth month, the Duke left Loyang, and the old man went his separate way.

Here is a suggestion that beyond the world of human arrangements (in which are vast differences of social position) is a realm of cosmological truth which links men according to some prior system of affinities and which breaks through the world of appearances from time to time. When it does, human connections can transcend the accidents of station. Clearly, socializing between high and low is a remarkable thing, otherwise there would be no story. Yet, even

26

though unusual, such closeness is not seen as defiling to the person of high status. The connection with the old man rather reflects credit on the Duke. That such a connection could be achieved may also have something to do with old age, when presumably status differences begin to lose their sharp outlines in the twilight of life. The story would hardly have the same appeal or plausibility if both men had been young. Finally, the appeal of the story seems to depend on the idea that, however steep a status gradient, it can be bridged by shared human characteristics. One pictures a rather jolly time between the two protagonists, despite the vast difference in their rank.

Trying to distill from these materials a set of principles that we can say constitute 'the Chinese view' of social stratification is surely risky, if for no other reason than that we have yet to describe such a unified Chinese view about *any* social question. At least one can say that the foregoing material is not in serious conflict with these conclusions:

1) Historically, Chinese views about social hierarchy have been closely related to the hierarchy of state office. Furthermore, only in the twentieth century has hierarchy been (however awkwardly) seen in terms of human groups rather than points on a scale.

2) Occupational status hierarchy has had a place in Chinese social theory, but it has been largely overshadowed by a political distinction, dividing the state sector from all others.

3) Status distinctions which denote the natural and hereditary inferiority of certain groups have existed, but have been subject to rationalization in the search for some human act which caused them, and it has been thought necessary that servile status be documented by some legal instrument.

4) Distinctions of wealth have been only loosely linked to other human characteristics and other systems of social differentiation. Moreover, a powerful fatalism underlay the view of how wealth was acquired. Beneath distinctions of wealth was seen to persist a set of universal human characteristics.

If these can be said to sum up the cultural background from which twentieth-century Chinese have viewed the question of class and hierarchy, we should guess that Chinese social theory would be somewhat uncomfortable with ideas of hereditary and immutable class status. We would further expect the political order to play a dominant role in defining any new system of classification that emerges.

In fact, the current Chinese system of social classification suggests just such an orientation. There are actually two systems in force: that of 'social role' (*chengfen*) and that of 'social origin' (*chushen*). Social role is defined in the official dictionary published in 1973 by the Chinese Academy of Social Sciences, as 'a person's most important background or occupational status before entering upon revolutionary work' (*geming gungzuo*), that is, before being assigned to a job. For instance, one's official 'social role' might be worker, or student. The important thing is that 'social role' can change. It is not ascribed by accident of birth, and may be different from that of other family members.

'Social origin', by contrast, designates (in the same dictionary) 'A person's status as determined by his early experience or his family's economic circumstances.'[18] Social origin is the designation by which most persons were formally categorized during the early 1950s (for instance, 'textile worker' or 'landlord'). It corresponds closely to 'class background', and ordinarily does not change as one's social activities or consciousness change.

The relative importance of 'social origin' seems to be in decline, as China's leadership moves toward a less conflictual view of internal social relations. Though there are doubtless current policy reasons for this tendency, a more profound reason may perhaps be sought in layers of Chinese consciousness about social classification which lie far back in history. So basic a component of man's social awareness does not change quickly or easily.

3

CLASSES, OLD AND NEW, IN MAO ZEDONG'S THOUGHT, 1949–1976*

Stuart R. Schram

It has frequently been argued that, with the passing of the years, Mao Zedong came to define class according to increasingly subjective criteria, until, during the Cultural Revolution, the quality of 'proletarian' was attributed only to those who were loyal to his person, or had thoroughly mastered his Thought. Others have put precisely the opposite view, to the effect that, with the turn

* The gestation of this article has been prolonged, and the main stages in the process must be briefly evoked if I am to give proper acknowledgement to those who, by their comments and criticisms, have stimulated me to develop and clarify the ideas presented here. It first took shape as a seminar paper on Mao's view of the 'new class', presented at Keiō University in Tokyo in June 1979 when I was Visiting Professor there. The participants on that occasion, especially Yamada Tatsuo and Linda Grove, made many useful points. This paper, in roughly the same form, was also given at Berkeley in August 1979, where the most suggestive reaction was that of Chen Ruoxi. The first draft of the version designed for inclusion in the present volume was presented in April 1982 to a seminar at United College, Chinese University of Hong Kong, when I was a guest of the college on the occasion of its Silver Jubilee celebrations. The participants there were so numerous, and so lively in their response, that it would be invidious to single out any individual for particular thanks. Subsequently, I visited China in April and May 1982, and again in September, and had discussions on issues related to the theme of this article with a number of theoretical workers in Beijing, Shanghai, and Nanjing. (These visits took place in the context of the British Academy–Chinese Academy of Social Sciences exchange agreement, and I am grateful to both institutions.) In particular, Liao Gailong and Su Shaozhi gave me copies of articles and speeches which are cited in the notes, and Liao Gailong commented in great detail on the draft of this chapter in the course of a two-hour conversation. I need hardly add that, since I do not share Professor Liao's ideological position, I did not agree with all of his criticisms, and have maintained in what follows many formulations to which he objected. He is therefore in no sense responsible for what I have written here, but the information and ideas he put forward have contributed significantly to the refinement of my interpretation in this final version, and for this assistance I thank him most sincerely.

to the Left at the Tenth Plenum in September 1962, symbolized by the slogan 'Never forget the class struggle!', Mao Zedong moved back toward a more objective definition of the protagonists in this struggle, stressing the harmful influence of the remnants of the old exploiting classes. Yet others argue that, in Mao's last years, 'class struggle' meant for him primarily the struggle against the 'new class' elements in the Party.

All of these views are so one-sided as to be largely misleading. It cannot be disputed that, by the early 1960s, three different frames of reference were taken into account in assigning class labels or 'hats' to people in China: (1) the socio-economic category of the individual, or of his family, before 1949; (2) political attitudes, as measured by behaviour, ideological stance, or a combination of the two; and (3) rank or status in the new society, and especially in the hierarchy of cadres and other privileged elements. The relative importance of these three aspects of the matter varied from time to time, but the position was never absolutely clear cut, either in Mao's thinking or in the way the criteria were applied in practice. This ambiguity resulted, no doubt, partly from the fact that Mao had some difficulty in making up his mind. It may also have persisted because the simultaneous existence of different standards was in some respects convenient to those who made and administered policy.

Before discussing Mao Zedong's discovery, at the time of the Great Leap Forward, that the bourgeoisie could be 'born anew' in socialist societies, which added an extra dimension to his thinking about problems of class in China, I shall begin by making a few observations about Mao's use, down to 1957, of the socio-economic and ideological frames of reference.

Regarding the significance of objective class origins, I should first of all like to make the point, with which others have dealt at much greater length, that there existed in the People's Republic of China from the early 1950s at least until the beginning of 1979 what has been called a 'class status system'. Although class labels were not supposed to be inherited, at least beyond the second generation, family origin remained, especially in the countryside, the main determinant of an individual's socio-economic position. Access to the Party, the PLA, to other desirable careers, and (in the case of men) to a desirable marriage partner was rigorously denied to children of landlords, rich peasants, and others of 'bad' class background.

The framework employed in this vast effort to define the class nature of each and every member of the Chinese people derived, of course, in the first instance, from Mao Zedong's analyses of the structure of Chinese society, and especially of Chinese rural society, from the 1920s onwards. Two points should be made at the outset about Mao's approach to classes prior to 1949, both of which have relevance for the subsequent development of his Thought.

First of all, Mao carried out his revolutionary activities in the context of a complex social structure derived from the co-existence of elements and strata dating from different historical epochs, and shaped both by indigenous and foreign influences. It included, in addition to a limited but rapidly growing number of urban workers, and Chinese entrepreneurs or 'national bourgeois', a small but extremely powerful landlord class, the peasants (rich and poor, landed and landless), and a rich variety of other categories, from artisans and hawkers to 'compradors' in the service of foreign capitalists, and from bureaucrats and militarists to monks, bandits and rural vagabonds.

The consequences of this situation are reflected in the concepts of the 'principal contradiction', and the 'principal aspect of the principal contradiction', which play so large a part in Mao's interpretation of dialectics. Marx, it is hardly necessary to point out, would never have posed the question, with reference to France or England in the nineteenth century, 'Which contradiction is primary today?' He took it as axiomatic that the key contradiction was that between the proletariat and the bourgeoisie, and that this would remain the case until the conflict was resolved by socialist revolution. Mao, on the other hand, saw it as his most urgent practical task to determine, in the light of what he regarded as a correct Marxist analysis, where the decisive cleavages should be drawn, both in China and in the world.

It is evident that he went about this task with a considerable degree of acumen, and a considerable degree of realism, since otherwise the movement he led, which based its strategy to a large extent on Mao's analyses of Chinese society, would never have survived and developed as it did. But at the same time, from the very outset,

Mao took account not merely of the objective situation, but of the possibility of modifying or re-shaping it through the conscious action of human beings.

The importance of this second dimension of Mao's pre-1949 approach to classes should not be exaggerated to make of him some kind of raving voluntarist lunatic, but neither can it be neglected. Thus, as early as the late 1920s, Mao put forward the view that an individual's objective class nature could be modified as a result of subjective transformation, brought about by indoctrination or by participation in revolutionary struggle. I have explored this theme on several occasions, most recently in an article published in 1981,[1] and I shall not repeat that discussion here. The evidence that Mao thought along these lines seems to me, however, conclusive. Such being the case, the potential ambiguity about class nature resulting from the simultaneous use of objective and subjective criteria not only antedates the Cultural Revolution, but in fact made itself felt two decades before 1949.

Apart from the idea that a 'qualitative change' could be effected in rural vagabonds or *youmin*, thereby turning them into proletarian fighters, Mao Zedong also displayed, in these early years, the tendency to juxtapose political and moral categories which was to feature so extensively in Chinese political culture in the 1960s and 1970s, though at that time he did not yet *define* class in moral terms. In the Gutian resolution of December 1929, after deploring the low standard of the existing Party membership, he proposed the following criteria for carrying out a more rigorous selection of new members in future:[2]

1) There should be no errors in their political outlook (including their class consciousness);
2) They should be loyal;
3) They should have a spirit of sacrifice, and be capable of working actively;
4) They should not seek to enrich themselves;
5) They should not smoke opium or gamble.

Four out of these five points refer exclusively to moral qualities. Only the first bears any relation to politics. If one were to interpret the 'class consciousness' (*jieji juewu*), which was to be without errors, as the consciousness inherent in, or related to, their *own* class, then this point might be seen as evoking indirectly social origins, as well as political attitudes. But in fact, earlier in the same text, Mao had stated that a *majority* of the soldiers in his army were lumpen-proletarians (*youmin wuchanjieji*), not workers or peasants; no doubt for this reason, he wrote that education, to raise the political level, was the most urgent task in the Party at present.[3]

Mao's view about the decisive significance of subjective factors was not in harmony with the ideas prevailing in Moscow. A Comintern directive of July 1931 asserted categorically:[4]

The hegemony of the proletariat and the victorious development of the revolution can be guaranteed only on condition that the Chinese Communist Party becomes a proletarian party not only in its political line but in its composition and the role played by the workers in all of its leading organs.

This passage was, of course, directed in the first instance against the excessively large place occupied by peasants in the Chinese Communist Party, but to the extent that Moscow was aware of the existence of *youmin* and former bandits in the Party (even if they had been 'born again' as a result of indoctrination), such elements would have been regarded with even more suspicion.

Even in articles such as 'Analysis of the Various Classes in the Chinese Peasantry and of their Attitudes toward the Revolution', published in January 1926, and the parallel piece 'Analysis of all the Classes in Chinese Society', which appeared in February 1926,[5] one can note the use of what might be called 'objective–subjective' criteria, i.e. of criteria which have a certain objective basis, but are sufficiently flexible to allow considerable scope for subjective judgment in their application.

It has been pointed out before that in these writings, Mao cuts reality into very thin slices, not simply on the basis of the relation of each category to the means of production, but according to the wealth or poverty of households, as measured by whether or not they can 'make ends meet'. There is, of course, an objective basis for such an approach, for many people in China in the 1920s literally did not have enough to eat, while others enjoyed abundance. But well-being is at least partially a subjective phenomenon. In 1926, this dimension of Mao's analysis was superposed on a set of categories (such as 'peasant landholders', 'semi-landholders', 'sharecroppers', etc.) which did relate to ownership of the land, but in later years, labels such as 'rich' and 'poor' became primary in the analysis of rural class relations, though various explanatory directives related these to land ownership and hiring of labour. This approach contained a further element of subjectivity to the extent that it allowed the multiplication of class distinctions – perhaps a necessary thing, in view of the complex, ambiguous, and shifting character of class relations in China, but nevertheless a point to be noted.

The central role in the Chinese revolution which Mao Zedong assigned to the peasants, both in theory and in fact, beginning in 1926, is too well known to require comment here. If he, and others, had not made such a sociological analysis, and devised a strategy based upon it, the Chinese Communists would almost certainly not have enjoyed the success they did. And yet, Mao stressed very heavily, in 1949, that though he had been obliged by force of circumstances to win victory in an unorthodox way, the Chinese revolution would henceforth take the orthodox course of the cities leading the villages.[6] Strenuous efforts were therefore made in the early years of the Chinese People's Republic to recruit more real flesh-and-blood workers into the Party, in order to improve its class composition. Then, in 1956, the more rigorous selection procedures formerly applied to non-workers were abolished in the new Party Constitution, on the grounds that, as Deng Xiaoping put it in his Report to the Eighth Congress, 'the former classification of social status has lost or is losing its meaning'. It is perhaps worth recalling the details of Deng's argument, for they provide the background against which Mao's views on class developed during the last two decades of his life:[7]

The difference between workers and office employees is now only a matter of division of labour within the same class ... Poor and middle peasants have all become members of agricultural producers' co-operatives, and before long the distinction between them will become merely a thing of historical interest ... The vast majority of our intellectuals have now come over politically to the side of the working class, and a rapid change is taking place in their family background ... [E]very year, large numbers of peasants and students become workers, large numbers of workers, peasants, and their sons and daughters join the ranks of the intellectuals and office workers, large numbers of peasants, students, workers, and office workers join the army and become revolutionary soldiers ... What is the point, then of classifying these social strata into two different categories?

To the extent that Deng here attaches more importance to subjec-

34

tive attitudes, and willingness to work for the revolution, than to family origins, his views are consonant with a continuing (though not a consistent) trend in Mao's thinking. But to the extent that he indicated class struggle within Chinese society was rapidly dying away, his ideas obviously go completely against the tide which was later to emerge, and to swamp the Party. That does not, of course, mean that Mao Zedong disagreed with him at the time. Even during the first upsurge of the Cultural Revolution, in October 1966, when Kang Sheng complained that the political report at the Eighth Congress had contained the theory of the disappearance of classes, Mao was honest enough to reply: 'I read the report, and it was passed by the congress; we cannot make those two – Liu and Deng – solely responsible.'[8]

How and why did Mao come to change his attitude toward classes and class struggle so dramatically that the man whose ideas he had endorsed in 1956 became, a decade later, the 'number one capitalist roader'? The general context is well known. An aspect which merits emphasis is the crucial generational change in China's educated elite, which was inevitable in any case, but was accelerated by the events of 1957. During the early years after 1949, both technical and managerial cadres were, of necessity, to a very large extent people inherited from the old society, 'bourgeois' in their social origins, and/or in the sense that they had been trained in the West or in universities staffed by graduates of European, American, or Japanese schools. Mao believed that the loyalty of these people could be gained, and that being already expert, they could be made red as well. The Hundred Flowers policies which Mao launched with his speech of 2 May 1956 were primarily designed to serve this aim of drawing the pre-1949 intellectuals into active participation in political and social life, improving their morale, and re-moulding them in the process. When these hopes proved unjustified, Mao began to place greater emphasis on training a new generation of intellectuals whose redness was not open to doubt.

Thus, in January 1957, noting that 80 per cent of university students in China were still children of landlords, rich peasants, upper middle peasants, and the bourgeoisie, Mao commented: 'This situation should change, but it will take time.' Such a tolerant and 'gradualist' attitude was in harmony with Mao Zedong's overall view of China's problems at the time, as expressed in the original version of his speech of 27 February 1957 'On the Correct Handling of Contradictions among the People', which stated flatly that class struggles had 'basically come to an end' in China.[9]

It is argued by some leading Chinese theoretical workers today that Mao's ideas of early 1957, as set forth in this speech, implied the replacement of class struggle by contradictions among the people (which cannot, generally speaking, be regarded as a form of class struggle) as the 'principal contradiction' in Chinese society after the socialist transformation of 1955–6.[10] Although Mao himself did not use precisely this terminology, there are passages in his speech of 27 February 1957 which appear to support such an interpretation. For example, he declared: 'It is precisely these contradictions [among the people] that are pushing our society forward'; since contradictions were, in Mao's view, the motor of change, the particular contradiction, or type of contradiction, which moves society forward ought logically to be the principal contradiction. Moreover, in the same passage, Mao went on to say:[11]

Contradictions in socialist society are fundamentally different from those in the old societies, such as capitalist society. In capitalist society contradictions find expression in acute antagonisms and conflicts, in sharp class struggle; they cannot be resolved by the capitalist system itself and can only be resolved by socialist revolution. The case is quite different with contradictions in socialist society; on the contrary, they are not antagonistic and can be ceaselessly resolved by the socialist system itself.

As late as 2 May 1957, an editorial in *People's Daily* which, according to a well-informed Chinese specialist, 'reflected completely Comrade Mao Zedong's views at the time' argued:

Following the decisive victory in socialist transformation, the contradiction between the proletariat and the bourgeoisie in our country has already been basically resolved, and the previous several thousand years of history of a system of class exploitation has been basically concluded.

As a result, the editorial stated, the principal contradiction in China was no longer that between hostile classes, but the contradiction between 'the demand to build an advanced industrial country and the reality of a backward agrarian country', and others of a similar nature.[12]

But in mid-May, Mao's attitude changed radically as a result of continuing harsh criticism, and he perceived among the members of the Party 'a number of' revisionists and Right deviationists, whose thinking was 'a reflection of bourgeois ideology inside the Party', and who were 'tied in a hundred and one ways to bourgeois intellectuals outside the Party'.[13]

Re-writing his February speech in June 1957, Mao qualified his original statement that class struggles were over by making it read: 'The large-scale, turbulent class struggles of the masses characteristic of times of revolution have basically come to an end, but class struggle is by no means entirely over.'[14] This was still a relatively soft position, but Mao progressively hardened it. Thus, in July 1957, as the Hundred Flowers campaign was being transformed into an Anti-Rightist movement, he asserted:

To build socialism, the working class must have its own army of technical cadres and of professors, teachers, scientists, journalists, writers, artists and Marxist theorists ... This is a task that should be basically accomplished in the next ten to fifteen years.

To be sure, he added that this new army would include intellectuals from the old society 'who take a firm working-class stand after having been genuinely remoulded', but it was plain that most members of this army were to be young people of good class background. 'The revolutionary cause of the working class', he added, 'will not be fully consolidated until this vast new army of working-class intellectuals comes into being.'[15]

As for the existing intellectuals, Mao warned them disdainfully:

Intellectuals are teachers employed by the working class and the labouring people to teach their children. If they go against the wishes of their masters and insist on teaching their own set of subjects, teaching stereotyped writing, Confucian classics or capitalist rubbish, and turn out a number of counter-revolutionaries, the working class will not tolerate it and will sack them and not renew their contract for the coming year.[16]

From this time forward, Mao increasingly saw 'ghosts and monsters opposed to the Communist Party and the people' everywhere.[17] As for the structure of society as a whole, on the eve of the Great Leap, Mao made, in his speech of 20 March 1958 at Chengdu, a curious statement to the effect that 'the reciprocal relations between people' were 'determined by the relationship between three big classes': (1) 'imperialism, feudalism, bureaucratic capitalism, the rightists, and their agents'; (2) 'the national bourgeoisie', by which he said he meant all the members of this class except the Rightists; and (3) 'the Left, that is to say the labouring people, the workers, the peasants'. To this last category, Mao added, more or less as an afterthought, the parenthetical remark: 'In reality there are four classes – the peasants are a separate class.'[18]

In his speech of 6 April 1958 to the Hankou Conference, Mao corrected one anomaly – the failure to single out the particular role of the peasantry – but continued to include the 'imperialists' among the classes existing in China. On this occasion, he put the matter as follows:[19]

there are four classes within the country, two exploiting classes and two labouring classes. The first exploiting class consists of imperialism, feudalism, bureaucratic capitalism, and the remnants of the Guomindang, as well as 300,000 Rightists. The landlords have now split up, some of them have been reformed, and others have not been reformed. The unreformed landlords, rich peasants, counter-revolutionaries, bad elements, and Rightists resolutely oppose communism. They are the Chiang Kaishek and the Guomindang of the present day, they are the enemy class, like Zhang Bojun. The Rightists in the Party are just the same . . . If you add up all these people, they come to roughly 5 per cent of the population, or about 30 million . . . This is a hostile class, and still awaits reform. We must struggle against them, and at the same time take hold of them . . . If we succeed in transforming 10 per cent of them, this can be accounted a success . . . After a few years, when they demonstrate a sincere change of heart and are genuinely reformed, their exploiting class hats can be removed.

An interesting point for our purposes is, of course, the statement that members of this rather heterogeneous collection of people making up the first and most hostile exploiting class can have their 'hats' removed when they have been genuinely reformed, i.e. that they will change their class natures. The second exploiting class, made up of the national bourgeoisie, its intellectuals, and part of the upper stratum of the petty bourgeoisie, including the well-to-do middle peasants in the country, Mao described as a vacillating and opportunistic class. As for the 'two labouring classes, the workers and the peasants', Mao remarked: 'In the past, their minds were not at one, and they were not clear about ideology or about their mutual relations.' And he added: 'The workers and peasants work and till the land under the leadership of our Party, but in the past we did not properly handle the problem of their mutual relations.'

Before proceeding further with this discussion of the relations between objective and subjective criteria, it is necessary to introduce the third dimension in Mao's view of classes in the 1960s: the notion that privileged elements among the cadres and intellectuals constituted an embryonic class. This trend was linked to the generational change referred to above, for it had long been understood that, because they were accustomed to a certain standard of living, intellectuals of bourgeois origin must be paid high salaries. This was extensively discussed in the Chinese press in 1956–7, and in January 1957 Mao himself defended what he called 'buying over' at a 'small cost' the capitalists plus the democrats and intellectuals associated with them.[20] Obviously the same considerations did not apply to the newly trained young people, who did not have such expensive tastes, and who might be assumed to have a higher level of political consciousness.

The main factor in transforming the whole framework of Mao's thinking about classes was, however, the radicalism which emerged in his thinking in the summer of 1957 in the context of the Anti-Rightist campaign, and which attained new and higher levels, and new and stranger forms, in the following years.

It might be said that at the time of the Great Leap, a decade before the events of May 1968, Mao grasped and illustrated the slogan which the students of Paris were later to make famous: 'L'imagination au pouvoir!' The difference was, of course, that he really *was* in power. I have spoken earlier of objective and subjective criteria for defining classes, but in the summer of 1958, fantasy rather than sober observation came all too often to be the criterion for defining truth and reality generally. In July and August 1958 in Beidaihe, Mao Zedong advocated the abolition of the wage system, and the introduction of a military-communist style of free supply system (*gonggeizhi*);[21] he was only dissuaded from going ahead with this plan because Zhou Enlai produced detailed estimates, based on materials from various ministries, to show that it would be ruinously expensive as compared to the wage system.

In the atmosphere of euphoria which reigned in the autumn of 1958, Mao Zedong was again carried away to the point of claiming that grain production had doubled, and would double again in 1959, so that there would be more than people or animals could eat, and the surplus would have to be used for industrial raw materials.[22]

Such illusions, though short-lived, caused many communes to abolish or diminish the role of workpoints, and to institute a free supply system for grain and other essential foodstuffs. One of those who set out to draw theoretical conclusions from this situation (or from the fantasies which were rampant at the time) was Zhang Chunqiao. Zhang expressed nostalgia for 'the pattern of military-communist life' which had prevailed in the heroic days of the past, characterized by the 'free supply system', and called for the immediate restriction and rapid elimination of material incentives, which corresponded in his view to 'the ideology of bourgeois right'. An editorial note, undoubtedly by Mao, which accompanied Zhang's article when it was reproduced in *People's Daily*, said his views were 'basically correct', but found the article 'one-sided' and 'incomplete' in its explanation of the historical process.[23] But although Mao probably thought Zhang was in too much of a hurry, the problem of 'bourgeois right', and of the elements in Chinese society who defended material incentives because they were attached to their own privileges, remained posed in his speeches and writings from this time forward.

I shall not seek to trace here in detail the emergence of the idea of 'new bourgeois elements' in Mao's thinking, but will simply mention a few basic turning points, and sum up Mao's conclusions, as he formulated them from the mid-1960s to the end of his life.

It cannot be too much emphasized that the Lushan Plenum of August 1959, culminating in the disgrace of Peng Dehuai' as well as the arrest and imprisonment of several middle-ranking officials who had dared to express support for his criticisms of the Great Leap policies, marked another decisive turning point in Mao's view of the political situation in China, and of his own role in it. Explicitly, Mao moved toward a greater emphasis on class struggle. Condemning Peng and his allies as anti-Marxist 'bourgeois elements' who had infiltrated the Chinese Communist Party,[24] Mao declared that the struggle at Lushan had been a class struggle, 'the continuation of the life-or-death struggle between the two great antagonists of the bourgeoisie and the proletariat in the process of the socialist revolution during the past decade', and predicted that such struggle would last 'for at least another twenty years'.[25] (In the event, Mao very nearly saw to it that it did.) But a further development, not formally stated or given ideological sanction at this time, was that henceforth Mao tended to regard any criticism of himself or his policies as literally equivalent to *lèse majesté*, and sought to ensure that all instances of this crime received an exemplary sanction.

Mao's growing conviction, from 1959–60 onwards, that the bureaucratic tendencies which not only he, but Liu Shaoqi and others, had long denounced in the Chinese Communist Party were not simply the result of a defect in 'work style', but reflected an incipient change in the class character of the Party and its cadres, was inspired to a significant extent by his observations regarding the Soviet Union. But the comments he made in 1960 regarding the emergence of 'vested interest groups' in a socialist society after the abolition of classes, although they occur in his reading notes on the Soviet textbook of political economy, were obviously intended to apply to China as well. Already at this time, he attributed to such people two traits which were to remain central to his ideas on this theme in later years. On the one hand, they were attached to their privileges, founded in the principle of distribution 'to each according to his work' – in other words, in what Zhang Chunqiao had called 'bourgeois right'. And on the other hand, they behaved like overlords. 'This animal, man, is funny', said Mao. 'As soon as he enjoys slightly superior conditions he puts on airs.'[26]

In January 1962, in a speech mainly stressing the need to continue the struggle against the old reactionary classes (landlords and bourgeoisie), which he said were 'still planning a comeback', Mao stated explicitly that in a socialist society, 'new bourgeois elements may still be produced'.[27] And in August 1962, at a preliminary meeting of the Central Committee in Beidaihe, prior to the Tenth Plenum, at which he proclaimed the slogan 'Never forget the class struggle!' Mao declared:[28]

In the book *Socialist Upsurge in China's Countryside* [which he had himself edited] there is an annotation saying that the bourgeoisie has been eliminated, and only the influence of bourgeois ideology remains. This is wrong, and should be corrected ... The bourgeoisie can be born anew; such a situation exists in the Soviet Union.

As it stands, this statement that the bourgeoisie can be 'born anew' leaves open the question, central for our purposes, of whether Mao means the old bourgeoisie can be re-born, or whether he is referring to the reincarnation of the soul or essence of the bourgeoisie in a new form, adapted to the conditions of a socialist society. In my opinion, he was talking about the second of these things, in other words about what Djilas and others have called the 'new class' – though to my knowledge, Mao himself never used that term. He seemed unable to make up his mind, however, in the mid-1960s, as to whether these 'new bourgeois elements' were merely isolated individuals, corrupted by the advantages drawn from the misuse of their status, or whether *all* cadres, because of the privileges and power they enjoyed, were prone to take on this character.

In the early 1960s he appeared to lean in the first direction, by stressing the corrupting effects of money, and advantages bought with money. Thus, while continuing to acknowledge that material incentives were necessary in Chinese society at the present stage, he argued that they should be subordinated to 'spiritual incentives' in the political and ideological domains, and that individual interests should be subordinated to collective interests.[29]

In the summer of 1964, Mao referred scathingly to material corruption throughout the Party. 'At present', he said, 'you can buy a branch secretary for a few packs of cigarettes, not to mention marrying a daughter to him.'[30]

The reference here to lower-level cadres would suggest that at that moment, shortly before Liu Shaoqi produced his 'revised later ten points', Mao did not wholly disagree with the view that the Socialist Education Campaign should be directed at the grass roots, as well as at the higher echelons. He was, however, particularly exercised about the attitudes and behaviour of the privileged urban elite. In a talk of June 1964 on the Third Five-Year Plan, he remarked:[31]

Don't strive for money all the time, and don't spend it recklessly once you've got it ... In accordance with our policy, bourgeois intellectuals may be bought when necessary, but why should we buy proletarian intellectuals? He who has plenty of money is bound to corrupt himself, his family, and those around him ... In the Soviet Union, the high-salaried stratum appeared first in literary and artistic circles.

The final confrontation between Mao Zedong and Liu Shaoqi took place in December 1964, when Mao, dissatisfied with what he perceived as the distortion and watering-down of his original strategy for the Socialist Education Campaign, put forward a new twenty-three-article directive which Liu refused to accept. On this occasion, he made a number of observations regarding the 'new bourgeoisie' in which power, rather than money, began to appear as the decisive factor.

It is perhaps worth noting in passing that, although the problem of status and wage differentials was obviously of very acute concern to Mao, he displayed toward it even at this time a relaxed and humorous attitude scarcely to be found in the writings of the glum and fanatical ideologists of the Gang of Four. 'This business of eating more and possessing more is rather complex!' he declared. 'It is mainly people like us who have cars, and houses with central heating, and chauffeurs. I earn only 430 yuan, and I can't afford to hire secretaries, but I must.'[32]

It is hard to resist reading this passage in the light of Mao's remark, earlier in the same year of 1964, 'Xuantong's monthly salary of a little over a hundred yuan is too small – this man is an emperor.'[33] One has the impression that for Mao, there existed, in addition to 'worker', 'poor peasant', 'son of revolutionary martyr', and so on, yet another *chengfen*: that of ruler. As for those who did not share this status with him, and with the former emperor, they could not be allowed to grow attached to their privileges.

In a discussion of 20 December 1964, he thus castigated once again those 'power holders' among the cadres who were primarily concerned about getting more wage points for themselves, and agreed that the 'hat' of 'new bourgeois elements' should be stuck on 'particularly vicious offenders' among them. He warned, however, against overestimating their number, and said they should be referred to as elements or cliques, not as 'strata' – still less, obviously, as a fully formed class.[34] A week later, on 27 December 1964, Mao declared that there were 'at least two factions' in the Chinese Communist Party, a socialist faction and a capitalist faction; these two factions thus incarnated the principal contradiction in Chinese society.[35]

Such formulations, and Mao's determination to direct the spearhead of the Socialist Education Campaign against 'those in authority taking the capitalist road', led, of course, directly to the confrontation with Liu Shaoqi and others in the Party, and to the Cultural Revolution. They do not in themselves make at all clear, however, where at this time Mao saw the bourgeoisie as mainly situated. His suggestion that the 'capitalist faction' in the Party was identified with it does not necessarily imply that 'new bourgeois elements' within the Party actually constituted it, as held in the mid-1970s. In looking for the answer to this question, let us consider further the problem of the relation between objective and subjective criteria for class status in Mao Zedong's Thought, as it presented itself on the eve of the Cultural Revolution.

In his speech of 30 January 1962 to a central work conference, Mao related the 'five bad categories' to the social origins of the individuals in question: 'Those whom the people's democratic dictatorship should repress', he declared:

are landlords, rich peasants, counter-revolutionary elements, bad elements and anti-communist Rightists. The classes which the counter-revolutionary elements, bad elements and anti-communist Rightists represent are the landlord class and the reactionary bourgeoisie. These classes and bad people comprise about four or five per cent of the population. These are the people we must compel to reform.[36]

It should be noted that this formulation refers to 'classes and bad people'. In other words, though the counter-revolutionaries and other 'bad elements' were said by Mao to 'represent' the landlords and the reactionary bourgeoisie, they did not necessarily come from these classes. Two passages from speeches by Mao during the period from the summer of 1962 to the spring of 1963, when the 'Socialist Education Campaign' was in the process of taking shape, stress more heavily the class origins of deviations within the Party, but at the same time underscore the continuing importance, in Mao's view, of transformation through education.

In a talk of 9 August 1962 at Beidaihe (in the course of a central work conference called to prepare for the Tenth Plenum), Mao said:[37]

The composition of the Party membership (*dangyuan de chengfen*) includes a large number of petty bourgeois, a contingent of well-to-do peasants and their sons and younger brothers, a certain number of intellectuals, and also some bad people who have not yet been properly transformed; in reality, [these last] are not Communist Party members. They are called Communist Party members, but they are really [members of the] Guomindang ... As for the intellectuals and sons and brothers of landlords and rich peasants, there are those who have been transformed by Marxism (*Makesihua le de*), there are those who have not been transformed at all, and there are those who have not been transformed to a satisfactory level. These people are not spiritually prepared for the socialist revolution; we have not educated them in good time.

In May 1963, on the eve of the promulgation of the first directive regarding the Socialist Education Movement (the 'First Ten points'), Mao defined the class composition of the Party quite differently, but discussed the problem of 'transformation' in very similar terms:[38]

With respect to Party composition, the most important class components are workers, poor peasants and farm labourers. Consequently, the main class composition is good. However, within the Party there is a large number of petty bourgeois elements, some of whom belong to the upper stratum of the urban and rural petty bourgeoisie. In addition, there are intellectuals, as well as a certain number of sons and daughters of landlords and rich peasants. Of these people, some have been transformed by Marxism-Leninism; and some have not been transformed at all. Organizationally they may have joined the Party, but not in terms of their thought. They are not ideologically prepared for the socialist revolution. In addition, during the last few years some bad people have wormed their way in. They are corrupt and degenerate and have seriously violated the law and discipline. The democratic revolution has not been thorough, bad people have wormed their way in. This problem requires attention, but it is relatively easy to deal with. The most important problem is the petty-bourgeois elements who have not been properly reformed. With respect to intellectuals and the sons and daughters of landlords and rich peasants we must do more work. Consequently, we must carry out education, and yet more education, for Party members and cadres. This is an important task.

It is evident from these two quotations that, although objective social origins remained important for Mao, inward transformation through political education was likewise an important aspect of the problem of class taken as a whole. If anything, the stress on 'transformation', i.e. on subjective criteria, is greater in 1963 than in 1962.

In May 1964, as the Socialist Education Campaign unfolded, Mao declared, at a meeting with four Vice Premiers:[39]

We must definitely pay very close attention to class struggle. The 'four cleanups' in the countryside is a class struggle, and the 'five antis' in the cities is also a class struggle ... Class status (*chengfen*) must also be determined in the cities. As for how such class lines should be drawn, criteria must be formulated when we come to do this work. We cannot take account only of [inherited] class status (*wei chengfen lun*). Neither Marx, Engels, Lenin nor Stalin had working-class family origins (*chushen*).

A directive on drawing class distinctions, undated but almost certainly from late 1964, discusses explicitly the relation between subjective and objective criteria.[40]

It is necessary to draw class distinctions ... Of the two, [objective] class status (*jieji chengfen*) and the behaviour of the person in question (*benren biaoxian*), it is the behaviour of the person in question which is most important. The main thing in drawing class distinctions is to ferret out the bad elements.

We must moreover clearly distinguish between family origins (*chushen*) and the behaviour of the person in question. The emphasis must be placed on behaviour; the theory that everything depends on class status alone (*wei chengfen lun*) is wrong, the problem is whether you take the stand of your class of origin, or whether you adopt a different class stand, that is, on the side of the workers and the poor and lower middle peasants. Moreover, we must not be sectarian, but must unite with the majority, even including a portion of the landlords and rich peasants, and their children. There are even some counter-revolutionaries and saboteurs who should be transformed; it suffices that they be willing to be transformed, and we should be willing to have them, one and all.

Although on the whole the views expressed by Mao in the passage I have just quoted set the pattern for the Cultural Revolution, there was, as everyone knows, sharp conflict, especially in 1966, between so-called 'conservative' Red Guards, who came from 'good' class backgrounds, and therefore stressed family origins in evaluating people, and the 'radicals' of various persuasions who stressed commitment to Mao and his Thought, as measured by behaviour, and even in subsequent years the position was frequently confused. I cannot go into these events here. In any case, the essential point for our purposes is that, while objective class origins were never regarded as *irrelevant*, and were given varying degrees of emphasis by different people at different times, high, and generally decisive, importance was attributed, during the Cultural Revolution, to subjective factors as the main criterion of class nature.

Lenin, for his part, had written in orthodox Marxist vein: 'The fundamental criterion by which classes are distinguished is the place they occupy in social production.' In November 1966, Mao's evil genius, Kang Sheng, said that Lenin's definition had proved inadequate, for class differentiation also fell under political and ideological categories, and in 1970 Kang stated more precisely:[41]

The existence of the capitalist class is particularly manifest in relations of

46

economic exploitation. In socialist society, although there are economic contradictions among the various classes, the existence of classes shows itself ideologically and politically.

But just where and how did the existence of classes thus defined 'show itself' in China, and what was the nature of class struggle in such a society? Before giving my views regarding these issues, I should like to discuss the interpretations of Zhang Chunqiao and Yao Wenyuan on the one hand, and Joseph Esherick on the other.

In grouping together for purposes of analysis the views of Esherick and those of the two leading ideologists of the Gang of Four, I do not mean to suggest that their ideas were identical, still less that Esherick has simply followed the line of Zhang and Yao. They do raise, however, several of the same questions. Moreover, while noting that Yao's argument 'is now most decidedly out of favour in China', Esherick expresses the opinion that it is 'generally consistent with much of Mao's thinking', though somewhat more one-sided than Mao's own approach, and characterizes it as 'one of the most important Chinese theoretical discussions of capitalist restoration'.[42] It therefore seems appropriate to look at Esherick's interpretation side by side with that of Zhang and Yao.

Two questions are central to any attempt to clarify the meaning of terms such as 'new bourgeois elements' or 'the restoration of capitalism'. First of all, did the 'bourgeoisie' in China, in the 1960s and 1970s, have its social roots primarily in the 'vested interest groups' of the new, socialist society, or in the surviving bourgeois and capitalist elements from the old society? Or, as I put it earlier, was the bourgeoisie mainly to be found within the Party and state bureaucracy, or were the 'capitalist roaders' in the Party merely the tools of, or the spokesmen for, the old bourgeoisie? Secondly, what sort of 'capitalist' system did the supposed partisans of 'restoration' want to establish?

Regarding the first of these questions, Esherick's position is quite clearly different from that of Zhang and Yao. He draws a sharp distinction between Lenin, who 'always identified the primary threat of capitalist restoration with the spontaneous capitalist tendencies of the "small-producer economy"', and Mao, who 'rarely shows anything comparable to Lenin's considerable antipathy toward the petty bourgeoisie', found the Bolsheviks' 'alliance with state capitalism ... and ... reliance on state power', resulting from fear of the petty bourgeoisie, an 'unfortunate policy', and therefore saw the main danger of restoration in the emergence of a new class in the Party and state bureaucracy.[43]

This approach leads Esherick to put forward the idea of the new bourgeoisie as a potential hereditary ruling class in a socialist society which has taken the road of revisionism and 'restoration'. He calls attention to a striking passage in Mao's notes of 1960 on the Soviet textbook regarding the defects of the children of cadres:[44]

The children of our cadres are a source of great concern. They have no experience of life and no experience of society, but they put on very great airs, and have very great feelings of superiority. We must teach them not to rely on their parents, nor on revolutionary martyrs, but to rely entirely on themselves.

Recalling Mao's disparaging comments in the 1960s, to Snow and others, about the defects of China's youth, Esherick concludes:[45]

Mao is concerned that the sons and daughters of cadres might inherit the status and privileges of their parents. Obviously, to the extent that this happened, a 'vested interest group' – by perpetuating itself over several generations – would transform itself into a class. The problem would thus be more than ideological; it would be a structural problem of the whole society.

In his view, Mao's conception of the 'unmediated authority over the means of production' enjoyed by cadres and technicians provides, at least by implication and in broad outline, a theoretical explanation of the process by which such 'new bourgeois elements' can transform themselves into a 'new bourgeois class' capable of passing on its control over the means of production to future generations.[46] The difficulty with this argument is that it fails to provide any serious analysis of the relation between such a bureaucratic stratum and the rest of society, or any real justification for calling it a class.

I submit that this whole vision of Chinese society today is, in fact, a metamorphosis of Marx's theory of the Asiatic Mode of Production. Esherick would surely reject the suggestion that he is following in the footsteps of Karl August Wittfogel, who characterized Mao's China as 'a stronger Oriental Despotism', but in my opinion his approach offers distinct parallels with Wittfogel's treatment of the imperial bureaucracy as a law unto itself, rather than as the emanation of the landlord class.

In essence, my criticism of Esherick can be summed up by saying that he confuses Mao's, and Lenin's, stress on the *primacy* of politics with the divorce of politics from the economic and social system. Indeed, he goes so far as to claim that Mao was 'not averse to treating the state as similar to a class'.[47]

I do not mean to suggest that an argument cannot be made for focussing on control rather than ownership of the means of production, and treating existing socialist systems as forms of 'state capitalism', ruled by a 'new class' or 'new bourgeoisie' defined in this context. From Djilas to Bahro, a great many people have made such an argument over the past three decades. Moreover, on the basis of all the available evidence, it appears that Mao himself leaned in this direction in his later years. Not only did he accept Kang Sheng's view that, in a socialist society, classes manifested themselves 'ideologically and politically' rather than in terms of relation to the means of production, but he actually did subscribe to the view, put forward in 1975–6, that in China the bourgeoisie was to be found primarily, or decisively, in the Party. Moreover, he accepted the logical conclusion from such a premise, namely that these 'new bourgeois elements' exploited the workers and peasants through the mechanism of the socialist system, i.e. of the state apparatus.[48]

Even if we conclude, however, that Mao held such a view in the early 1970s, he did not, to my knowledge, produce a systematic argument to justify it – indeed, by that time he was probably incapable of doing so. And Esherick, though in some respects he has correctly grasped Mao's instinctive reactions, does not make such an argument for him in the article under discussion.

The study by Richard Kraus, *Class Conflict in Chinese Socialism*, which reached London only in mid-1982 when this article was in the final stages of revision, is a far more important contribution to the subject in general than Esherick's article. On many aspects of the problem of the relation between stratification based on class origins, and 'class as political behaviour', Kraus offers extremely subtle and illuminating analyses. I believe that he errs, however, as does Esherick, in arguing that in his later years, Mao defined class primarily in terms of the privileges, and the control of the means of production, derived by cadres from their relationship to the state. Nor does he, in my opinion, put forward even as cogent an analysis as Esherick to justify this view.[49]

On the problem of the relation between the old and the new bourgeoisie, Zhang and Yao adopt in the last analysis the opposite approach from that of Esherick. Both of them discuss at considerable length the selfish and corrupt behaviour of privileged strata among the leading cadres, in terms derived from Mao and not unlike those used by Esherick. At the same time, however, they treat these as a 'bunch of extremely isolated persons', who are largely the tools of those remnants of the 'overthrown reactionary classes' who desire the restoration of capitalism in the literal sense. If the role of 'bourgeois right' and material incentives is not restricted, writes Yao Wenyuan:[50]

capitalist ideas of making a fortune and craving for personal fame and gain will spread unchecked; phenomena like the turning of public property into private property, speculation, graft and corruption, theft and bribery will increase; the capitalist principle of the exchange of commodities will make its way into political and even into Party life, undermining the socialist planned economy; acts of capitalist exploitation such as the conversion of commodities and money into capital, and labour power into a commodity, will occur ... When the economic strength of the bourgeoisie has grown to a certain extent, its agents will demand political rule, demand the overthrow of the dictatorship of the proletariat and the socialist system, demand a complete changeover from socialist ownership, and openly restore and develop the capitalist system.

If Esherick's analysis is theoretically questionable, this one is impossible to accept on practical grounds. Was the pre-1949 bourgeoisie really so powerful in China, a quarter of a century after the revolution? Above all, how could the 'new class elements' within the Party, who revelled in their power and perquisites under the existing order, willingly participate in the restoration of actual capitalism, involving the private ownership of the means of production? Surely they must have realized that, in such a system, they would be very ill-equipped to compete with the 'real' capitalists of yore, and would soon lose their privileged position?

But, although both Esherick's analysis of the 'new class' and that of Zhang and Yao are, in my opinion, inadequate and unacceptable, both build explicitly on tendencies apparent in Mao's own writings from the late 1950s onward. The problem lies, perhaps, in the fact that Mao not only contradicted himself on many occasions, but frequently intended his words to be taken as metaphor or parable,

50

rather than literal truth. Let me return, then, once again, to Mao's own ideas during his last years.

As noted above, Mao appears to have agreed with the view propagated in 1975–6, according to which the 'bourgeoisie' as a whole was to be found primarily within the Communist Party. To begin with, this formulation implies that, in some meaningful sense, the privileged elements in the Party and the remnants of the bourgeoisie as it existed before 1949 (or before 1955) belong to a single class, since if we were talking only about the 'new class', this would, by definition, be located almost wholly within the Party. Such was, I think, indeed Mao's view. I should like to suggest a parallel here with his attitude toward the relation between classes and political behaviour in 1926. At that time, he had treated the enthusiasm of each group for the revolution as directly proportional to the degree of misery suffered by that particular stratum of Chinese society. Similarly, I would say that, in his later years, Mao established an almost linear proportion between the material advantages enjoyed by various groups or individuals, and the degree of revisionism or 'capitalism' they might be expected to manifest in their thinking. From this it might follow that, if Mao did not believe that the majority of those members of Chinese society who were in some sense 'bourgeois' were to be found in the Party, he did see the Party as the nesting-place for the biggest, most virulent, and most threatening members of the 'bourgeoisie'.

As I argued earlier, the view which seems to predominate in the rather contradictory analysis of Zhang and Yao, to the effect that the 'bourgeois' elements in the Party are, in large part, simply the spokesmen or tools of the old exploiting classes, cannot be taken seriously. There is, to my knowledge, no evidence that Mao ever formulated such a proposition, and his approach was undoubtedly closer to that of Joseph Esherick. On the other hand, I do not think he ever really answered, any more than Esherick does, the question of how the bureaucratic stratum he disliked so much could transform itself not only into a ruling class, but into an hereditary ruling class.

To a large extent, Mao's primary concern was with the resurgence in China, after the revolution, of 'bourgeois' attitudes such as attachment to money, pleasure, and privilege. Such deviations would, in his view, be encouraged by inequality of material rewards – hence his support, qualified or not, for the campaign of 1975 against

51

'bourgeois right'. But in the last analysis he was more concerned with the struggle to transform 'hearts' or 'souls'. If he focussed his attention on 'bourgeois elements' in the Party, this was partly because such people enjoyed more of the privileges likely to corrupt them, and more of the power and influence which would enable them to corrupt others.

At the same time, it should be stressed that in Mao's view, the source of corruption was not merely the rewards of power, but power itself. In one of the very last directives published in his lifetime, Mao was quoted in May 1976 as saying that revolutions would continue to break out in future because 'Junior officials, students, workers, peasants, and soldiers do not like big shots oppressing them'.[51] There is no way of verifying the authenticity of this text, but it sounds very much like the irrepressible Mao. Although he remained committed to the need for leadership, and for a strong state, he was plainly sceptical that anyone – except the emperor himself – could be trusted with power.

Whatever our conclusions regarding the nature of the 'new class' and its place in Mao's scheme of things, however, the 'class status' of the overwhelming majority of the citizens of the Chinese People's Republic would necessarily continue to be determined by their family origins, and/or by their subjective attitudes. Beyond any doubt, Mao was fully responsible both for the use of inherited class status, or *chengfen*, as the basis for something not far short of a caste system, governing the lives and prospects of all Chinese citizens, and for superposing on this institutionalized system for assigning class labels an ongoing process of evaluating thought and behaviour which to some extent eroded or cancelled out the basic system, and to some extent reinforced it.

About the system based on inherited class status I shall say no more. It is a complex historical, cultural, and sociological phenomenon which has already been the subject of several studies by scholars.[52] This system was to a substantial degree dismantled in January 1979, for reasons which have been spelled out at length in the Chinese press, and are not unlike those given by Deng Xiaoping in 1956 for the elimination of class discrimination from the Party statutes.

About the role of subjective criteria I would like to say a few final words. The manifestation of this approach, so characteristic of Mao over half a century, are to be found everywhere during the Cultural Revolution decade. To mention only a few aspects or symptoms, there was the emphasis on 'a great revolution which touches people to their very souls', in other words, which constitutes a process of subjective transformation leading to a new political identity. There was the whole range of ideas and policies summed up by the slogan, 'Fight self, oppose revisionism', with the implication that 'bourgeois' tendencies were to be found even in the hearts of veteran revolutionaries and proletarian fighters, if not in the Chairman himself. There was the idea, put forward by Mao in December 1968, that the sons and daughters of urban workers should be given 'a profound class education' by the peasants in the country-side.[53] And finally, there was the stress on devotion to the Leader and his Thought, symbolized by the value of 'loyalty' (*zhong*). Not only were 'proletarian revolutionaries' such as the Red Guards to learn by heart the 'Little Red Book', so they could repeat a suitable saying on every occasion and thereby demonstrate their mastery of Mao Zedong Thought. They were also to be 'boundlessly loyal to Chairman Mao', and this quality above all others was the touch-stone for distinguishing genuine from sham revolutionaries in the China of the late 1960s and the early 1970s.

In the *Zuozhuan*, under the ninth year of Duke Cheng, it is written: *Wusi, zhong ye*. Loosely translated, this can be taken to mean 'He who is selfless is truly loyal [to the ruler].' The Chinese, in Mao's last years, read this equation both backwards and forwards. On the one hand, he who was genuinely selfless, who was willing to serve the people like Lei Feng as a 'rustless screw', was a true and loyal disciple of Chairman Mao and a genuine proletarian revolu-tionary. But conversely, he who was loyal to Mao Zedong and Mao Zedong Thought became, by that very fact, selfless and proletarian, and endowed with all the other revolutionary virtues. In this respect, as in the use of the parallel with Qin Shihuang, Mao truly moved, at the end of his life, from expressing Marxist ideas in a language accessible to the Chinese people to a somewhat eclectic position in which traditional values and ideas played an increasingly large part.

One or two statements by Mao on the relation between class and nation are of interest here. In March 1958 at Chengdu, he declared: 'First classes wither away, and then afterward the state withers away, and then after that nations (*minzu*) wither away, it is like this in the whole world.'[54] Talking to Edgar Snow on 18 December 1970, Mao put the matter as follows:[55]

What is a nation (*minzu*)? It includes two groups of people (*liang bufen ren*), one group consists of the upper strata, the exploiting classes, a minority. These people know how to speak [effectively], and to organize a government, but they don't know how to fight, or to till the land, or to work in a factory. More than 90 per cent of the people are workers, peasants, and petty bourgeoisie; without these people, it is impossible to constitute a nation (*zucheng minzu*).

Mao's remarks of 1970 illustrate once again his tendency, in his later years, to see class struggle as a conflict between a small group of 'big shots' and the people as a whole. But they also underscore, as does his comment of 1958, the fundamental importance he attached to the nation as a primary form of social organization.

I do not mean to suggest, of course, that we should draw from these tendencies the conclusion, commonly put forward by the Soviets and their supporters, Trotskyites of various persuasions, and others, that Mao was, after all, nothing but an old-fashioned Chinese peasant leader with very little Marxism about him. Although he consistently strove to adapt Marxism to Chinese conditions, and although the imprint of Chinese culture was always plainly visible in his writings, his Thought, from the mid-1930s to the mid-1960s, nevertheless appears primarily as a revolutionary ideology of Western origin.

The fact remains that, during the Cultural Revolution decade especially, the synthesis toward which Mao had been bending his efforts for many decades largely fell apart, at least as regarded his own ideas and attitudes. Moral and political criteria drawn from the *Zuozhuan* and similar sources thus loomed very large in 1976, when Mao, as he put it to Edgar Snow, 'saw God', or 'saw Marx' (or perhaps both of them), and a new era opened under his successors. To avoid such neo-traditionalist deviations, while continuing to attach positive value to aspects of the Chinese heritage, is one of the more delicate imperatives in the process of separating the positive elements of Mao Zedong's Thought from the 'errors of his later years' in which the current leadership is now engaged. The objective or (as the Chinese themselves would say) scientific character of the criteria employed henceforth for determining social class, and the extent to which anything resembling an hereditary caste system is repudiated not only in theory but in fact, will be important touchstones for the success of this whole operation of placing the Chinese revolution and Chinese society on a new, more modern, and more democratic basis.

4

THE DECLINE OF VIRTUOCRACY
IN CHINA

Susan L. Shirk

When Mao Zedong led the People's Liberation Army into Peking in 1949, he brought with him extraordinarily ambitious plans. He aimed to achieve national self-reliance, build a new state structure, and modernize the economy, but even more, he wanted to transform Chinese society. Mao intended to create a just and moral social order in which everyone, even the illiterate peasant, was deemed equally worthy of social respect; in which individuals were motivated by the desire to serve the people rather than by self-interest; and in which people cooperated rather than competed. The scope and boldness of Mao's vision was awesome; it captured the imagination of people inside and outside China. In most societies the government's role is much more limited and political leaders manage people's selfish and competitive drives rather than trying to change them. But Mao was determined to transform people, to make them more virtuous, and he believed that it was the responsibility of the Communist Party to lead people toward virtue.[1]

Since the death of Mao and the defeat of his radical allies in 1976, talk about moral transformation is seldom heard in China, and political pessimism and cynicism are more pervasive than most observers would ever have believed. For example, students in one college class, when asked on a Young Communist League questionnaire to indicate whether they believed in socialism, capitalism, religion, atheism, or fatalism, overwhelmingly (85 per cent) chose fatalism; no one chose socialism.[2] Newspaper articles with titles like 'On Some Understanding of the Superiority of the Socialist System' and 'Marching into the 1980's Full of Confidence' try to defend socialism and the Communist Party to those who have fundamental doubts about them.[3] Other articles describe shocking examples of cynicism: e.g., when a youth fell through the ice while skating, bystanders taunted the soldiers who tried to save him by shouting, 'Big soldiers, run fast, it's time to win a medal', and derided the old worker who joined in the rescue by saying, 'He just wants to join the Party.'[4] According to the official press and interviews with Chinese citizens, there is a 'crisis of belief' in China today, especially among members of the younger generation who were raised under socialism.

More than thirty years after Liberation we must conclude that Mao's crusade to transform social consciousness has left people more rather than less alienated from one another and from the state. How can we explain the failure of the Maoist vision? Facile conclusions about the intractability of human nature or the universal imperatives of economic growth will not suffice. Rather we must seek an explanation in the nature of revolutionary regimes, such as that which Mao founded, which attempt to purify society.

A revolutionary movement coming to power (whether as a communist state, as in China, or a religious one, as in Iran) tries to transform society by taking control of the distribution of opportunities and awarding the best opportunities to those who exemplify the moral virtues of the movement.[5] But as Michael Walzer says, by using state power in this way, the leaders 'freeze' the revolution.[6] The noble endeavour is stymied not just by the practicalities of political rule and economic development or by the gradual erosion of revolutionary enthusiasm, but by the social ramifications of the reign of virtue.[7]

This paper will argue on the basis of the Chinese case that regimes which attempt to bring about the moral transformation of society by awarding life chances to those who are the most morally virtuous are inherently unstable. If social systems are differentiated by their principle of occupational selection, then a system like that in China might be called a 'virtuocracy' in contrast with 'meritocracies' which select according to professional or intellectual ability, and 'feodocracies' which select according to ascriptive status such as caste, class origin, race, native region, sex, or religious origin. Even in a virtuocracy, merit and ascriptive status may also be considered when people are assigned to occupational roles, but a major criterion is a person's moral worth. No one who is not judged morally acceptable is allowed to succeed. As the Chinese put it, everyone must be 'red' as well as 'expert'.

I will argue that virtuocracy is inherently unstable because it produces opportunism, sycophancy, patronage, avoidance of activists and privatization within social organizations, and thereby alienates people from one another and the regime. The chapter begins by laying out the objectives of virtuocracy and the properties of virtuocratic distribution, especially the vagueness and subjectivity of standards of moral worth. Then I describe the effect of virtuocratic distribution on social behaviour before the Cultural Revolution. I go on to consider the Cultural Revolution decade (1966–76) as the apotheosis of virtuocracy and to analyse the social consequences of this movement which made political criteria the sole basis for selection and promotion. Then I analyse the distribution policies which have emerged in China since 1976 as a political response to the virtuocratic practices which have prevailed in the past. Many recent policy changes especially in educational selection, work payment, and job promotion represent the decline of virtuocracy and the rise of meritocracy in China. In the final section of the chapter I examine the resistance of Communist Party officials to the meritocratic trend and speculate about the future of virtuocracy in China.

THE NATURE OF VIRTUOCRACY

A regime's choice of a principle of occupational selection has profound social ramifications. The choice of how to distribute life chances is made very explicit in an authoritarian system like China's where there is no education or labour market. Government bodies make all decisions about educational and job selection and promotion. The political leadership must decide on what basis to assign opportunities: Randomly? By election? By birth? By professional or intellectual merit? By moral virtue? In practice there are three major principles of occupational selection: virtuocracy, meritocracy, and feodocracy.[8] These three principles parallel Max Weber's three types of authority: charismatic (virtuocratic), bureaucratic (meritocratic), and traditional (feodocratic).[9] Each principle implies a different mode of managing the frustration of those who fail to win the more desirable opportunities, and structures different rules of the game in which people pursue their goals.

58

The decision of revolutionary leadership to introduce virtuocratic criteria into educational and occupational selection and promotion serves its political interests in several ways. First, it is a means to bring about *social transformation*. By rewarding political commitment, activism, egalitarian attitudes, and cooperative behaviour, the leaders of the Chinese revolution create incentives for all citizens to strive to realize these moral values.

Second, virtuocracy facilitates the leadership's efforts at *mass mobilization for economic development*. If the country is poor, economically backward, and lacking in capital and technical resources, one way to increase productivity is by mobilizing underutilized labour power. Virtuocratic appeals seem most appropriate to mass mobilization strategies of economic growth. Calls for volunteers to work longer, harder, or under more arduous conditions offer chances for people to prove their virtue. And it is easier for organizations to substitute cheap moral rewards for expensive material ones when rewarding virtue than when rewarding merit (the virtuous are satisfied – or have to pretend to be satisfied – with praise).

Third, virtuocracy contributes to the processes of *political consolidation and legitimation* in a post-revolutionary regime. Virtuocracy is much more amenable to political control than is distribution according to merit or ascriptive status. Because the definition of political virtue is broad and flexible, elites can use the virtue standard to promote their loyal supporters and demote those who are potential threats.[10] The creation of a political ladder of success helps isolate and weaken commercial, intellectual, or noble groups whose power derives in part from meritocratic or feodocratic status values. For example, the requirement that all college applicants be evaluated politically as well as academically makes it more difficult for intellectuals to build power bases in schools and universities, and for bourgeois families to maintain their traditional advantage over worker and peasant families. Virtuocracy is an important source of regime legitimation for a new regime. The revolutionary leaders have already demonstrated their virtue by risking their lives to overthrow the old regime. The egalitarianism of virtuocracy also helps legitimate a new system; the groups – in the Chinese case the peasants and workers – who did poorly under the old meritocratic or feodocratic rules, see that virtuocracy offers them a chance to get ahead.[11]

Thus, distribution according to virtue became a crucial element in the Chinese revolutionary leaders' strategy of social transformation, development mobilization, and political legitimation, which together formed a coherent radical alternative to Western capitalist strategy and came to be called 'the Maoist model'.[12] The consequences of virtuocracy, however, were not what Mao and his colleagues had intended. During the period of post-revolutionary stabilization, virtuocratic selection came to incorporate more criteria of intellectual-professional merit and family background. As Weber predicted, 'In its pure form charismatic authority may be said to exist only in the process of originating. It cannot remain stable, but becomes either traditionalized or rationalized, or a combination of both.'[13] The attempt to impose virtuocratic rules and the tendency to mix standards of virtue, merit, and family origin in practice engendered social conflict and estranged people from the regime.

These negative consequences stem first of all from the competitiveness of the opportunity structure in China. In all societies there is competition for the occupational roles which people prefer, but the competition is particularly intense in countries like China which have opportunity structures with the following three characteristics.

Limited opportunities

Although elite positions are limited in all societies, in systems like China which restrict the growth of the modern urban sector by controlling labour allocation and rural–urban migration, the desirable opportunities are particularly scarce.

High stakes

When the level of economic development is low, as it is in China, there is a vast disparity in living standards between the countryside and the city. There is therefore a social consensus that status divides along the rural–urban line: the winners get to work in the city while the losers have to struggle along in the countryside. The combination of migration controls and rural–urban disparity in living standards produces a 'stratification of places'.[14] People prefer white collar jobs to blue collar jobs, skilled blue collar jobs to unskilled blue collar jobs, industrial jobs over jobs in the service sector, but any urban job is seen as better than working as a peasant (or even as a factory worker) in the countryside.[15]

Monolithic distribution

If all school and job assignments are made by state organs and there is no education or job market, then there is only one mobility game for people to play and no alternative routes to success. Under these conditions, occupation is the primary determinant not only of income and consumption levels but also of social respect and political influence. If, as in China, there is little job mobility, then school graduation is the decisive point of career embarkation; competition among students is very intense because they know they will have no second chance. The more job mobility there is in adult work units, the more competitive will be social relations within these units.

When virtuocratic selection rules were imposed on this competitive opportunity structure in China, the result was social acrimony and the widespread perception that the contest was unfair. This result can be explained by three features and one tendency of the reign of virtue.

Most important are the *vague and subjective standards* of virtuocratic distribution. It is intrinsically difficult to devise a clear and objective test of moral excellence. It may be easy to tell the very bad from the very good, but degrees of virtue are much more difficult to measure.[16] All the standards of virtue must be behavioural, for example, how enthusiastically people respond to political directives, what they say in meetings and mutual criticism sessions, whether they volunteer for unpleasant tasks. The only way to judge thought is to evaluate behaviour. But there are many different ways to assess behaviour: one can take the act at face value, examine the effect of the act, or infer the motive. For example, if one wants to criticize someone with good outward behaviour, one can claim that the action had a bad effect and thereby 'demonstrate' that the person had bad intentions.[17] Because the link between thought and behaviour is problematical, people in a virtuocracy run the constant risk of having their actions misconstrued.

The vagueness and subjectivity of virtuocratic standards also make it easy to cheat. Compare a contest of political purity to one of intellectual or athletic skill: in a mathematics examination or a foot race the standards are clear and unambiguous, and the outcome can be seen by everyone; therefore contestants cannot win by fakery.[18] In political competition the rewards for the virtuous inevitably attract opportunists and it is impossible to devise a method for screening all of them out.[19] Because it is so difficult to distinguish the sincere activists from the false ones, there is considerable leeway for arbitrary judgments on the part of the authorities.[20] The inevitable promotion of opportunists into elite positions disillusions even sincere believers.

The subjectivity of evaluations of virtue means that political competition comes to be pervaded by playing up to authority as well as by opportunism. People try to demonstrate their moral zeal by flattering teachers or bosses or by running to them with tales of their fellow-students or fellow-workers.

A second divisive feature of the virtue contest is that it is judged by *judges within the group* as well as by outside authorities. In the Chinese virtuocracy people's moral character is evaluated by fellow-students and fellow-workers as well as by teachers or bosses. The politically excellent are recruited into vanguard organizations, the Young Communist League (YCL) and Chinese Communist Party (CCP); membership in these elite groups signifies moral achievement and is weighed heavily in university admissions, promotion to leadership posts, and distribution of housing and major consumer items. League and Party members are supposed to be well-integrated in the peer group, to be the friends and helpers of their classmates or colleagues. But they are also supposed to make moral judgments of their peers: they are consulted when the authorities write the annual or biannual conduct evaluations which are placed in each individual's permanent dossier; and they decide who is pure enough to enter the League or Party. Because they have the power of political judges, League and Party activists are avoided by many of their peers; for the security-conscious the safest strategy is to keep activists at arm's length.

The subjectivity of evaluations of virtue also permits virtuocratic elites within organizations to monopolize the advantages of the chosen few. Party and League members are supposed to take the lead in revolutionizing all citizens, but in fact they are reluctant to throw open the doors and relinquish the distinction of vanguard status. In Max Weber's terms the Leninist strategy of social transformation results in a 'sect' (an organization only for the truly righteous who pass a moral trial to enter) superimposed upon a 'church' (an organization open to all which is aimed at trying to save all souls, to make everyone a better person).[21] And the members of the sect (the Party and Youth League) are responsible for leading the church (the entire society, or at least 'the people' who are capable of salvation). The members of the elite sects, who are understandably ambivalent about expanding group membership and diluting their special advantages, find it easier to exclude people under virtuocratic rules than if they were operating under objective meritocratic or feodocratic standards. When aspirants find their actions continually unappreciated and misinterpreted by the activist peers who judge them, they grow frustrated and alienated from the system.

All things being equal, the type of individual competition least destructive of group cohesiveness is one in which winning and losing are intrinsic to the activity. For example, in a foot race, no judge is necessary because the winners are determined by the race itself.[22] If a judge is necessary, then social divisiveness is minimized if the standards for determining winners and losers are clear and objective, and if the judge is an authority figure outside the group; this is the case in all school academic competition and some work competition in factories. The type of competition most destructive of social unity is one in which the standards are vague and subjective and the judges are members of the groups, as in political competition.[23]

The third feature of virtuocratic competition which generates social conflict is *mutual harm*. In China and other revolutionary regimes virtue is defined by actions that are costly to one's colleagues. The virtuous are required to watch over others and to criticize them in public discussions and to authorities. Mutual surveillance (what the Puritans called 'holy watching')[24] and mutual criticism are central to the political life of virtuocratic institutions. Everyone is expected to participate. As one informant observed in an interview, 'The main difference in the political atmosphere on the Mainland and Taiwan is that on Taiwan everybody was supposed to say nothing while on the Mainland everybody was supposed to say something.' In order to minimize the divisiveness of the criticism process people usually criticize only the minor shortcomings of other group members. But those trying to prove their virtue have to violate these informal norms; in order to make themselves look good, they have to make others look bad. Criticism sessions are effective tests of political commitment because people recognize that social loyalties are a strong force in public, face-to-face encounters. To speak out against a colleague in a criticism session tells the authorities and your peers that you put political principles ahead of loyalties to your friends.[25]

As long as opportunities are limited, all competition – both virtuocratic and meritocratic – is zero-sum. One student's high examination grades decreases other students' chances for university admission; one worker's overfulfilment of production targets lowers the probability of promotion for all his fellow-workers. But in political competition the activist must choose a particular person whose chances for success he or she is going to downgrade by public criticism.[26] The necessity of choosing a specific victim makes virtuocratic competition seem to participants to be more threatening and mutually destructive than meritocratic competition.

There is a tendency for meritocratic and ascriptive (feodocratic) selection criteria to appear increasingly attractive in a virtuocracy, and groups who stand to gain under these other criteria become increasingly able to advocate their use. This is because it is difficult to devise standards for evaluating virtue which are not vague, subjective, and subject to abuse. Examination scores and family class origins are much clearer and simpler bases for selection than is revolutionary virtue.

Except for the 1966–76 period, there has been little support in China for totally abandoning intellectual and vocational standards in university admission or job promotion. Even Mao, who went further than anyone else in stressing the dominance of virtue over skill, urged followers to 'unite politics and technology', and derided people 'who had no professional knowledge' as 'pseudo-red, empty-headed politicos'.[27] Therefore the policy was to combine judgments of political virtue with examination scores or work performance records. Because in practice virtue was so difficult to measure, academics were often able to put more weight on meritocratic criteria, arguing that students actually manifest 'redness' in expertness.[28] And industrial managers intent on fulfilling production targets would often assign positions to employees on the basis of professional skill and productivity.

In a virtuocracy where opportunism is endemic, the argument for the use of an ascriptive test to cull the phonies from the true believers is very persuasive. Given the subjective standards of virtue and the populist egalitarianism of Marxism, it is possible for certain groups in a communist system to claim that although redness is achieved and not innate, some people are more predisposed toward it than others.[29] Compensatory favouritism for groups which were discriminated against in the past seems fair and just. Virtuocratic elites, who claim to represent the 'have-nots', often include themselves in the list of those who deserve special treatment. For example, in China, cadres and soldiers by identifying themselves with peasants and workers have been able to take advantage of 'affirmative action' policies. These policies not only give their children preference in educational and occupational selection, but also provide *legitimacy* for this preferential treatment (whereas back-door tactics are impossible to legitimize and have to be kept under cover). The groups who benefit from this belief in 'natural redness' – especially officials and their children – are always tempted to establish policies which judge people solely on the basis of birth status. But if they succumb to this temptation, those not blessed with innate virtue will give up in defeat, and one of the most powerful weapons of social transformation will have to be abandoned. Therefore a virtuocratic elite attempts to maintain an ambiguous combination of behavioural and ascriptive criteria for distributing opportunities. The Chinese regime's ambiguous 'class policy' which has been summarized in the slogans 'pay attention to origin (*chengfen*) but don't pay exclusive attention to it', and 'put the major stress on (political) behaviour', has been interpreted differently over time, with the relative emphasis shifting from political (and academic) achievement (1960–2) to class background (1963–4) and back again to achievement in 1965. The Cultural Revolution did not resolve this ambiguity.[30]

THE SOCIAL CONSEQUENCES OF VIRTUOCRACY

In a virtuocratic state with monopolistic control of job selection and promotion, everyone, even the aeroplane pilot or nuclear physicist, must pass a moral test. Not all people have to be virtuous – more is expected of the military officer or government official than of the engineer – but no one who has shown the slightest sign of deviance is allowed to succeed. This means that everyone has to partake of virtuocratic competition to a certain extent, if only to protect themselves from taint. Everyone must find a way to adapt to a social environment characterized by virtuocratic competition.

The general patterns of adaptation described below – opportunism, sycophancy, patronage, avoidance of activists, and privatization – appear in all Chinese organizations, work units as well as schools.[31] The specific behaviour patterns characteristic of particular organizations vary, however, according to the structure of virtuocratic competition and the rates of mobility within these organizations.[32] For example, although political competitiveness among high school students is intense because graduation is the point of career embarkation, it probably is less intense in rural schools (because only a tiny percentage of rural graduates will have a chance to escape to the city through the army or college) than in urban schools (which may send as many as 80 per cent of their graduates to university). Political competitiveness is also probably less acute in adult work units than in schools because of the low rates of career mobility within these work units. Andrew Walder has found, however, that workers and employees in Chinese factories must nevertheless compete to demonstrate their political loyalty in order to obtain the welfare benefits (housing and jobs for relatives in particular) which are allocated by factory leaders according to subjective virtuocratic criteria.[33]

Opportunism

Opportunism is inevitable in a virtuocracy. The career rewards for political involvement provide incentives for people to become activists, and the lack of hard objective standards for evaluating virtue makes it impossible to distinguish the opportunists from the genuine believers merely on the basis of outward behaviour. When opportunists gain political recognition, it demeans activists in the eyes of their peers.

Not all activists are the objects of social opprobrium, however. Non-activists try to differentiate the sincere activists from the hypocrites by applying traditional, rather than official, standards of behaviour. Ironically the pressures generated by the communist regime's political efforts to transform Chinese society have heightened people's appreciation of the traditional virtues of honesty, sincerity, and loyalty.[34] Where the air is filled with 'empty talk' (*kong hua* – false statements made in order to go along with or rise up in the system), people come to put a premium on speaking honestly. Where people are rewarded for presenting themselves as political zealots, those who admit their doubts are admired. And where one person's political success is accomplished at another's expense, people who stand by their colleagues are esteemed. The possibility of political opportunism under virtuocracy makes people acutely sensitive to the sincerity–hypocrisy dimension of social life.[35]

The activists respected as sincere are usually those who are relatively confident of success and who therefore can afford to temper ambition with loyalty to their peers. They do not have to report trivial mistakes or exaggerate their public criticisms of others. They can warn their friends in advance that they will speak against them in a criticism meeting. The activists despised as hypocritical opportunists are usually the less confident ones who have to go overboard to convince the authorities of their revolutionary zeal. They play up to their superiors, exaggerate their criticism of others, fill their talk with political rhetoric, and rush around performing conspicuous good deeds.[36] Established League and Party members who are reluctant to expand the circle of activists (because they want to monopolize the advantages of their elite status) often encourage the stereotype of the neophyte as hypocrite.[37]

Sycophancy and patronage

The subjectivity of standards of virtue means that people play up to the authorities who evaluate them and who allocate school admissions, jobs, promotions, and welfare benefits. Aspiring activists tell tales on their peers in order to demonstrate to superiors that they put political loyalty ahead of friendship. Sycophantic behaviour – what Chinese students scornfully deride as 'patting the horse's rump' (*pai ma pi*) – alienates activists from their peers.[38] In a virtuocracy underlings also are motivated to agree with and praise superiors rather than give them an honest appraisal of the situation. The communication of information upwards, a problematic process in any hierarchical organization, becomes all the more so in a virtuocracy.

From the perspective of organizational authorities, the subjectivity of virtuocratic standards allows them to become patrons who can reward their activist-followers. Almost everything in China – housing and consumer goods as well as education and job opportunities – is in scarce supply and is allocated by authorities in schools or work units, based, at least in part, on political criteria. As Andrew Walder has noted in his study of political control in Chinese factories, shortages place great power in the hands of the authorities who distribute these goods.[39] Under virtuocracy, they can reward their loyal followers (and thereby provide incentives for all the rank and file to comply with their wishes) by claiming that these followers have good political thought.

Avoidance of activists

While political activism can gain one great rewards, it also entails grave risks, especially for people who lack political self-confidence. Becoming an activist not only takes a great deal of time and effort, but also requires making oneself conspicuous, 'taking the lead', which is potentially dangerous if one is vulnerable to political criticism. In a system like China's in which the definitions of good and bad behaviour are broad, imprecise, and frequently changed, the safest approach for the politically unsure is to avoid attracting notice. But even those who do not pursue an activist strategy have to keep a clean political record. A minor mistake such as reading traditional novels disclosed in public criticism or a politically irreverent remark reported to the teacher or work group head, might be marked in your permanent record and ruin your life chances. Therefore, the behaviour of activists who need to criticize peers to prove their fervour creates real costs for those who are trying to protect their reputations from taint. This conflict of interests leads to tension and separation between activists and non-activists.

Whereas leadership in other systems is usually defined by a set of behaviours that benefit group members – for example, staying up late to put up decorations for a dance, writing articles for a union newspaper, organizing a picnic for a congregation – the definition

68

of leadership in China includes behaviours damaging to group members, such as public criticism and reporting errors to the authorities. Although it is in any individual's interest to impress the teacher or cadre by criticizing a colleague, it is in everyone's interest *not* to be the target of public criticism. Peer group norms therefore accept striving for success as necessary, but condemn people who harm others by making major criticisms of them in public, especially people who use exaggerated rhetoric in their criticisms. In order to prove their political zeal, activists have to violate these norms. Therefore, all but the most politically self-confident try to protect themselves by keeping activists 'at arm's length'. By avoiding activists they minimize the risk of activists discovering something about them which could be used in criticism sessions.[40]

Privatization

As of 1966, on the eve of the Cultural Revolution, virtuocracy in China had produced distrust and division within organizations, but as yet little alienation from the values of the revolution. If the reign of virtue led to opportunism, playing up to authority, and harming others the blame was placed on the participants or on the faulty implementation of policy and not on the basic premise of virtuocracy. The revolutionary virtues of selflessness and serving the people were revered, and it was considered entirely proper that the Communist Party try to shape people into this mould. Since people had internalized the official moral creed, many of them felt like deviants because they could not satisfy its stringent demands. Because the official morality did not recognize the legitimacy of any self-interest, people were ashamed of their ambitions and were constantly on guard lest their 'selfishness' be discovered by others.

The pressures of political competition and the self-perception of deviance lead people to seek out a friend with whom they can validate their beliefs and express their true selves.[41] Under a system in which anyone can gain career advantage by betraying a friend, loyalty to friends becomes more highly valued. When people see others all around them being forced to cultivate instrumental relationships, the expressive quality of friendship is made more vivid. Thus, virtuocracy generates privatism as well as social conflict. In a non-virtuocratic system with an autonomous economic sphere, most of the hustling for careers takes place in business, and people can express their moral sentiments in politics. But in a monolithic virtuocratic state like China, the competition for careers permeates the political sphere, polluting it with conniving and opportunism. The contamination of political life by careerism detracts from the emotional and moral hold of politics; people divert their moral sentiments from public life into the private world of friendship and family.[42]

Yet because people in China genuinely revere the official political values this retreat into the private haven of friendship, although consoling, is not ultimately satisfying. People yearn to overcome the tension between private loyalties and political beliefs. Mao Zedong may have intuitively understood this tension between privatism and political commitment generated by virtuocracy and responded to it by launching the Cultural Revolution and creating the Red Guards. During the Cultural Revolution the routines of selection and promotion which had infected politics with opportunistic competition were abolished; politics regained its romance; and the private morality of friendship and the public morality of politics were merged as Red Guards fought both to protect their friends and to realize the noble values of the revolution.

THE APOTHEOSIS OF VIRTUOCRACY: THE CULTURAL REVOLUTION

In the mid-1960s Mao Zedong diagnosed the most serious ills of Chinese society fifteen years after Liberation: the growth of bureaucratic elitism and class privilege, the persistence of bourgeois intellectual, artistic, and social values, and the degeneration of revolutionary elan into privatism and opportunistic competition. He diagnosed these maladies not as lingering vestiges from tradition but as the products of the current system. His prescription, however, was the intensification rather than the dismantling of virtuocracy. He advocated more political education, more mutual criticism and struggle, more mass mobilization, and more promotion of activists as the remedies for China's problems. By strengthening virtuocracy he hoped to counter the threats of meritocracy and feodocracy. He saw meritocratic practices such as academic examinations and industrial skill hierarchies as the basis for the continuing dominance of bourgeois groups in academic and some economic institutions. He viewed the feodocratic practice of class favouritism as largely responsible for the growth of a lazy, complacent elite of officials who were more concerned about opening doors for their children than serving the people.[43] The problems of selfish ambition, opportunism, and privatism he analysed as the consequences of too little rather than too much virtuocracy.

Mao's decision to lead a second revolution to purify Chinese society had disastrous consequences. The revival movement not only damaged the nation's economy and international position, but also destroyed people's trust of one another and their leaders. When the Cultural Revolution began, many people – especially youth – eagerly enlisted in the crusade to defend revolutionary ideals against the evils of selfishness and competition.[44] But ten years later there appeared to be few people who still believed that it was possible to realize these ideals through political action.

The virtuocratic crusade backfired because it was carried out not by a leader of a reform movement who could offer followers little more than spiritual redemption, but by the leader of the state who could use the weapons of power and opportunity to induce moral transformation. What was at stake for participants was not just their moral reputations but their life chances as well.

Therefore political competition did not disappear but instead became more cut-throat. All behaviour was construed as an expression of revolutionary commitment or opposition. Peasants who sold more grain to the state, workers who volunteered to work overtime, rural cadres who constructed Dazhai-type terraced fields, even if they were impractical in their locales, were all praised as 'red' (good); anyone who did not join in these campaigns or who questioned their logic or justice was condemned as 'white' (bad). At the same time, the gap between rewards and penalties was increased in order to arouse more enthusiastic commitment. A person deemed morally excellent might be catapulted to a high leadership position overnight, while someone accused of serious political sins would be stripped of all responsibilities, brow-beaten and sometimes physically abused in struggle meetings, and sent to do hard labour. Everyday life became a minefield of risks; one never knew when a colleague might try to protect him or herself by making a preemptive attack on one. As a result, although

SUSAN L. SHIRK

extreme virtuocracy increased outward political conformity, it exacerbated the problems of individualistic calculation and social conflict.

The triumph of virtuocracy over meritocracy also appeared to lead to less rather than more equality of opportunity. The consequences of abolishing all meritocratic protections were clearest in university admissions. The system which combined entrance examination with political screening was replaced by a recommendation process in which the applicant's fellow-workers or peasants determined who was the most worthy of university education. The recommendation method was designed to 'place the "moral" aspect in the forefront'[45] and to operate to the advantage of peasants and workers. In fact the subjectivity of the process and the absence of objective screening actually favoured officials who could wield personal influence. Local elites in rural villages where traditional patterns of power and deference persist were the major beneficiaries. Many production brigades recommended the son (rarely the daughter) of the brigade leader. At the same time, higher level cadres were able to exploit their connections to get their offspring into university through the 'back door'. University professors now say there were more children of workers and peasants enrolled in their departments before the Cultural Revolution than afterward.

Within work organization the vagueness and subjectivity of virtuocratic criteria allowed faction leaders to promote their favourite followers.[46] Because they were completely unconstrained by objective requirements of merit or birth, they could sponsor their followers into higher positions by defining virtue in terms of personal loyalty.[47] Even officials who made an earnest effort to promote the truly virtuous tended to promote their relatives and friends because it was possible to detect sincerity and insincerity only in those with whom one was most familiar. The more that leaders used their appointment powers to promote their personal supporters the more virtue seemed to people to be just a cover for self-interest.

Factional conflicts at the upper as well as the lower levels of leadership further deepened people's cynicism about virtue. Attacks on the motives and attitudes of Liu Shaoqi, Deng Xiaoping, Lin Biao, Chen Boda, Jiang Qing, and the many other top-ranking

72

leaders who were purged from office in rapid-fire succession, were so unconvincing and inconsistent that they naturally made people sceptical. Political competitors assume the mantle of the public interest in all systems, but in a virtuocratic state like China this tendency is pronounced. Character assassination is the standard technique of virtuocratic politics; it is necessary to impugn a rival's motives and character.[48] During the 1966–76 period, the gap between the rhetoric of political competition – filled with the language of moral claims – and the reality of Beijing power struggles seemed to widen. Citizens came to believe that their national leaders were just as hypocritical as some of the activists in their own schools and work units.

By the mid-1960s virtuocracy in China was eroding because of its divisive social effects. The extreme pursuit of virtuocracy during the Cultural Revolution accelerated this process so that by 1976 many citizens were estranged not only from one another but also from their leaders. People came to see that at national as well as at local levels, it was not really virtue that was rewarded but the ability to ingratiate oneself to a powerful patron. Mistrust was so widespread that the virtuocratic basis of regime legitimation was threatened.

THE MERITOCRATIC BACKLASH

After Mao Zedong's death, the defeat of the Gang of Four, and the return to power of Deng Xiaoping in 1976, there was a dramatic shift to meritocracy in China. This shift was initiated by Deng and the leaders allied with him who believe that the extreme virtuocracy of the Cultural Revolution decade led to economic disaster. It harmed productivity because 'giving prominence to politics ... rewarded the lazy and punished the diligent'.[49] It resulted in poor economic decisions because many of those selected as managers were politically reliable but technically incompetent. Managers had to worry more about becoming the target of political criticism than about producing economic results, thus they tended to stress sheer hard work and death-defying spirit rather than careful planning and technical skill.[50]

Multiplying the economic costs of virtuocracy were its social costs which were borne directly by ordinary citizens. There is today

73

a strong popular backlash against virtuocracy. The widespread enthusiasm for meritocratic standards stems mainly from their clarity and objectivity. After years of experience with the vague and subjective criteria of virtuocracy, people in China feel a strong need for a fairer process of distribution. Their experience with the use of political criteria has strengthened their belief in the norm 'to each according to his work'.[51]

Signs of the new meritocracy appeared everywhere. On a 1980 visit to Sichuan I found factories using academic tests (in mathematics, Chinese language, politics, and physics–chemistry) to select new workers and assign them to jobs. Technicians and engineers moved up the ladder of rank and salary according to their performance on technical examinations. The 40 per cent of workers who received wage increases in 1980 had their skills and knowledge assessed in written and practical examinations designed specifically for their job category. There was a rage for piecework which by 1980 had already spread beyond the industrial sector: in beauty parlours hairdressers were paid according to the number of heads of hair they cut, and in some hospitals, doctors and nurses were paid according to the number of patients they treated. Party cadres were warned to upgrade their technical skills and prepare for competency tests in the future.[52] New Party cadres were to be selected mainly from among graduates of universities and secondary technical schools instead of from among workers and peasants with little education.[53] More military officers were being recruited through special army schools rather than through the ranks, and demobilized soldiers with no technical expertise were having a harder time finding civilian jobs.

The meritocratic trend was clearest in educational selection, of course. Academic examinations were once again required for admission to secondary schools and universities; oral interview examinations were even used for selecting six-year-olds to attend elite key primary schools. Although applicants were still required to pass a political screening, the examination results were weighed much more heavily.

People believe that meritocratic evaluations are fairer than political ones: they measure actual individual achievement whereas political assessments can be won through family influence or fakery. According to the press, many people said, 'In the past, gaining

74

admission to a school depended upon a relationship. Now gaining admission to a school depends upon a student's own ability. If our sons and daughters fail the entrance examination, we yield willingly.'[54]

The tendency for virtuocracy to degenerate into favouritism and back-door deals caused people in work units to devise meritocratic practices which allow little scope for local authorities to exercise their own judgment.[55] Monthly bonuses were determined by counting the number of pieces produced by each worker (or by each small group) or by adding up the points earned by each worker for meeting various production targets (such as output, quality, conservation of materials and energy, and safety). The pieces produced or the points earned were recorded daily in the work group, so the relative standings at the end of the month were clear, unambiguous, and not subject to manipulation by factory leaders.[56] The distrust of local cadres was also reflected in the 1980 procedure for allocating wage increases. Points for fulfilment of production targets of output, quality, etc., were added up to determine a worker's contribution; then points were subtracted for violations of labour discipline, excessive sick leave and chronic tardiness which were the quantitative measures of labour attitude. These point totals were then combined with the worker's scores on the written and practical technical examinations which were based on national standards.[57]

The trend toward quantitative meritocratic measures also stemmed from the desire to eliminate the subjectivity and divisiveness of peer judgments. One of the most repellent aspects of virtuocracy was the requirement that colleagues evaluate one another. In 1978, when factories began to replace the principle of 'to each according to his virtue' with 'to each according to his work', there were no clear standards for comparing employees' work and distribution decisions were made democratically by work groups. According to factory workers, the allocation of bonuses and wage increases which resulted from group 'evaluation and comparison' (*pingbi*) inevitably were based on subjective impressions (*yingxiang*) and reflected personal relationships and factional loyalties. It was difficult, moreover, for people who expected to work together everyday for entire lifetimes to engage in face-to-face criticism; the lack of labour mobility intensified the concern for group harmony. Therefore when the stakes were relatively low, as they were with

75

bonuses (which constitute a maximum of 15 per cent of basic wage), workers often devised egalitarian solutions to the distribution dilemma (giving everyone the same bonus, or, if there were rules against that, rotating high and low bonuses among group members).[58] The distribution of wage increases by group evaluation caused more group conflict because there were higher stakes involved. The 1980 point system was supposed to minimize ambiguity and therefore divisiveness in group distribution, but even with it, group evaluations were acrimonious and protracted. Meritocracy may be less ambiguous and mutually destructive than virtuocracy, but the translation of meritocratic principles into specific distributive outcomes remains a difficult process.[59]

The renunciation of virtuocracy involved not only a turn to meritocracy but also a redefinition of ascriptive criteria for career distribution. The national leadership abolished reverse discrimination against people of bad class origin, but rather than totally eliminating ascriptive partiality and making all career contests universal, it instead institutionalized the practice of work units hiring the children of their own employees. Under the replacement (*dingti*) policy, when an employee retired his or her son or daughter is given a job in the unit. Employees' offspring were also favoured when factories recruited new workers. This kind of ascriptive favouritism turned work units into guild-like institutions in which membership could only be inherited. It also gave city-dwellers a virtual monopoly on the best job positions and closed the city gates to rural-dwellers. If these policies of ascriptive exclusivity are sustained, there will be more limitations on social mobility and more inheritance of occupational status in post-revolution China than in the traditional, pre-1949 society. Although family favouritism runs counter to the meritocratic trend it is a quick answer to the urban unemployment problem and is popular with city-dwellers.

PARTY RESISTANCE AND THE FUTURE OF VIRTUOCRACY

The turn to meritocracy presented Deng Xiaoping with some political advantages and some new challenges. It gained him the support of some groups while alienating others. On the positive side, meritocratic policies lend Deng the support of the intellectuals whom he needs to carry out the technical modernization of the economy, and of the foreign banks and companies whom he needs to relieve China's shortage of investment funds and foreign currency. The shift away from virtuocracy toward meritocracy has also earned Deng popularity with ordinary citizens, especially in the cities (where access to education is widespread), but probably even in the countryside (where access to education is more limited). The Maoist vision of a communist utopia was very appealing, but people now seem to feel that it was not worth the price of constant anxiety about being politically attacked by neighbours or fellow-workers. Years of experience with the realities of virtuocratic competition seem to have convinced people that state-led moral crusades are futile. People also seem persuaded by the meritocratic defence of inequality: that it is based on differences in individual achievement and is therefore fair 'distribution according to work'. As the example of other societies makes clear, under the meritocratic principle of equality of opportunity, those who lose contests tend to blame themselves rather than the rules or the judges, even if (like Chinese peasants) they in fact do not have an equal chance because their home environment or educational preparation is inferior.

Although the moves away from virtuocracy were popular, they also created severe problems of legitimation for Deng Xiaoping and the rest of the Party leadership. Because citizens no longer find credible virtuocratic 'masks' of purity and altruism, leaders now claim legitimacy on the utilitarian basis of competence.[60] Deng Xiaoping and his colleagues must convince people that everyone will benefit from their rule because their policy judgments are technically rational and conducive to the improvement of standards of living. When speculating about the prospects for China's economic success in the next decades it is important to remember that the basic problem of any large, centrally planned economy is that even with the smartest, most public-spirited officials it is impossible to manage the huge number of interrelated decisions which must be made.[61] The combination of meritocracy with authoritarian control of the economy legitimates individualism and competition and weakens the ideological basis for unity and loyalty without gaining any of the economic advantages of market systems.

Leaders who claim legitimacy on the basis of competence rather than virtue are vulnerable when they fail to deliver on their economic promises. According to the Chinese press, recent vacillations in economic policy and its inability to meet the expectations of the populace for higher living standards (expectations which Deng himself elevated by exaggerated promises) have caused many people 'to feel frightened and disturbed' that China is 'retreating' rather than progressing.[62] To assuage this fear, local cadres have been urged to carry out special 'education on the economic situation' to:

let the masses know what great efforts the state has made since the Gang of Four was smashed, and especially since the Third Plenary session, to solve problems in the people's living standards, despite the country's economic difficulties.[63]

The turn to meritocracy has also required the Chinese leadership to confront the issue of the superiority of socialism in the context of China's relative economic backwardness. Many people are now asking the question, 'China's economy has been developing so slowly, how can we say that socialism is superior?'[64] Under virtuocracy Party leaders could claim that China was superior to capitalist countries because it was more cooperative and egalitarian. But under meritocracy, egalitarianism has turned into an epithet, and it has become much more difficult to defend against the widespread belief that 'capitalism is superior to socialism'.[65] One line of rebuttal emphasizes that China's low living standard 'has not been brought about by the socialist system but by a number of historical and objective factors' such as 'a large population but little land'.[66] Another line of argument is that there is a trade-off between prosperity and security, and that although people in capitalist countries like the United States may be more affluent, they are always 'worrying that there won't be enough money when they get old or if they lose their jobs'.[67] Still another approach to the crisis of confidence in socialism is the revival of patriotic appeals. Press articles refer to China as 'our motherland' much more often than in the past, and plead with readers 'not [to] disregard our motherland simply because it is poor, as we should not disrespect our mother just because she is ugly'.[68] The victory of the Chinese women's volleyball team in international competition in 1981 became the occasion for a major campaign to stir up patriotic sentiments.

By 1981, meritocracy was causing serious political strains and Party leaders were able to reassert themselves by reviving virtuocracy.

Once again political reliability is the first requirement for selection and promotion.[69] Criticism, self-criticism, and political education have been reinstituted in schools and work units. Iconoclasm in literature and art has been strongly attacked. And, in the ideological realm, it is now argued that China over-reacted to the Cultural Revolution. Because the Gang of Four made the error of 'placing the role of spirit above everything', after they were overthrown people made the opposite mistake of ignoring the role of the spirit.[70] Because the schools had previously overemphasized politics and neglected academic study, after 1976 they 'overstressed intellectual development to the neglect of ideological education and political orientation'.[71] Because of the previous 'leftist mistake of neglecting the individual interests of the masses' people have recently 'tended to go to the other extreme of neglecting the interests of the state'.[72] Tapes and books with 'reactionary and pornographic content' filtered in from abroad and 'poisoned' people.[73] People started to 'look for money in everything' and took the pursuit of money as the sole aim in life.[74]

The return to virtuocracy serves the political interests of the top Party leadership in several ways. First, it addresses the legitimation problem by reminding people that 'material civilization' is not as important as 'spiritual civilization', and that although materially speaking, China may be inferior to other countries, in the spiritual realm, she is superior.[75] Second, it addresses China's problem of economic scarcity by substituting moral incentives, which are cheap, for material ones, which are more costly.[76] And, probably most important, it restores to the Communist Party its leading role.

Party cadres had felt threatened by meritocracy and had fought hard to resist it. Partynomial[77] systems always have to tolerate a certain degree of meritocracy in the economic realm, but when the domain of meritocracy is expanded – to education, administration, and even to the internal processes within the Party itself – those who draw their authority from virtuocracy must fight back. Merito-cratic policies diminished the power of Party officials over selection and promotion, and thereby weakened their control over sub-ordinates in factories, offices, and other organizations. If people know they will be evaluated on a meritocratic basis, according to their work output or examination grades, they have less reason to comply with the wishes of Party cadres and may even dare to flout them. Meritocracy also threatened the ability of Party officials to pass down their economic and social status to their children through education. Although children from cadre families continued to do well on entrance examinations, they were usually surpassed by the children of intellectuals. The turn from virtuocracy to meritocracy also was experienced by Party cadres as a direct loss of social status. Newspaper articles urging that technically skilled intellectuals be recruited into the Party must have made Party veterans, most of whom are generalists with no educational credentials and little technical competence, feel that they had been passed by. As national goals shifted from social transformation to economic modernization, the political elite saw themselves being eclipsed by the intellectual elite. The Party leadership recognized that the only way to regain social respect and political power was to return to virtuocracy and restore its role as guardian of socialist virtue. The reestablishment of criticism practices and political education returns to the Party its traditional function of political remoulding. The reintroduction of the criterion of political reliability into university admissions and job promotions enables Party cadres to reassert their control over subordinates and rebuild their informal patron–client ties.

Will this virtuocratic revival succeed? Can a socialist state restore the reign of virtue at the same time as it pursues an ambitious programme of economic modernization?[78]

The newest version of virtuocracy is in some ways more popularly appealing than earlier ones. The definition of political virtue is 'softer' and more respectful of traditional values than in the past. Under the umbrella of 'spiritual civilization', Maoist slogans such as 'serve the people wholeheartedly', 'the individual must obey the organization', 'serve the public and others without any thought for self', and 'fear neither hardship nor death',[79] are combined with traditional Confucian moral desiderata such as 'diligence and bravery, honesty and sincerity, endurance and industriousness ... support for parents and respect for the aged'.[80] The return to traditional moral themes and the attack on foreign immorality must resonate with the culturally conservative and xenophobic sentiments of some members of the older generation and the peasantry.[81]

There are also new rules of virtuocratic competition designed to make it less acrimonious. For example, the 'three do not's' for behaviour with the Party say 'do not seize on another's shortcoming and blow it up, do not put labels on people, and do not use the big stick'; they 'forbid the wilful exaggeration of anyone's mistakes, cooking up charges against him and attacking him politically and organizationally and even persecuting him'.[82] There are also warnings not to turn all disagreements into a struggle between two lines and in criticism of art and literature to criticize specific works rather than making wholesale attacks on artists and writers.[83] (Of course, no matter how sincere this effort to moderate political competition may be, as long as opportunities are limited and virtuocratic selection criteria prevail, people will be motivated to denigrate one another's characters in public criticism.[84])

Another reason why the recent revival of virtuocracy may be accepted by the public is that it is combined with meritocracy in selection and promotion (much as it was before the Cultural Revolution). There is no suggestion that academic or technical examinations will be abolished; to the contrary, several 1982 articles analysing bureaucratic selection practices in traditional China argued that the meritocratic method of 'selection by examination' was preferable to the virtuocratic method of 'appointing the recommended'.[85] Point systems and piecework continue to be the main bases for distribution of bonuses in factories.

We may predict, nevertheless, that the restoration of virtuocracy will be stymied by some powerful social and political forces. The intellectual elite will be a major source of opposition. Because, ironically, the anti-intellectual persecutions of the Cultural Revolution raised the stature of intellectuals, their prestige and their influence on mass public opinion are greater than ever. Their numbers are being expanded by the proliferation of training programmes for managers, undergraduate and graduate programmes, and foreign exchange programmes that the government has fostered as part of the economic modernization effort. Their social bargaining power has been enhanced by the recognition of the top leadership that technical expertise is a critically important component of the material base for economic development.[86] The intellectual elite is likely to demand as the price of its economic contributions meritocratic standards for educational selection and job assignment. They will argue that if China wants a strong, modern economy, it can not afford to return to a situation in which Party cadres can overrule experts and in which scarce resources are wasted by educating or granting responsibility to incompetents. To bolster their arguments they are likely to refer to the example of Western countries which have achieved economic modernization through meritocracy and democracy. In this, they will be supported by Western businessmen who want to run their joint-ventures according to meritocratic rules and who worry that their investments could be jeopardized by political interference.

Virtuocracy will be resisted at the mass level as well as by the intellectual elite. As long as school and job selection and promotion are based in part on evaluations of political virtue, the social consequences described earlier in this paper – i.e., opportunism, sycophancy, patronage, avoidance of activists, and privatization – will continue to detract from people's wholehearted commitment to politics. Political cynicism was exacerbated by the Cultural Revolution, so that a situation like that which has for a long time prevailed in the Soviet Union and Eastern Europe has now emerged in China: what is favoured by the Party is condemned by the masses and what is condemned by the Party is favoured by the masses.[87] Before 1966 young people were genuinely stirred by stories about the young martyr, Lei Feng; now they laugh at the efforts of the Party to resuscitate Lei Feng as a model.[88] In criticism meetings people now instinctively sympathize with the person who is being criticized rather than ostracizing him or her.[89] Individuals who are singled out by the Party as politically advanced workers or students are ridiculed and socially isolated as a result of this 'honour'.[90]

At the same time, the control motive underlying the Party's enforcement of virtuocracy has become more transparent. It is obvious to people that the Maoist ideas that are now being revived have become symbols of loyalty rather than guides to action, or as Chalmers Johnson has put it, more 'totem' than 'thought'.[91] Virtue has come to be defined as support for the Communist Party at a time when the prestige of the Party is probably at its nadir, due largely to rampant corruption among Party cadres (which has been reported in the press with remarkable candour).[92] Political evaluation is seen as a device for screening out trouble-makers rather than a measure of revolutionary enthusiasm. If the Party continues to keep itself in power by enforcing virtuocratic standards, the disjunction between official values and informal norms is likely to grow even worse. The future of this volatile amalgam of virtuocracy and meritocracy in a system which combines Party rule with economic modernization is very much in question.

5

DESTRATIFICATION IN CHINA

William L. Parish

To those thirsting for a truly egalitarian society, China once seemed
to provide new hope. From the start of the Cultural Revolution in
1966 through the fall of the Gang of Four in 1976, there was a radical
attempt in China to reduce the authority of teachers, technocrats,
and older administrators, to narrow the income gap between high
and low status positions, to reward with moral rather than material
incentives, and to substitute political commitment for achievement as
a basis for educational advancement and later occupational placement. Since 1976, the new leadership in Peking has begun systematically to dismantle this experiment in destratification. In schools,
achievement measured by exams has become the principal basis
for promotion. Young political activists who rose to power during
the 1966 to 1976 decade have been shoved aside and demoted.
Experienced teachers, technocrats, and other bureaucrats have been
restored to authority. Salary increases have been reinstituted for
some higher level positions, and the talk is all about how China,
still being a socialist rather than a full communist society, needs
material incentives to reward workers relative to effort.

The radical experiment of the 1966–76 decade and its subsequent
reversal pose two questions. First, during the radical decade did
China really become all that different from other societies? How
much was just propaganda puff and how much was real change?
Second, to the extent that there was change, what has brought about
the recent counter policy? Did the radical attempt at destratification
really cause problems for the society? Or, is the new policy simply
the result of the pre-1966 bureaucratic and intellectual elite, the
'new class' in Djilas' terms, trying to restore its privileges?

DATA

This paper attempts to deal with these two questions using data from interviews conducted in Hong Kong with 133 emigres from fifty cities and towns scattered throughout China.* Most of these emigres left China, some illegally as refugees, others legally with exit visas between 1972 and 1978, thus providing data on Chinese society at the end of the radical destratification experiment and at the start of the restratification policy. The unit of analysis is not the emigre him or herself, for they surely are a biased sample – too young, too many males, too many intellectuals, and so on. Rather, the units of analysis are, first 2,865 of the emigres' former neighbours for which we have such census characteristics as education, occupation, and income. These characteristics provide the answer to the question of how egalitarian China became in its radical decade. Second, the emigres provide data on their work units and how their fellow workers responded to the attempts to narrow income discrepancies and to replace material with moral incentives. These data help answer the question of whether there were real pressures from below which would favour an attempt to restratify the society and to provide more material rewards.

The emigres hold a range of political opinions. Some of those with legal exit visas, who can and sometimes do go back for visits, remain defensive about washing China's dirty linen in public. They hesitate to mention negative events in their past experience. Others, more often the refugees, are committed to doing just the opposite. The primary check on veracity is to press for concrete details of daily life in the emigre's former neighbourhood and work unit. Questions about the age of a neighbour's child, his education, and current occupation are likely to be immune to political position. Questions about recent events in the emigre's former work unit are less immune to bias. But by sticking to concrete events, one develops a picture of the 1966–76 decade which is generally consistent across emigres of different persuasion and which, by the way, is more moderate than the extremely negative story presented in today's official press.

Additional checks on veracity and the representativeness of our

* Funded by National Science Foundation Grant #SOC–7707888 A02 and National Endowment for the Humanities Grant # RC–25746–76–1200.

sample are possible. The part of the sample which covers the drainage basin of the West River running through Guangdong and Guangxi – the Lingnan Region – includes the widest range of occupations, cities and towns of different sizes. When weighted by population size to approximate the distribution of cities shown in the atlas for this region, several regional figures closely approximate figures reported in official media for cities scattered throughout the nation. For example, the average household size in our weighted sample is 4.4 persons per household, and this falls exactly between the reported figures of 4.3 and 4.5 in two official studies. In our sample, 76 per cent of the urban labour force is employed in state firms, while in official reports for 1977 a not too dissimilar figure of 79 per cent is given. In our weighted sample, 45 per cent of the non-agricultural labour force is in mining and manufacturing while in the media 48 per cent are reported to be in these two industries. In our weighted sample, the average monthly wage around 1975 was 46 yuan in state-run firms and 39 yuan in collectively-run firms. The official figures for 1977 were 50 and 39 yuan for these same sets of firms. And most importantly for the present discussion, there are some comparable figures for the distribution of per capita income. In our weighted sample, the richest 10 per cent of all individuals get 18 per cent of all income while the poorest 40 per cent get 29 per cent. The implicit figures in an official survey for these same two groups are 15 and 30 per cent, respectively.[1] Thus, in the economic area, with which we are most concerned, sample and published results are quite similar. It is on the basis of this similarity and on the basis of good results in an earlier village study using the same study techniques that we are so bold in generalizing from the results that follow.

The traditional hope for socialist societies has been that they would reduce overall inequality of personal conditions and give formerly dispossessed groups a new chance to participate fully in society. The counter fear has been that socialist societies would only substitute one elite for another, shoving new groups to the bottom and denying them equal opportunity for social mobility. How has China developed in terms of this twin set of concerns about overall inequality and opportunities for mobility? And, in considering equality of condition, how does China distribute both income and material goods?

INCOME

The Chinese system for distributing income was not born afresh in either 1949 or in the 1966 radical reforms. It borrowed both from China's own past and from the Soviet Union, with later patching and amending by the new revolutionary government.

Starting in 1949, former high government officials were expelled from office. In time, landlords and capitalists lost their property and some professionals lost their private practice. But many people including engineers, doctors, and professors were kept on at salaries similar to what they had been earning before. In 1956, the Soviet wage system was adopted. The old revolutionary free supply system was abandoned for a strict grading of administrative personnel into over twenty salary grades, of technicians into seventeen grades, and workers into eight grades, plus prizes and bonuses for exceptional performance. The Chinese were never very happy with this imported system, and began to soften some of its harder material aspects soon after its adoption. By the late 1950s, in the Great Leap Forward, the use of piece rates in industry was sharply curtailed. By 1963, the top salaries for government officials were reduced from some 600 yuan a month to a little over 400 yuan a month – compared to an average worker's salary of about 50 yuan a month. Yet, the system remained essentially intact until the 1966 Cultural Revolution when radicals gained control of the government and tried to restore the revolutionary equality and elan of the pre-1949 revolutionary period. All piece rates, bonuses, and prizes were eliminated. Higher and middle salaries were frozen, and some managers and administrators were demoted for a time. The only general promotions after 1963 were around 1971 and 1973, and then they were given only for a minority of low-wage, medium-seniority workers. There were no merit raises. A few political activists moved into leadership positions, but in theory even they were to retain their old worker salaries. Thus, the system we are sampling in the early 1970s is one which has been largely constant since the early 1960s except for the promotions of some low-wage workers and the elimination of bonuses for workers at all levels.

What was the net result of this system for income inequality? By the early 1970s, China was considerably more equal than other

Table 1. *Urban income inequality by type of country and measurement unit*[a]

| | % Proportion of total income received by: | | | | | | | |
| | Poorest 40% of the population | | | Richest 10% of the population | | | Gini index of inequality | |
	HH	PC	EAP	HH	PC	EAP	HH	EAP
China[b]	25	29	28	21	18	19	.25	.20
Developing market states[c]	15	15	11	32	33	43	.46	.54
Socialist states[d]			26			19		.22

[a] The measurement units are: HH = households by total household income; PC = population by per capita household income; and EAP = economically active population by personal income.
[b] The three Chinese weighed samples include 305 households, 1,374 total population, and 899 economically active population.
[c] Nations with a 1970 gross national product of US $1,200 or less, giving a total of 23 nations for HH, 3 for PC, and 3 for EAP mean figures.
[d] Five nations – see Table 2.

Sources: China – 1972–8 Chinese urban survey; others – Shail Jain, *Size Distribution of Income* (Washington, DC: International Bank for Reconstruction and Development, 1975).

88

developing societies. Those states which remained under a market system provided less for their urban poor and more for their rich than did China (Table 1). The poorest 40 per cent of China's urban households got 25 per cent of the total income distributed in cities, while in twenty-three developing market states, the poorest 40 per cent got only 15 per cent of urban incomes. A similar story is repeated with other measures of income distribution. China's expropriation of income-earning property in the 1950s, its restricted wage scales, and policy of equalization after 1966 had a definite impact on the urban distribution of income.[2]

But how did China compare with other socialist states which have also expropriated property and forced people to move into the public sector? Was the expropriation of property and socialization of labour sufficient to produce China's level of equality? Or did it take the special measures of the Cultural Revolution to produce China's income distribution? On the whole, China was slightly more equal than the average socialist state (see Table 1, last row). And in state by state comparisons, China was at least as equal as the most egalitarian states of socialist Europe (Table 2). Under Stalin in the 1930s and 1940s, Russia was a highly inegalitarian society. Egalitarian reforms in the late 1950s and mid-1960s narrowed income gaps in Russia, but still in 1970 Russian workers at the ninetieth percentile were earning 3.2 times as much as those at the tenth percentile. The states of Bulgaria, Czechoslovakia, and Romania were considerably more equal with the high-income earners receiving only 2.3 or 2.4 times as much as the low-income earners. China was at least as equal or more equal, with high-income earners receiving only 2.3 to 2.2 times as much as low-income earners. Given that economic development tends to increase equality and that the European socialist states used for comparison are all much more highly developed, the Chinese accomplishment is impressive. China is not a copy of the Soviet Union which it mimicked for a time in the mid-1950s. While the Soviet Union was becoming more equal in the 1960s, China moved even faster to avoid the more inegalitarian aspects of the Soviet model and to adopt reforms of its own to become one of the most egalitarian of socialist states.

The overall distribution of income among individuals is more revealing than the distribution of income among occupational groups. Much of the inequality in income is among people in the

Table 2. *Income distributions in socialist states*

	Decile ratios[a] ca. 1970	Gini index ca. 1964
USSR	3.2	—
Poland	3.2	.26
Yugoslavia	—	.24
Hungary	2.6	.21
Bulgaria	2.4	.21
Czechoslovakia	2.4	.19
Romania	2.3	—
China: economically active population	2.3	.20
China: state-employed population	2.2	.21

[a]Decile ratio = ratio of earnings by workers and staff at the 90th percentile to earnings by workers and staff at the 10th percentile.
Sources: 1972–8 Chinese urban survey; Shail Jain, *Size Distribution of Income* (see Table 1); Peter Wiles, 'Recent Data on Soviet Income Distribution'; *Survey*, 21, 3 (1975), p. 33.

same occupation rather than between occupations. Nevertheless, the distribution of income by occupational group provides a visual characterization of how resources have been distributed (see Figure 1). In China, there is no self-employed group of doctors, lawyers, and engineers to boost professional incomes. Yet (1) higher professionals are second in income only to (2) government administrative cadres (*xing-jeng gan-bu*). Next, (3) teacher, accountant, nurse, and other lower professional incomes are considerably lower. Personal incomes continue roughly on down through (4) factory and store managers (*ye-wu gan-bu*); (5) office clerks, postmen, cashiers, and sales clerks; (6) drivers, transport workers, and other skilled workers; (7) barbers, cooks, waiters, and other service personnel; (8) ordinary and semi-skilled blue collar workers; to (9) street cleaners, apprentices, housemaids, and other unskilled and casual labourers. With minor exceptions, this progression is similar to that found in other states. It is somewhat flatter than that found in the United States – Chinese labourers on the bottom make 46 per cent as much as

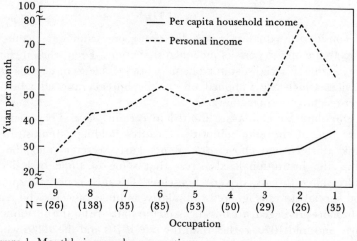

Figure 1 Monthly income by occupation

1 = High professionals   6 = Skilled manual
2 = Administrative cadres   7 = Service workers
3 = Low professionals   8 = Semi-skilled
4 = Managerial cadres   9 = Unskilled
5 = Clerical and sales

Source: 1972–8 Chinese urban weighted sample, economically active males.

administrators and managers while US labourers have a mean income only 31 per cent as high as administrators and managers.[3]

This describes the personal or individual distribution of income. The distribution of income by household is somewhat different. With many women working and with some co-resident sons working as well, family income has been averaged among several labourers working in different types of jobs. The result has been a per capita household income distribution which has been considerably more equal than the personal income distribution (Figure 1). It has been only the higher professionals with exceptionally few children and the administrators with their high personal salaries who have stood out from the rest of the population. It is this relatively equal distribution of per capita household income which is a frequent referent in later analysis.

CONSUMPTION

In considering equality in socialist states, one cannot rest content to examine only reports of income distributions. Even when income is available in socialist states, one may not be able to buy goods and services which are siphoned off by the bureaucratic elite before ever reaching the open market.

Our data for China are limited in certain ways. They include only one of the elite minority of cadres holding administrative ranks thirteen and above – the county Party secretary and above. Thus the institutionalized access that some of these high level cadres have to cars, drivers, household servants, cooks, banquets, and special stores is ignored.[4] Similarly, military officers, who tend to be more privileged, are missing. And our data are for the puritanical early and mid-1970s rather than the late 1970s and the 1980s when liberal economic policies made it easier to finagle the system. Nevertheless, as in the sample surveys for other societies, we include a wide array of workers and officials, including some middle level city and Party officials. If there is a systematic bias, and if the early part of the 1970s was not quite so equal as it was supposed to have been, then that should appear in our data and in the comparisons to other societies using similar kinds of survey data.

Housing is one good that could have been distributed in favour of administrative officials. By the 1970s, only a small proportion of housing remained private in the major cities, and the rest was allocated either through one's neighbourhood housing office or work unit. The waiting lists for residential units were long. A young couple having registered to marry could easily expect a one to three year wait before a place would open up for them, and many gave up and simply moved into cramped quarters with their parents. Our more cynical informants argued that personal connections could be used to gain better housing allocations from the neighbourhood housing office. Others asserted that favouritism played no role, noting that people with larger apartments at times had been forced to accept in those in greater need. Leaders, these informants argued, got slightly better places only because they had more money to pay the rent and because they were around in the 1950s when more places were available.

The statistics on housing density and facilities give qualified

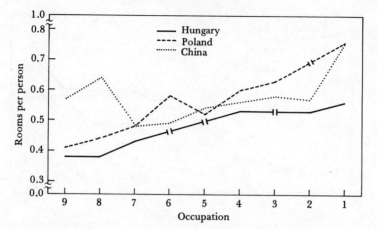

Figure 2 Housing density by occupation

China	*Poland and Hungary*
1 = High professionals	1 = Intelligentsia
2 = Administrative cadres	2 = Professional non-manual
3 = Low professionals	3 = Technicians
4 = Managerial cadres	4 = Clericals
5 = Clerical and sales	5 = Physical–mental workers
6 = Skilled manual	6 = Foremen, etc.
7 = Service workers	7 = Skilled
8 = Semi-skilled	8 = Semi-skilled
9 = Unskilled	9 = Unskilled

Sources: 1972–8 Chinese urban survey, economically active males; Walter D. Connor, *Socialism, Politics, and Equality* (New York: Columbia University Press, 1979), p. 284.

support to the egalitarian description of Chinese urban housing. The number of rooms per person (always less than 1.0 in these countries) rose less steeply or regularly with occupation than in Poland or Hungary (see Figure 2). Similarly, personal income in China was less tightly linked to housing density. The correlation between rooms per person and personal income was .19 in China while it was .24 and .33 in Finnish and Polish cities.[5] Neither were bathing and toilet facilities so closely linked. The absolute figures are not strictly comparable. Chinese bathing facilities may include just a tub in one's own kitchen or in the toilet. And our figure on toilet facilities is the inverse of the number of households using the

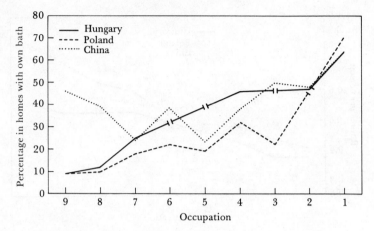

Figure 3 Bathing facilities by occupation

China	Poland and Hungary
1 = High professionals	1 = Intelligentsia
2 = Administrative cadres	2 = Professional non-manual
3 = Low professionals	3 = Technicians
4 = Managerial cadres	4 = Clericals
5 = Clerical and sales	5 = Physical–mental workers
6 = Skilled manual	6 = Foremen, etc.
7 = Service workers	7 = Skilled
8 = Semi-skilled	8 = Semi-skilled
9 = Unskilled	9 = Unskilled

Sources: 1972–8 Chinese urban survey, economically active males; Walter D. Connor, *Socialism, Politics, and Equality* (New York: Columbia University Press, 1979), p. 284.

same toilet, which is often a communal facility. It is, however, the differential between high and low status occupations which is of most interest, and this shows both a more irregular and a more equal pattern than in other socialist states (Figures 3 and 4). These figures all point towards relative equality of housing conditions in China.

Other more detailed tabulations show that this was a qualified equality, however. The most important determinants of both housing density and housing facilities are the administrative level of the city in which the dwelling was situated, the ownership of the dwelling, and per capita household income (Table 3).[6] Dwellings

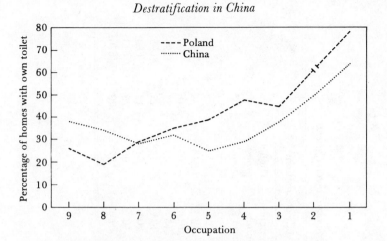

Figure 4 Toilet facilities by occupation
Proportion of households with own toilet in Poland and toilets per household
= inverse of number of households per toilet in China.

China	*Poland and Hungary*
1 = High professionals	1 = Intelligentsia
2 = Administrative cadres	2 = Professional non-manual
3 = Low professionals	3 = Technicians
4 = Managerial cadres	4 = Clericals
5 = Clerical and sales	5 = Physical–mental workers
6 = Skilled manual	6 = Foremen, etc.
7 = Service workers	7 = Skilled
8 = Semi-skilled	8 = Semi-skilled
9 = Unskilled	9 = Unskilled

Sources: 1972–8 Chinese urban survey, economically active males; Walter
D. Connor, *Socialism, Politics, and Equality* (New York: Columbia University
Press, 1979), p. 284.

in Peking and provincial capitals had fewer and smaller rooms but
better facilities. Privately owned and occupied houses (more common
in small towns) were better all around except for water and bathing
facilities. Greater income bought larger, but not necessarily better-
equipped dwelling space. Once these elements were controlled
in regression equations, higher professionals and government
administrators are shown to have fared no better than anyone else
in getting space and rooms for their family. They fared somewhat
better in getting a kitchen, toilet, and bath to themselves, for these

95

Table 3. *Housing by city and individual characteristics (metric regression coefficients)*

Dependent variables	Administrative level of city	Self-owned house	Per capita household income	Male occupations		R^2	N
				Government administrator	Higher professional		
Living area per person (square metres)	− .33	4.04*	.186*	.42	− 1.15	.34	(662)
Rooms per person	− .02*	.20*	.009*	− .01	− .05	.18	(730)
Room differential[a]	− .11*	.87*	.018*	.18	.03	.32	(396)
Kitchens per household	− .04*	.23*	.001	.13*	.17*	.15	(696)
Toilets per household	.08*	.16*	.002*	.20*	.31*	.12	(680)
Water in building	.16*	− .20*	.000	.10	.08	.29	(645)
Own bath	.18*	− .04*	.001	.07	.27*	.20	(576)

[a] See the text for explanation of indices.

*p ≤ .05.

Source: 1972–8 Chinese urban survey, economically active population.

Destratification in China

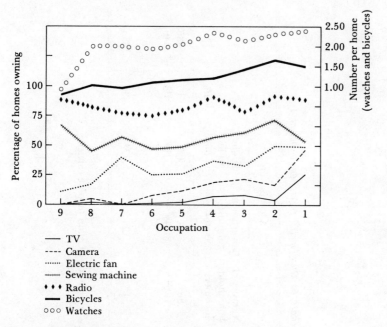

Figure 5 Family possessions by occupation

1 = High professionals	6 = Skilled manual
2 = Administrative cadres	7 = Service workers
3 = Low professionals	8 = Semi-skilled
4 = Managerial cadres	9 = Unskilled
5 = Clerical and sales	

Source: 1972–8 Chinese urban survey, households classified by occupation of male income earner, total N = 433.

often came in official quarters in which they were housed. In the 1970s, then, Chinese urban housing did not contribute seriously to material inequality. Partly as a result of occupying better official quarters, rather than public or private housing, higher professionals and government administrators had somewhat better kitchen, toilet, and bathing facilities. But they shared meagre space and few rooms just like everyone else.[7]

What of differences in other areas? Were administrative and technical elites able to gain special access to scarce goods? Or did the distribution system serve everyone equally? Some goods were

Table 4. *Family possessions by selected characteristics (metric regression coefficients)*

Dependent variables	Administrative level of city	Per capita household income	Number of household members	Occupation		R^2	N
				Government administrators	Higher professionals		
Watch and/or radio	.09	.02*	.26*	.21	.03	.15	(336)
Bicycle and/or sewing machine	.02	.01*	.16*	.54*	.31	.08	(340)
Fan, camera, and/or TV	.13*	.01*	.11*	.23	.79*	.30	(333)

*$p \leq .05$.
Source: 1972–8 Chinese urban survey, households classified by occupation of main income earner.

much easier to buy and more widely distributed than others. Though still rationed, bicycles were common, as were watches and radios (Figure 5). Of all households, 92 per cent had at least one watch and 76 per cent a bicycle. The variability among households came more in the number of bicycles and watches owned rather than in the presence or absence of these goods (see the right hand scale of Figure 5). Sewing machines, electric fans, cameras, and televisions were scarcer. Sewing machines, like bicycles, continued to be rationed through work units. Electric fans, cameras, and televisions were unrationed and high priced.

Visual inspection of the data in Figure 5 suggests that the distribution of consumer goods deviated only slightly from the per capita distribution of income. There was a somewhat wider gap between higher and lower level occupations in the possession of the scarcer fans, cameras, and televisions. But the more common, and frequently rationed, goods such as watches and bicycles were relatively equally distributed among the population.

This problem can be examined in greater detail with statistical controls. Large families with a good income in major administrative cities acquired the most possessions (Table 4). Once these background conditions are taken into account, we see that neither administrators nor professionals have been able to get more of the widely available watches and radios. Administrators have acquired more of the slightly more scarce sewing machines – an item that has been rationed. But they have not done as well as professionals in acquiring the scarcer, unrationed items of fans, cameras, and televisions. Among middle level officials, then, we get a picture of only minimal interference in the state distribution system. Administrative position has not led to significantly more material rewards in addition to salary. This distribution of material goods seems more equal than in some other socialist states. And these findings suggest that there is little reason to amend the conclusion drawn from the income data that urban China has been exceptionally egalitarian.

EQUALITY OF OPPORTUNITY

The discussion of equality of condition by itself is excessively static. By focusing on inequality at one point in time it misses change in the stratification system that was only beginning to emerge under the post-1966 radical reforms. It deals neither with whether the old under-classes were beginning to rise in society nor with whether a new elite class had begun to reproduce itself.

Class labels

In China, from the early 1950s to late 1970s, it was not too hard to tell whether the old class order was being inverted, since everyone carried a class label marking their class origin. In cities, the process of class labelling was never completely systematic, but in a series of political campaigns in the early 1950s, families gradually began to be identified with a label such as capitalist, merchant, peddler, worker, or poor peasant. Professionals, minor bureaucrats, and other intellectuals took the nebulous label of 'staff' which remained a relatively neutral label through the early 1960s. Other labels were more highly charged, with worker and poor peasant being the more esteemed labels while capitalist, landlord, and 'bogus staff' (for higher level bureaucrats in the previous government) labels were officially despised. Some labels could be earned, including the positive one of 'revolutionary cadre' if one or one's father became a substantial administrative official and the negative ones of 'counter-revolutionary' or 'rightist' if one was found in error in one of the myriad of political campaigns of the 1950s. The precise emphasis on these labels ebbed and flowed with the political wind, but with Mao Zedong's injunction to 'never forget class struggle', they were never forgotten.

From the radical's point of view, one's class label should affect all one's life chances, from education, through occupation, to one's rate of pay and promotion. In the early years of the regime, the educational differences among those of different class labels did narrow quite rapidly (Figure 6).[8] Continuing a process begun by the 1930s and slowed only by the Japanese invasion in the 1940s, urban residents of peddler, worker, and peasant origin began to approach the educational level of the formerly dominant capitalists, staff, and similar classes. By the early 1960s, in the children's generation, class was even less of an indicator of educational achievement. Yet, while the gaps between people of different class origin were narrowing, the rank order of educational accomplishment remained, with one major exception, the same. By the early 1960s, the children

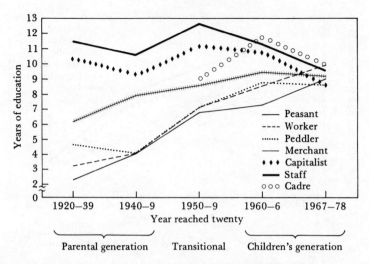

Figure 6 Years of education by class label and year reached age twenty

Source: 1972–8 Chinese urban sample.

of the new elite administrative cadres began to get the most education, attending elite boarding schools, which later in the Cultural Revolution came to be attacked as 'little treasure pagodas'. And with admission as much by rigid academic exams as by recommendation, the cadre children were often joined in these special schools by the sons of old professional and other intellectual staff members as well as by the sons and daughters of former capitalists. China was falling short of the goal of inverting the old class order and in danger of quickly adding a new elite class on top of the old. Worker, peasant, and peddler children continued to get fewer years of education and were relegated to second level schools which often combined work with study and had smaller budgets than the elite schools.

The issue of educational sorting came to a head in the 1960s as the state began to run out of urban jobs for new school graduates. The early 1960s was a time of retrenchment with many unprofitable factories being closed in the wake of the 1958–9 Great Leap. Much as in Western academia today, most of the best jobs in China had been taken by a young cohort in the 1950s. In the 1960s, that earlier cohort was far from retirement. There was little career mobility, and very few openings at the bottom for new entrants into the labour

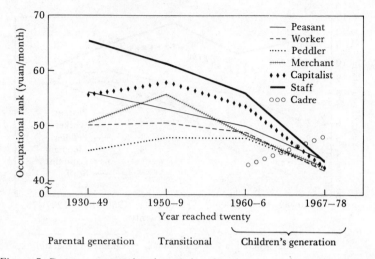

Figure 7 Current occupational rank by class label and year reached age twenty

Source: 1972–8 Chinese urban sample.

market. Those jobs which continued to be given, were again given to a goodly extent on the basis of academic merit and recommendations from one's middle school. And as in other societies, the children of the old elite, doing the best in school, continued to get the best jobs (see Figure 7).[9] The pre-1949 order was never thoroughly inverted even in the first years of the regime. Capitalist parents from the 1930–49 generation were hindered in getting and keeping the best jobs. But their children regained part of their lost advantage in the 1950s and continued it into the 1960s (Figure 7).

Meanwhile, the children of workers and peasants got the worst jobs or no jobs at all. With increasing urban unemployment, the administration turned to sending youth to the countryside, and it was often the worker and peasant children with poor academic records who were sent first. Under these circumstances, there was ever more serious debate over the proper emphasis on academic achievement, political commitment, and class origin. Emphasis on political commitment or on 'serve the people' might be ideal, but it was hard to measure and the children of intellectuals and capitalists, it was feared, were good at dissembling proper attitudes.

Class origin had its drawbacks as well, as some very committed people would be left behind.

Nevertheless, the answer of the Cultural Revolution was that academic excellence was to be abandoned since it selected careerists and people of bad class origin. Class origin was to be the principal screening device, with staff children now being declared suspect along with capitalist and other bad class children. After initial screening on class origin, promotion was to be on the basis of political commitment which could best be measured by how one performed at lengthy stints of factory and farm work both while in school and for a number of years afterwards. Work periods during school were increased, and the total number of years of pre-university education were abbreviated from twelve to nine or, in some places, ten years. University enrolment was drastically curtailed.

There were loopholes in the university admission and urban job selection procedures which relied on class origin and recommendation by leaders in the work unit where one proved dedication to serving the people. Urban children of intermediate class origin could get themselves declared peasants after a few years in the countryside and re-enter urban universities under new peasant quotas. Cadres could get their children favoured by intervening in the recommendation process, and increasingly in the 1970s the press accused them of doing just that – of 'going by the back door'. Nevertheless, the new policy had much of its intended effect. Everyone moved rapidly toward the new norm of nine years education (see the final points in Figure 6). With special schools closed, and exams watered down, worker, peasant, and other good class children were simply passed through the school system for their allotted number of years. Staff and cadre children continued to do somewhat better than the rest, but capitalist children were more positively discriminated against and lost their former favoured position.

Similar trends took place in the occupational world. The few urban jobs that were open tended to be worker jobs or similar ones with low starting salaries (Figure 8). Indeed, jobs as blue collar workers in factories began to be esteemed. Even the children of intellectuals and capitalists began to seek blue collar factory jobs, as such jobs provided both relief from the rigours of the countryside and long term security free from the dangers of political attack which so threatened bureaucrats, teachers, and other intellectuals.

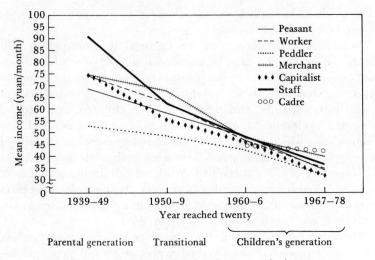

Figure 8 Current income by class label and year reached age twenty

Source: 1972–8 Chinese urban sample.

As was intended, capitalist and other bad class children suffered the sharpest reversal, losing their favoured occupational positions to others. Staff and other intellectuals' children got jobs no better than peasant children. And, as unanticipated, but later signalled in the press, cadre children gained in the occupational world the advantage they had formerly gained in education.[10] With the minor exception of cadre children, the new radical policies were having their intended effect of narrowing and inverting the class order.

Some of the regression towards mean educational levels and mean occupational levels seen in Figures 6 and 7 could have occurred just as a matter of course as a few elite sons and daughters fell into lower positions and a few low status children became educated and rose into higher positions. That is, the observed process could represent no more than individual social mobility which left the greater social order unchanged. Also, some of the apparent decline in occupational levels and income could be no more than the in-experience of the young who had yet to rise into the prime of their occupational careers. Can we show that more than this was

104

Table 5. *Average socio-economic status by generation*

	Generation				
	I	II	III	IV	V
			Chinese sample		
Year reached age twenty	1930–9	1940–9	1950–9	1960–6	1967–78
Mean age in 1972–8	*59*	*50*	*40*	*31*	*24*
Index of mean					
1. Years education	100	93	135	141	135
2. Occupational rank	100	93	96	89	75
3. Income	100	88	73	57	43
N (occupation)	(84)	(162)	(222)	(233)	(294)
			American sample		
Age in 1962	*55–64*	*45–54*	*35–44*	*25–34*	
Index of mean					
4. Years education	100	107	114	118	
5. Occupational prestige	100	99	105	101	
6. Income	100	111	107	88	

Sources: 1972–8 Chinese urban sample, economically active population; Otis Dudley Duncan, David Featherman, and Beverly Duncan, *Socioeconomic Background and Achievement* (New York: Seminar Press, 1972).

Table 6. *Social variability by generation*

			Generation		
	I	II	III	IV	V
Year reached age twenty	1937–9	1940–9	1950–9	1960–6	1967–78
			Chinese sample		
Coefficient of variation[a]					
1. Education	.88	.80	.49	.36	.21
2. Occupational rank	.32	.29	.29	.28	.26
3. Income	.65	.44	.28	.22	.26
			American sample		
Coefficient of variation					
4. Education	.34	.29	.27	.25	
5. Occupational prestige	.58	.56	.55	.58	
6. Income	.91	.88	.71	.70	

[a]Coefficient of variation = standard deviation mean.

Sources: 1972–8 Chinese sample, economically active population; Otis Dudley Duncan, David Featherman, and Beverly Duncan, *Socioeconomic Background and Achievement* (New York: Seminar Press, 1972).

106

occurring – that Chinese policy intervention was indeed able to reshape the social order?

A comparison with trends in the United States suggests that more was occurring – that there was positive social intervention. The data are for individuals rather than class groups. In the US, average occupational prestige and average income levels have been relatively constant across generations (Table 5, rows 5 and 6). Educational levels have risen steadily (row 4). But in China, there has been a sharp decline in both occupational rank and income (rows 2 and 3). After rising for a time, average educational levels began to decline in the late 1960s. The Chinese pattern is distinctive.

Patterns of variability about these averages also support our earlier generalizations of narrowing status differentials (Table 6). Expressed as the standard deviation of a distribution divided by its mean, the coefficient of variation shows the extent to which there is great inequality in a population or a wide spread between those with much and little education or much and little income. A high figure indicates great spread or great inequality – a small figure the reverse. In the US, the variability in occupational prestige remained relatively constant across time. Inequalities in education and income declined only slightly. In China, in contrast, there has been a very sharp narrowing of educational and income inequalities, and occupational inequalities declined slightly as well. The reshaping of the social order in China, then, was more than just apparent; it was real, with old inequalities being drastically reduced and with education, occupation, and income levels being brought down at the same time.

Parental occupation and education

Children in China have been influenced not only by the class label which marked their fathers' position as of about 1949 but also by their fathers' current occupation and education. Class label is an imperfect indicator of occupational status which shifted quite radically for some people after 1949. Examination of father's current education and occupation and the status attainment of children age 16–39 (the generation that reached maturity since 1949) provides a better estimate of the extent to which post-1949 status groups are reproducing themselves.

Table 7. *Determinants of educational achievement and income by year reached age twenty (metric regression coefficients)*

Dependent variables	Father's			Child's				R^2	N
	Educa-tion	Occupa-tion	Class label[a]	Age	Sex	Educa-tion	Occupa-tion		
Education[b]									
Pre-1966 cohort	.22*	.46*	1.09	.10	1.12*	—	—	.38	(117)
Post-1967 cohort	.05	.00	.09	.12*	-.23	—	—	.10	(165)
Occupation[b]									
Pre-1966 cohort	-.41	.29*	7.79*	.55	5.95*	1.30*	—	.31	(117)
Post-1967 cohort	-.20	.16*	-.54	.92	1.52	.60	—	.16	(165)
Income[b]									
Pre-1966 cohort	-.28	.03	.93	.65*	2.16	.06	.42*	.37	(117)
Post-1967 cohort	.05	-.07	2.08	.71*	-.13	-.29	.33*	.22	(165)

[a] Class dichotomized with the old high status labels of staff, merchant, and capitalist = 1, the others = 0.

[b] Education = years of education. Occupation = mean income of thirty-two occupational groups. Income = yuan per month.

* $p \leq .05$.

Source: 1972–8 Chinese survey, economically active population, non-farm, age 16–39.

108

Table 8. *Determinants of status attainment by country (% change coefficients)*[a]

Dependent variable and country	Age	Sex	Father's Education	Father's occupation[b] Upper non-manual	Lower non-manual	Skilled worker	R^2	Mean
Years of education								
China	5*	2	2*	4	4	4	.26	9.6
Poland	−1	−2	2*	21*	21*	3	.18	9.0
Finland	0	−8	5*	32*	20*	4	.29	8.4
Norway	0	9	3*	28*	19*	1	.26	10.0
Income								
China	14*	4	2	1	2	7	.26	39
Poland	5*	41*	2*	15*	12*	6*	.24	367
Finland	8*	45*	7*	17	7	5	.23	156
Norway	7*	32*	2	11	10	1	.22	385

[a]Metric (unstandardized) regression coefficient divided by the mean education and income of each county to indicate what percentage change about the mean is induced by one unit's change in an independent variable.

[b]Dummy variables with semi-skilled and ordinary workers being the deleted referent.

*p ≤ .05.

Sources: 1972–8 Chinese urban survey, economically active population, age 16–39, N = 329; Erik Allardt and Wlodzimierz Wesolowski, eds., *Social Structure and Change: Finland and Poland* (Warsaw, Poland: Polish Scientific Publishers, 1978), p. 174. Finnish sample age 25–44, N = 215. Norwegian sample age 25–44, N = 174. Polish sample age 30–9, N = 6,800.

109

The data are divided between children who reached age 20 by the start of the Cultural Revolution in 1966 and those who did so afterwards. Prior to 1966, even if in muted form, the Chinese process of status attainment resembled patterns found around the world (Table 7). Fathers in higher paying positions with more education produced children who got further in the educational system. Better positioned fathers produced sons who got better jobs, and, as we have already seen, those with negative class labels continued to do well in the occupational world. Better education and better jobs were turned into higher incomes for high status families. The patterns are familiar. Familial influence over the education and status attainment of children is difficult to erase.

After 1966, however, the Chinese came very close to doing just that. The numbers confirm what informants often report – that after 1967 there was very little that an upper-middle class parent could do to help his children succeed in school or find a better job once they were out. A note of extreme unpredictability was introduced. Education was no guarantee of occupational success (Table 7, row 4). Government policy to break the reproduction of status groups was indeed effective, and it had the side effect of reducing male advantages in education, occupation, and income as well.

Comparison of China with other countries further confirms China's unique position. Even when the pre-1966 generation is included, there has been extraordinarily little intergenerational transmission of status in China (Table 8). Whether compared to the socialist state Poland or the market states Finland and Norway, upper status Chinese parents have been able to do very little to improve their children's future. Indeed, the factor which stands out most clearly in the Chinese figures is that to get ahead, the best thing a Chinese child could have done was to be born early, getting educated and employed in the 1950s before the vigorous destratification policies of the 1960s.

EVALUATION

What are we to make of these changes? The Chinese press is busy these days castigating the 1966–76 destratification regime. Trying to justify their own regime, they have every reason to do so. Can we, using reports of emigres who lived through these years, draw our own conclusions? The reports by emigres vary by social group, each responding in the area where their interests were most severely affected.

Not surprisingly, intellectuals and others in authority were the ones most alarmed by the 1966–76 decade. They objected vehemently to the capriciousness of justice during the decade, fearing that some previously forgotten aspect of their past might be brought up by this or that rebel faction to be used against them. In 1968–9, significant numbers of families with negative class labels were re-accused of political crimes and dispatched to the countryside. Whole families never before exposed to rural life suddenly had to make do with drastically lower incomes and grain diets in villages where they were not always welcome. Back in the city many others were demoted or remained under a cloud of suspicion. With the judicial system in shambles, as a result of its being attacked as a source of obstructive rules that protected bourgeois privilege, there was no avenue of appeal for what were felt to be unjust charges and punishments meted out by *ad hoc* rebel groups and non-judicial administrative bodies.

The upper status groups were also very concerned about what was happening to their children. Their concern originated over the fear that they could not provide their children an adequate education or job. But this concern became much more general as the negative consequences of both the rural sending-down programme for youth and the new education system became more apparent. With all but one of the children in a family required to go down, virtually everyone became involved. Even after 1949, the norm of family life had continued to be that children supported their parents financially, or at least sent token amounts signifying the duties owed by a loyal child. But after being sent to the village, children in their late teens and early twenties were not able to earn their keep. They could not cope with the heavy demands of physical labour in agriculture nor earn the extra income off family pig, private plot, and other sidelines which is necessary to economic survival in so much of rural China. Many had to turn to their parents for a monthly allowance to make ends meet, an action often interpreted as personal failure. Others drifted back into cities to lounge aimlessly about the streets. Younger children were not immune. Seeing no point to studying when they faced only a future in the countryside and when there were neither serious exams nor teachers with any authority, school children ceased studying and joined their older siblings in the street. Boys began smoking by the sixth or seventh grade. There was an outburst of bicycle thefts, pickpocketing on buses, rumbles by gangs protecting their turf, and in one year a wave of school window smashings. Though still tame by Western standards, to Chinese parents accustomed to juvenile obedience and complete safety in the streets, these crimes were exceedingly threatening.

There was little that intellectuals could do about either their own personal or their children's situation. Considered politically suspect – part of the 'stinking ninth class', the lowest of the low, in political jargon – they could not overtly resist. Instead, many turned to just soldiering on with the job – going through the motions but avoiding responsibility for actions that might get them in trouble. In new collective leadership arrangements, managers tried to pass the buck to others, or so we are told by both the press and emigres. Teachers abandoned discipline and strict academic standards lest they earn the enmity of good class children or new supervisory committees that could attack them. Intellectuals withdrew effort from work and rushed home to spend their time raising flowers, goldfish, and birds or to engage in other diversions. In some circles of Canton City, this new flurry of hobbies came to be known as the 'mass movement' because it rose from below rather than descending from above as did all the other political movements of the time. Alternatively, it was known as the 'army, air force, navy' activity, with grasshoppers being the army, birds the air force, and goldfish the navy. Untold hours which might have been spent on work were diverted to other activities.

Not all these concerns and responses were restricted to higher status groups. With their children likely to join gangs or other deviant activity, working class parents were as much alarmed by some of the consequences of China's radical decade as anyone. Workers were also directly affected by events at their place of work, and these events provide an acid test of the consequences of the Cultural Revolution. Workers along with peasants were supposed to be major beneficiaries of the Cultural Revolution. And workers, along with peasants, were supposed to embody the revolutionary virtues which everyone else in society was to emulate. In industry, they were to lead the way as moral replaced material incentives and political replaced technical leadership.

The elimination of piece rates, bonuses, and merit raises severely curtailed material incentives, as did the elimination of demotions and firings for non-performance on the job. Political study and small group criticism and self-criticism were to provide daily and weekly moral encouragement. Quarterly and annual lists of outstanding workers and work groups, with small red flags by their names, red banners to hang on the wall, commemorative tea mugs to take home, and photographs at the entrance to the factory were the symbols that were to replace the monetary rewards of the past. China had always tried to instill some level of political commitment in the average worker, but the Cultural Revolution made this attempt more massive. On the average, groups of a dozen or so workers in a single work group under a foreman met two or three times per week for an hour to half-hour's study after work. Every month or so the whole factory assembled for a meeting led by the factory's Party secretary and factory head. In both total factory meetings and work group meetings, the worker heard at least as much about the latest policy line from Peking as about concrete production problems. Though many workers were not interested in the details of these policy lines, a few political activists could be counted on to pick up current political themes and discuss them vigorously. Even the more reticent were forced to join in at times. 'Usually, only a few would do most of the talking and others would just listen', said a worker from a scrap steel plant, 'but periodically everyone would have to speak out on what their understanding of an article was.' Even if the worker's expressed 'understanding' was just a rehash of yesterday's editorial in the *People's Daily* or the Party secretary's speech from the day before, new policies were quickly disseminated to the total factory population.

When this system worked well, such as before the Cultural Revolution, workers were concerned as much about building a strong nation and a new way of life as about their individual economic welfare. This appears in a comparison to work in Hong Kong by an emigre from a lock factory.

Hong Kong workers have no aspirations other than earning more money. Chinese workers pay much less attention to money. Prior to the Cultural

113

Revolution, being influenced by communist thought, young workers in China were much more concerned about the collective good, the future of the nation, and so on. They were very idealistic.

Similarly, those emigres who could have left legally in earlier years because of foreign kin ties report that in the difficult Great Leap years of 1959–61, when they seldom had enough food to fill their stomachs, they nevertheless served contentedly and never thought of leaving because of a sense of participating in a common cause of building a new nation.

Despite this early idealism, emigres report paradoxically that idealism was increasingly absent in the wake of the Cultural Revolution. With an ideology of class struggle, in which one group necessarily attacks another, workers became wary of making political mistakes or speaking to the wrong person, lest they themselves be attacked. Workers began to shy away from frank political discussions, preferring to mouth the correct slogans when necessary and otherwise stick to safer mundane topics of family life and everyday events of the work place. With the emphasis on political commitment rather than high productivity for building a strong nation, some of the former unity of purpose was lost. And without frank political discussion it could not be easily regained. Where factions were left over from the most turbulent 1967–8 years, these too continued to inhibit unity in the early 1970s, and in a few places (now ballyhooed by the press) led to outbreaks of violence and work stoppages in 1975–6.

Moral incentives also proved incapable of being the sole support for work effort. Productivity began to decline, especially among the new Cultural Revolution generation of workers. In the lock factory:

There were quite a few lazy ones, at least during and in the wake of the Cultural Revolution. People would arrive late and then go out to shop once they were there. We had study meetings daily after work for about half an hour. In these meetings the work group head would sometimes bring up the name of someone who was constantly late and lagging on the job. Occasionally, even the Party secretary for the whole factory would look up someone who was lazy and have a little personal talk. Nevertheless, if one's name were brought up just in a study meeting after work, one would not worry about it, for most workers already having worked many years felt secure in their job.

114

Some of the problems of laziness were exacerbated by a generous health benefit system. In a scrap steel plant:

After the Cultural Revolution many people were taking a day off from work – some were taking off on their own affairs, some for illness, some were just lazy. Some with doctor acquaintances got [dubious] sick certificates. One gets full pay for sick leave only after eight years of work. [But] if one uses just two hours in going to see a doctor, there is no deduction in pay. So many workers who were late for other reasons would simply say that they had been to see a doctor.

A similar situation is reported in other factories, particularly among young workers who had come of age in the Cultural Revolution rather than in the more spartan work-committed 1950s and early 1960s.

With great security of work and little incentive to perform effectively, workers began to agree informally to control output, punishing the rate busters and hiding output much as in Western industry. In a metal works factory:

Every work group has a set amount it was supposed to produce each day. If the group fell short, the leaders might call the group into a meeting to discuss why they fell short. But in their hearts everyone knew the number they were supposed to complete, and once through they would start drinking tea, telling jokes, and so on. The group leaders did not care as long as the daily quota was met. Since there was no longer any bonus, there was no reason to keep working past the quota. Everyday we would just produce a little more or less than the quota so as to average out around the quota or just slightly above it. When we got near the end of the year, there were meetings to discuss the work quotas for next year. Workers were not willing to report too high a level since this would make it hard for themselves. So it took several meetings to hammer out an agreement.

In a textile factory:

The factory set output quotas per group and per person. The workshop head kept a record of personal output. But the quotas were fairly easy to meet and some would stretch out their work so that they just did the quota and no more.

This pattern will sound familiar to readers who know Western industry, yet the Chinese have had one technique for breaking this pattern that is generally unavailable in the West. They could use political activists, who out of political commitment or a desire to

115

toady to leaders chose to side with management rather than their fellow workers. In a scrap steel plant, which our informant estimated to be a fifth Party members, Youth League members, and other activists (a rather high proportion):

The activists were faster workers than the others. Except for production drives, things were pretty calm, but when the factory started a production high tide the workers sped up, not because they were personally enthused but because when one's neighbour speeds up one would look politically backward if one did not keep up with him. And one does not want to stand out as a potential target.

The activists did not always have such an easy time of it, however. The work of the activists could make them sufficiently unpopular for them to be excluded from normal social relations and for their personal influence to be weakened. In the scrap steel factory. 'We were more careful in talking when the activists were present.' In the metal works factory where workers tried to keep quotas low, 'There were some activists calling for higher quotas [at the end of the year]. But with others not supporting them they could not get agreement on this. They were somewhat isolated.' And in the lock factory:

The activists got a little more information on quotas and they would respond to these calls by speeding up a little about the time of the month we had overtime. Some of the other more timid workers would speed up to emulate them, but only while the supervisors were present. As soon as the supervisors left the room, everyone except the activists would slow down again. The bold workers would speak to the activists, saying things like, 'Eh, you're trying to make shop head, huh?'

Political activism and more general political campaigns provided the Chinese factory manager an extra handle on worker effort, but one that fell far short of the radicals' goals of remaking society on a worker–peasant base.

Emigre workers were decidedly ambivalent about the events of these years. Some experienced them as rather comfortable. Since the early 1950s, Chinese state factories have had several warm, embracing features that are reminiscent of large Japanese enterprises. With lifetime employment and a wide range of fringe benefits including health care, pensions, hardship allowances, and occasionally housing and vacation tours, work units provided a strong sense of security. Work units are further involved in personal life by being the source of purchasing coupons for bicycles, watches, and sewing machines and approving and disapproving marriages and divorces as well as controlling family planning. Union and work group leaders often visit seriously ill workers at home or in the hospital or delegate fellow workers to do the same. With lifetime employment and little mobility among jobs, workers come to know each other well. Workers often inquire about the health of one's family members. The absence of similar concern among Hong Kong workers often leads to invidious comparisons by emigres. In the Cultural Revolution, with it being even more difficult to discipline workers or demand performance by varying material reward, some workers found life in the factory even more comfortable. The pace of work, they report, was much slower than before the Cultural Revolution and considerably slower and less hectic than the pace they find in capitalist Hong Kong factories where the piece rate reigns supreme. Fear of political attack concerned a few, but overall they reported a general feeling of security and some warmth. If short term worker security and freedom from stress is the goal, then there was something to recommend in the Cultural Revolution years.

If the goal is long term national growth, however, one's evaluation may be quite different. And since that was the goal of many older workers who had come of age in the 1950s, they were often distressed by what occurred in these years. They shared the goal (held most strongly by intellectuals) of making China strong and able to stand up to the Western world for the first time in a century. This was one of the major rewards the revolution was to bring and a goal in which everyone could participate regardless of social background or depth of political understanding. They were distressed by the diversion from this goal and by rewards to workers who did not contribute to its attainment.[11] Material rewards themselves had an evaluative content. Income was a symbol of personal worth, and either equal income for all or pay increases to young, less productive workers were indicating worth for the wrong people. Old workers began to think more of their own income levels. Having remained constant since the late 1950s or early 1960s, even while there was mild inflation and family responsibilities were growing as children reached maturity, the incomes of older and middle age workers were perceived as increasingly inadequate. And, in disgust, some old workers began to protest in the only way they knew how – through slacking off in their own work.

Older workers were particularly distressed by young political activists who rose to power over them. To them, these were not people to be respected. The workers in a restaurant had a poor impression of the new Party secretary, an army veteran appointed to the restaurant in 1966. His problem was that 'He couldn't talk without politics spilling out while at the same time he had no under-standing of concrete work problems.' In a water plant, an older worker reported that the old Party members who entered the Party before 1966:

> were the backbones of production. They had a lot of prestige among workers. The workers relied on them to solve all sorts of production problems. But those joining the party after the Cultural Revolution were all unacceptable. They were political upstarts who got into the party mostly by attacking others in political campaigns. We thoroughly disliked them.

This feeling was exacerbated by many of the new recruits being former peasants whose only qualification was that they had served for a time in the People's Liberation Army, where they acquired political legitimacy but not the technical competence so respected in factories. Political skills divorced from technical skills were not respected.

Neither were workers overly impressed with the Cultural Revo-lution's efforts to bring leaders and led closer together through requirements that cadres work at least once a week on the shop floor and that workers, technicians, and managers combine in special three-in-one technical innovation groups. Work on the shop floor was useful at times. Some emigres expressed admiration for leaders who wore patched clothes, avoided bureaucratic airs, and dealt with actual production problems – again, the respect of production skills. The irony of this politically inspired programme was that many non-political managers who did not necessarily have good political credentials were already at work on the shop floor. It was the political managers, the Party secretaries, and their like, who had to make a special effort to come to the shop floor. And with some political managers being so unskilled at jobs needed on the shop floor, workers who would otherwise never have thought that executive officers should do production work began to think

118

of their political leaders as hypocritical bumpkins. The widely touted three-in-one technical groups tended to have been formalistic. If they functioned at all, they tended to bring together skilled repair workers and technicians who would have been talking to one another anyway. These programmes too, then, were less effective than might have been anticipated. Most emigres indicated a 'ho-hum' attitude towards these participatory innovations.

CONCLUSION

There are, then, definite costs to a programme of radical destratification. Not all parts of the 1966–76 Chinese programme may have been necessary. The unpopular rural sending-down programme for youth with so many negative consequences might have been avoided in China, and can be easily avoided in countries without China's urban unemployment problems. Other features seem less avoidable. If the goal is not only to narrow the gap in material well-being between haves and have-nots, but also to invert the old class order and break the chain of inheritance between privileged fathers and privileged children, then large segments of the Chinese programme may be necessary. The education system will stress goals other than academic excellence. Technical, legal, and all other kinds of professional expertise are likely to be questioned. Zealotry of one sort or another will have to be tapped. The costs in ill-will and lessened productivity may well not seem worth the rewards in increased security for lower performance workers or in increased feelings of righteousness for principled idealists.

More intermediate models may well appear to provide a better compromise between the goals of equality and those of national economic growth. Prior to 1966, China had already achieved a significant degree of equality while continuing to maintain popular support and growth. Income gaps were significantly reduced while material goods were rather equally distributed relative to income. Within this narrow range, if the retrospective judgments of emigres can be trusted, material rewards were effectively linked to performance. And there was a judicious admixture of moral reward and idealistic commitment – not commitment to pure political ideals of class struggle or the ultimate egalitarian state, but to the goal of national growth for the sake of a strong people and nation –

119

the very goals to which the Party leaders are now appealing.

Existing theories about the functional necessity of stratification are too simplistic.[12] They fail to specify the degree of inequality necessary for what kinds of occupations under what kinds of conditions. They give too little attention to job sorting and work reward devices other than the individualistically material.[13] They fail to note how existing elites develop public rationalizations and other devices to protect their privilege and the privilege of their children, thus reproducing a given stratification system regardless of changing societal needs. Yet, in spirit, the functional theories may still be correct. And in China and several other socialist states such as Czechoslovakia and Cuba, which have retreated from radical destratification, we may well have critical tests of the extent to which differential reward is necessary for societies in the modern world. Judging from these experiments, the prospects for radical destratification on a societal scale are not encouraging. The prospects for more moderate equality such as found in the states of Eastern Europe or in China before 1966 are more encouraging. If these are the proper models of what is possible, then egalitarian states of the future will not break the chain of generational inheritance any better than do capitalist societies, but they will provide a significant degree of equality of condition and a degree of security for those on the bottom that deserves serious study.

6

THE CLASS SYSTEM IN RURAL CHINA: A CASE STUDY

Jonathan Unger

For the first three decades after the establishment of the People's Republic, class labels strongly influenced the life chances of each and every Chinese. A class label did not refer to a person's current income nor to his or her relationship to the means of production. It did not, in short, denote class membership in the existing socioeconomic structure. Rather, a class label had been affixed to each household in the early 1950s after the revolution's victory, categorizing the family's economic position under the *ancien régime*. During the next thirty years these capsule designations weighed heavily in determining social and political statuses; and nowhere was their impact more strongly felt than in the countryside. This paper explores the political functions served by these class labels in peasant China, the sources of popular support for their use in the 1960s, and the reasons for the system's ultimate disintegration in the late 1970s and early 1980s.

Illustrations of how this 'class system' operated shall be drawn from a community called Chen Village, in South China's Guangdong Province. During 1975 to 1976, again in 1978 and most recently in 1982, two dozen emigrants from this village were interviewed in Hong Kong about the recent history of the community, their own lives there, and the lives of neighbours.[1] Most of the quotes and descriptions of the following pages are based on their reconstructions of the period from the mid-1960s through the mid-1970s, the decade in which 'class' distinctions were most clearly and forcefully felt in Chinese villages.

With a population of slightly more than 1000, Chen Village is somewhat larger than the average community in the region. It contains a single lineage, as do many of the villages in its immediate district. By Guangdong standards its residents are neither rich nor poor. It is not an outstandingly progressive village (Chen Village has never been designated a model for its commune) but neither has the village gained a reputation as politically backward. Interviewees from the village felt that its internal 'class' stratification was typical of the villages in the surrounding district. Based on my reading of the Chinese media, there is no reason to assume that their impression is in any sense misleading for China as a whole.

THE 'CLASS' STRUCTURE IN CHEN VILLAGE

During land reform in 1950, a workteam of cadres sent by the Party had carried out careful investigations to determine how much property each Chen family had owned on the eve of the revolution. The apex of the village's socio-economic pyramid had been occupied by a small number of landlords and rich peasants. Below them was a considerably larger number of middle peasants who owned enough land to be basically self-sufficient. But the bulk of the village population had consisted of tenants who owned only small plots (or no land at all) and landless labourers.[2] All of those at the bottom of the pyramid subsequently were grouped together under a 'poor-peasant' label (see Figure 1).

During land reform this traditional pyramid was shattered. Economic exploitation was eliminated from Chen Village and the rest of the Chinese countryside. But in the process new socio-political distinctions were created. The pre-revolutionary class designations were stored in dossiers, and eventually a new system of the caste-like rigidity was devised on the basis of these files.

The former poor peasants were placed officially at the top of a new inverted pyramid (see Figure 2), on the grounds that they could be counted upon to support revolutionary change. But the government wanted to broaden its popular appeal beyond this category and eventually granted almost the same privileged status to the former lower-middle peasants (who make up approximately a quarter of Chen Village's population). Before Liberation, the main source of the lower-middle peasants' earnings had been their own small landholdings, but they had had to supplement their income by renting additional land or by hiring themselves out as

The class system in rural China

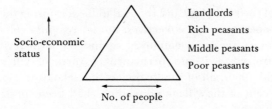

Figure 1 Pre-land reform

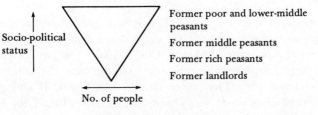

Figure 2 Post-revolution

part-time labourers. They, too, had benefited from land reform.

Together, during the decades to come, they and the former poor peasants were to comprise the village's 'good-origin' (*chengfen haode*) families.[3] Indeed, in the mid-1960s the Party reaffirmed and strengthened the lower-middle peasantry's good-class credentials by establishing a Poor-and-Lower-Middle-Peasants Association in Chen Village. Though a poor-peasant label continued to be recognized locally as superior, good-class Chen Villagers thereafter became accustomed to referring to themselves as being of 'poor-and-lower-middle-peasant' (*pinxiazhongnong*) status. This term was used as if it denoted a single 'class' category. In most respects it did.

Between 80 and 85 per cent of the families in Chen Village belonged to this privileged stratum of former poor-and-lower-middle peasants. Another 10–12 per cent belonged to the middling stratum of former middle and upper-middle peasants.[4]

During and after the land reform, there had been fears in Beijing that the old village elites might informally retain influence over local affairs. This fear had prompted repeated official efforts through the mid-1950s to discredit and isolate the overthrown classes. Landlords were targeted during land reform, and the rich peasants were stripped of their property and residual influence during the organization of cooperatives and collectives. But for reasons explored below, the temporary measures employed against the former village elites became transformed into permanent fixtures of village society. By the mid-1960s, all of the 'bad-class' households in Chen Village (4–5 per cent of the village population) had been consigned to an outcaste status.[5]

A household was bad class when it was headed by a 'four-bad-categories element' (*si lei fenzi*), defined as a landlord, rich peasant, counter-revolutionary (none in Chen Village), or 'rotten element' (*huai fenzi*). Among these, the true pariahs were the village's two former landlords: 'They were treated like lepers. If you greeted them your class stand was considered questionable. They had no friends. They didn't dare to talk to each other, either.' The former rich peasantry, though facing stiff discrimination, never suffered this degree of isolation and unremitting contempt.

As the titles connote, the remaining two types of 'four-bad elements' (the rotten elements and counter-revolutionaries) were not categories based upon economic class origins. They included people who, even if poor peasants before land reform, had been designated village bullies (*e-ba*) in the employ of the Guomindang or landlords. More significantly, these categories also covered people who had committed serious felonies or political errors after the Party came to power. A good origin peasant thus had to bear in mind that the punishment for a major transgression could be a permanent four-bad-element 'hat'. The prime example from Chen Village was a former bandit-turned-guerrilla who had been rewarded after Liberation with a petty post in urban government. Caught in an act of theft, he had attacked and injured his supervisor. The offender was officially branded a 'rotten element' and sent back to Chen Village to face lifelong discrimination.

As a symbol of polluted status, during the 1960s and 1970s the dozen or so elderly 'four-bad elements' (the designation included their wives and widows) had to sweep dung from the village square before mass meetings were held there. To symbolize further that most of them were irredeemably among the damned, they were not permitted to attend any political sessions or participate in Mao Study groups. If a production team was caught concealing the size of its harvest in order to reduce the government's grain quotas, a four-bad member of the team could expect to be pinned with part of the blame; he or she was deemed to be a corrupting influence on better-class teammates. In most of the various political campaigns of the 1960s and 1970s, bad-class villagers became the targets of struggle sessions, to remind the audience of past exploitation and the persistence of 'bad-class' hostility toward the new order. During the Cleansing of the Class Ranks campaign of 1968–9 (by far the fiercest campaign in Chen Village since land reform), fifteen out of the twenty campaign victims who spent time in the village jail were either 'four-bad elements' or their close relatives.[6] A number were beaten in the highly emotional climate of the struggle sessions.

The poor and lower-middle peasants' suspicions of the 'bad elements' were, if anything, fuelled by this maltreatment. Many of the good-class peasants reasoned that if they themselves had been so miserably treated they would want to seek vengeance. This rationale allowed some villagers to indulge in a hysteria that conveniently reconfirmed and underscored the bad elements' status as 'class enemies':

After a period in which they'd been struggled against, we became very careful when walking in the lanes at night. Who knows? If they couldn't get over the humiliation might they not club you down in the dark? It's a custom in the village at such times to put some fish in the wells, to test whether there's any poison in the drinking water.

The young people from bad-class homes were not themselves 'elements'. The government had never given them political 'hats' placing them under the 'dictatorship' and supervision of the masses. They have always held the various rights of citizenship; they could vote in team elections and attend Mao Study sessions. The official rhetoric consistently has held that these young people, like those from all other class categories, were politically 'educable' and could be 'united with'. Alongside this rhetoric, however, the government implicitly endorsed the argument that world views were hereditary: that the thinking of bad-class children had been dangerously contaminated by their parents. 'Actually', commented a former Chen Village cadre, 'you should be more on guard against the landlord's son. The old landlord himself is already just a useless old stick.' Official discrimination was invited against all bad-class descendants by noting their father's class origin label prominently in their personal dossiers. In keeping with traditional Chinese practices, class origin labels are hereditary only in the patriline, and the sons of the bad-class sons (but not the children of bad-class daughters) bore the stigma in turn. Even had they left Chen Village, the dossiers and labels of the bad-class grandchildren would follow them through life.[7]

Many of the bad-class descendants grew up burdened by confused feelings of inferiority. A rich-peasant grandson from Chen Village, now in his late twenties, recalls that even when he was just a small child,

I didn't quarrel much. People called me 'landlord son' [sic]. I felt inferior, hopeless, as if things were beyond my control. It was so unfair. Take me; I was born after the peace [n.b. he does not, as most Chinese would, use the word 'Liberation' here]. Even if my parents had done something wrong, exploited other people, why should I be discriminated against? I felt inferior, never dared to do anything. Even before I got involved in any quarrel, I'd already say to myself: 'eh, the only thing I can do is to live with my head down' ... Usually at school the teachers treated me like any other kid. But if I did something wrong and got a scolding, they'd bring out my class background: 'You mean you side with your parents rather than the poor-and-lower-middle peasants?!'

Most bad-class young people quietly kept to their own kind. A good-class peasant from another village observed in 1976:

Ordinarily, the young children of the four-bad elements get together in the evenings. Those of good-class background separately get together. They make up different social sets. The poor-peasant kids don't hate the others, but they're worried to visit with them.

Why did this system of rigid discrimination persist in Chen Village into the 1960s and 1970s? Certainly, the Party's reasoning of the early 1950s no longer held. By the mid-1950s, Party leaders had already concluded, I think correctly so, that the former rural elites were nearly powerless. They no longer controlled any private or lineage properties and had been excluded from the networks of political power which the Party was erecting on the basis of the new cooperatives and collectives. Accordingly, in 1956 the Party leadership's assumption was that the period of class struggle was drawing to a close.[8] Class origins – the younger generation's especially – no longer were to be rigidly taken into account.

This being the case, was the reintroduction of harsh class policies in the 1960s merely in response to the desires and demands of the peasantry? Certainly, in the case of Chen Village in the 1950s, and even into the 1960s, some of the good-class peasants did feel a strong personal hostility toward some of the four-bad elements. As a former Chen Villager remarks: 'Those old folks really felt it. They'd experienced it. They knew what landlords were like before.'[9] But the perpetuation of class discrimination beyond the fifties had to be rooted in more than just these personal antagonisms. Had revenge been the main spur, discrimination should have faded with the passage of time as memories grew dimmer and new generations emerged. Yet quite the reverse occurred. The stress upon 'class feelings' and the rituals of class hatred were stronger in the 1960s and 1970s than in the 1950s.

Why? The discrimination against the tiny minority of bad-class people was partly a consequence of renewed state sponsorship. But the Chen Village peasants did cooperate fully. Could it be, then, that discrimination against an outcaste group was in accord with the deepest cultural traditions and attitudes of people in this region?

CULTURAL ROOTS?

Certainly historical antecedents can be found; the practices of any society are necessarily coloured by its traditions. Confucian thought did stress that social stability depended upon a hierarchic ordering in human relations. Early Chinese religious thought contained notions of collective retribution through the patrilineage; descendants were often thought to be paying through ill fortune for the transgressions of their parents or grandparents. The premise existed, too, of collective legal guilt. In imperial law, punishments for the most serious crimes sometimes extended to relatives of the perpetrator, even collaterals much removed. These traditional notions of social order and of collective religious and legal guilt were still evident in rural thought during the 1960s. An interviewee who had been a leading member of Chen Village's public security committee turned implicitly to all of these arguments when she

127

justified to me the treatment meted out to the four-bad elements' relatives during the village's Cleansing of Class Ranks campaign of 1968.

In considering these historical legacies, however, the essential point to note is that late-imperial China did not have any strong traditions of caste or estate-like structures (see Chapter 2). The Chinese imperial state drew distinctions among its subjects only at the upper and lower fringes of the social system. Those of the elite who had passed the imperial examinations were exempted from many of the taxes and obligations imposed upon ordinary souls; but these privileges were, in theory, also obtainable by the bright sons of humble parents. At the very bottom of the social system certain pariah groups were permanently banned from taking the examinations. People in this category (such as boat people and entertainers) were often deemed to be unfit even to associate with ordinary Chinese. But these socially degraded groups constituted only a small fraction of 1 per cent of China's total population. Moreover, they were social isolates, outside the fabric of respectable community life; and, as much to the point, their pariah statuses were upheld by imperial dicta rather than by popular sentiment. Thus, with the Yongzheng emperor's emancipatory edicts of 1723–35, all but the culturally and occupationally distinct 'boat people' of South China melted easily into the general populace.[10] Indeed, during recent centuries, against the realities of grinding poverty and limited life chances, it had been a belief of the *laobaixing*, 'the ordinary people', that upward mobility was an intrinsic right, available to those with luck and wits.[11] It was a social myth which helped to legitimize and protect the status quo.

Isolated exceptions existed, such as the hereditary slaves (relatively few in number) maintained as symbols of prestige by wealthy members of powerful lineages.[12] But Chen Village, like most peasant communities, did not share in that practice; it was far too poor. In Chen Village all men were Chens; and, notwithstanding the richer households' economic exploitation of their poor agnates, religious and social beliefs held that all Chens were equal before the common ancestors.[13] The weight of traditional attitudes precluded notions of sharp hereditary distinctions within the village.

In short, the intellectual and emotional support for a new system of hereditary strata did not stem from cultural antecedents in Chen

128

Village. Instead, for a complex set of reasons, the Chen peasants were responding favourably to a new system of beliefs and behavioural norms fostered by the Party.

UNDERPINNINGS OF DISCRIMINATION: PARTY TACTICS AND THE SELF-IMAGE OF THE GOOD CLASSES

The Party's initiatives of 1956 to dampen the significance of class origins had been relatively shortlived. For one thing, by the early 1960s the top Party leaders apparently feared that the gratitude of former poor and lower-middle peasants was rapidly subsiding. Closely associated with the Chinese concept of gratitude, *bao-en*, are notions of debt and loyalty. In the early sixties, Mao and Party officials felt it was essential to remind the peasantry of this debt. Mao's directive of late 1962 – 'Never forget class struggle' – was propagated at a time when the nation was just recovering from the terrible economic depression caused by the Great Leap Forward. The peasants were not to judge the government in terms of the present difficulties; through 'class education' they were to bear in mind that life was still better than before land reform.

They were to keep constantly in mind, moreover, that the great divide in China was not between themselves and their leadership but between the masses and 'class enemies' who wanted to destroy the new society. During the Four Cleanups campaign in Chen Village (1965–6), the Party pushed this message with greater emotional force than ever before. It portrayed a Manichean world of righteous classes – the agricultural and industrial proletariat led by the Party – pitched in combat against the dark forces represented by the suspect classes.

A new workteam of Party cadres had come into Chen Village to carry out the Four Cleanups. To reinforce the legitimacy and significance of class distinctions, the cadres laboriously reinvestigated the 'class' designations of each household. Repeatedly in meetings, the peasants were urged to recall who had owned precisely how much property before land reform. 'But there purposely were very few changes in class labels', one of the workteam's helpers recalls:

It only involved the different gradations of middle peasants. For example, a landlord can *never* become a rich peasant, can *never* change, even if the land reform had been wrong. A case of a middle peasant could be corrected because it was less 'political' in its implications than that of a bad-class family ... But [even here] the workteam's assumption was that unless the evidence strongly contradicted the household's 'class' appellation, the land reform's appraisal would continue to be considered correct. The workteam wanted few alterations, because the Party wanted to pursue class struggle.

Class struggle required that the lines differentiating each category of household be reaffirmed, unchanged and sacrosanct.

As a result of the Four Cleanups, cadres in Chen Village became even harsher in their dealings with the four-bad households. Party officials had learned in the campaign that if they did not always exhibit an ostentatiously firm class stand, they might leave themselves open to attack. As one villager put it, 'Of course they'd prefer to be more on the left than the right. Who'd dare to do anything that might later open them to accusations of having had relationships with bad elements?' Being harsh took on the colouring of political merit.

Villagers who wanted to get ahead politically followed the village cadres' lead. The more activist and righteous a person wanted to seem, the more loudly he or she would harangue the four-bad elements at struggle meetings. It became a contest among ambitious young activists.

But all this does not adequately explain 'class struggle' in Chen Village. For not just the village's cadres and young political activists participated but also, voluntarily, the bulk of the unambitious ordinary peasants. They *believed* in the strict class distinctions and in the legitimacy of class antagonisms. Class struggle, in short, entailed more than what we have described thus far. The Party had provided the good-class peasantry with a complex set of emotional justifications and material reasons for discriminating against the bad-class households. Two concepts drawn from Max Weber's work – specifying two quite different ways in which groups can claim superiority – help to explain the appeal of the Party's messages.

In the Four Cleanups campaign, the cadre workteam had been teaching the poor and lower-middle peasant households that they constituted what Weber has called a 'negatively privileged' status group.[14] These are under-groups, like the Jews and early Christians, whose dignity is sustained by the belief that as a group they have a providential mission and a special place before God. The workteam organized public 'remember the bitterness' reminiscences and 'remember the bitterness' meals consisting of wild vegetables and roots. In these ways the peasantry ritually relived the worst deprivations of pre-Liberation times. They were told that their former sufferings (or those of their parents or grandparents) had granted them a superior moral value, with sacred responsibilities. They were the 'revolutionary masses' – the former wretched of the earth who had been entrusted with a mission to usher in a better future for China and the world. As such, they stood in a special, intimate relationship with Chairman Mao, 'China's Saviour'.

These messages of the Mao Study sessions provided the good-class peasants with new feelings of importance and self-pride. But there was a catch involved. To justify their new-found status, their behaviour would have to conform to the Party's ideological image of them. As one young man from Chen Village commented:

When Mao Study was pushed in the 1960s the good-class kids in our village felt a responsibility to be progressive. You know, all those slogans and ideas praising the reliability of the poor and lower-middle peasants.

In this system of beliefs, the pariah classes served an important function as negative emulation models. They represented the mirror image of the good classes' proletarian virtues. The more that the good-class peasantry painted the bad-class households in black colours,[15] the more their own purported 'redness' stood out in contrast.

In addition to the beliefs that they were a Chosen People, Party teachings simultaneously encouraged the good-class peasants to adopt the mythology of what Weber calls a 'positively privileged status group'. These are groups such as aristocracies, whose claims to superiority lie in 'this world', usually on the basis of a glorious inherited past and an innate superiority of genealogy. The poor and lower-middle peasants had become, within the village, an over-group in 'this world'; in the words of one peasant, 'they feel they're the masters of society'. As a credential of their superiority some even proudly traced the purity of their poor and lower-middle peasant ancestry back four generations to establish a 'blood-line' (*xuetong*) of 'naturally red' pedigree.

Weber points out that such beliefs in inherited superiority usually are employed to justify the monopolization of scarce goods and resources.[16] This was certainly the case in Chen Village. Be it in schooling, medical care, or job opportunities (e.g. an army career), the good-origin villagers could claim priority over their workmates of questionable origin.[17] Remarked an emigré from the village in 1975: 'Even if you go to Canton from the village to see a doctor, you don't have to stand so long in line; you show them your Poor-and-Lower-Middle-Peasant Association card.'

EXAMPLES OF GOOD-CLASS ADVANTAGES

The 'class line' – a Chinese term meaning privileged access to goods and services on the basis of one's class status – was pushed most strongly in rural China in the years between the end of the Cultural Revolution in 1968 and Mao's death in 1976. But during these years, the application of the class line varied noticeably from one village to the next. The reason was that the class line was brought to bear precisely where local shortages in goods and services were most pronounced. Interviews with former schoolteachers from six Guangdong villages indicate, for instance, that villages which could not provide enough primary-school places enacted a strong class-line admissions policy. This policy gradually weakened as primary schooling expanded, but in these same villages a strong class line in admissions was again applied as the competition to get into local middle schools increased.

In the same fashion, in some villages class-line decisions began to affect even the selection of teachers. In the 1950s, at a time when there was no real contest for middle-school places, many former landlord and rich-peasant families pushed their sons through the educational system as the only means of providing for their futures. Where their services were needed, they became primary-school teachers without any local protest. But as education expanded in the 1960s and early 1970s, large numbers of good-class peasants began to qualify to teach primary school. For the first time, teachers of unsavoury class origins were suspected of spreading bad ideas among their poor and lower-middle peasant pupils. A good class background soon became the indispensable qualification for new teachers. In fact, the incumbent bad-class teachers in some villages were dismissed *en masse* to make room for good-class candidates. But in areas where teacher shortages still existed, a very different perception of the bad-class teachers sometimes prevailed. An

132

interviewee from Canton who had been sent to settle in the country-side was recruited to be a teacher even though his father was a former capitalist:

Nobody cared about that, because they had a shortage of teachers in the village junior middle school. Even after I tried to run off to Hong Kong and got caught, the village leaders still wanted me to go back to teach in the school. They told me, 'Don't worry about that little incident. The poor and lower-middle peasants still trust you.'

In short, the class line could be turned on or off, depending on the local needs of the good-class peasantry.

They gained benefits from the class system in other respects as well. The privileged status of good-class men gave them an advantage in acquiring brides. This could be even more important to them than access to schools or jobs.

Peasant bachelors often needed this advantage. There is evidence of a demographic imbalance (with more young men than young women of marriageable age) in certain parts of rural China, in-cluding Chen Village, well into the 1970s. (This imbalance may be due to a persistence into the 1950s of the traditional strategy of female infanticide or neglect when food supplies were limited.[18]) In these circumstances, young men were more than willing, if need be, to accept a bride of questionable class heritage. Since the official policy decreed that class labels are passed only through the patriline, these good-class bachelors knew that their children would inherit good credentials irrespective of their mother's origin.

Notwithstanding this, a woman's class status still made some difference to a prospective groom.[19] Accordingly, women who married hypergamously did not usually rise very far above their origin. If a poor or lower-middle-class peasant family could not find a satisfactory bride for their son within the circle of good-class households, they normally approached a middle-peasant family. Middle peasants who could not find marriage partners within their own category would look for brides among the bad classes.[20]

Though the shortfall of rural women was only a few percentage points, this was enough to dim very substantially the marriage prospects of the bad-class men. Such men came, after all, from the least marriageable 5 per cent of the rural population. Bad-class parents faced the prospect that none of their sons would be able to marry. This situation, ironically, was the converse of pre-Liberation times, when it was the poor peasants who did not always have the financial wherewithal to see their sons married.[21]

To keep the family line alive, bad-class households began resorting to a special strategy. 'Just about the only way a landlord son can get married', noted a Chen Villager, 'is through a swap with another household ... Both families sacrifice their daughters to keep the incense burning [i.e. to sustain the male line].' Normally such exchanges were arranged with other bad-class families. But this was not always the case. One of Chen Village's landlord families traded brides with an impoverished poor-peasant family whose only son was dim-witted and ugly. This exchange of sisters between two categories of despised grooms was practised often enough to warrant a special derogatory title – a 'potato skin/taro root exchange'.[22]

CAUGHT IN THE MIDDLE: THE MIDDLE PEASANTRY AND SENT-DOWN URBAN YOUTHS

The bad-class peasants in Chinese villages comprised only a small proportion of the population. Thus the poor and lower-middle peasants benefited most from their advantages over the upper-middle and middle peasants, who were considerably more numerous than the bad-class elements. The poor and lower-middle peasants usually stood first in line for the most coveted jobs, such as teaching. The middle peasants also lost out in the competition for the most desirable brides; in Chen Village they generally had to pay higher brideprices, to offset their lack of status. Middle peasants could become brigade cadres and even village leaders. But to rise politically, a middle peasant had to be especially capable and exceptionally activist. Success was only likely when there were no good-class competitors of comparable ability. As one villager observed:

Our production team accountant was a politically active upper-middle peasant. Nobody else wanted the job; and this fellow seemed honest; and with so many poor and lower-middle peasants in our team we didn't worry that he would cause trouble – would turn the sky upside down.

The middle peasantry did not really object to the discrimination against the four-bad elements. In fact, many of them shared the common prejudices against the outcaste households. But the middle peasants wanted the class line drawn in a manner that placed them securely in the camp of the 'masses'. They wanted to be treated on terms similar to the good classes. They were wary of periods when the government pushed the rhetoric of class struggle. They knew that when emotions were stirred up against the suspect classes, arguments about 'reliability' could be employed against themselves as well.

Many of the eighteen million youths who came from the cities to settle in China's countryside in the 1960s and 1970s encountered difficulties similar to those which affected the middle peasantry. Like middle peasants, they did not bear the brunt of overt prejudice, but they were frustrated by the wall of class labels.

A contingent of fifty youths from Canton, mostly of middle- and bad-class origins, arrived in Chen Village in 1964. Initially, as outsiders without any fixed niche in the hierarchy of village class statuses, they were simply referred to by the ambiguous label 'students', which did not carry a class connotation. In this way the young people could be used to fill such high-status roles as Mao Study counsellors or cashiers, for which the peasantry themselves did not have the necessary skills. But there were too few opportunities in a small village for the majority of these former students to be upwardly mobile, and as a consequence these young outsiders became intensely competitive among themselves. Seeing this, in 1965 the Four Cleanups workteam in Chen Village followed the Party's new policies on class and granted the most desirable posts to a few of the urban youths who had good class origins. The peasants, following suit, began to view the urban-born youths in terms of their family statuses.

The bad-class families in Chen Village had always been too timid to protest against their own maltreatment; furthermore the middle peasants always had to keep in mind that they were stuck in the village and might bear the consequences for the rest of their lives if they protested against class-line favouritism. But Chen Village's middle-class youths of urban origin did not face such constraints. Young, unattached, unencumbered by village ties, and highly achievement-oriented, they were exasperated when they discovered that their expectations were being thwarted. By upbringing, they found it difficult to accept a second-class status.

Whenever protests have erupted in China against the official distribution of privilege, it is usually people in just such circumstances (quite often middle class) who have been involved (e.g. the Hundred Flowers movement of 1957). During the Cultural Revolution, these urban, middle-class teenagers became the Rebel Red Guards in Chen Village (just as middle-class high-school students formed the core of the Rebel Red Guards in China's cities).[23] In the village, the young Rebels attacked the Four Cleanups workteam, the village cadres and an official Red Guard group composed exclusively of good-class youths. Their claim was that their ardent 'devotion to Chairman Mao' proved that they were the true defenders of the revolution, in contrast to the good-class, but 'suppressive', local power-holders.

After the Cultural Revolution of 1966–8, peasant youths from Chen Village graduated from the local junior high school in rapidly growing numbers. To make room for them the sent-down youths of middle-class origin were eased out of whatever posts they still held. They became the victims of the same demographic process which was costing many bad-class teachers their jobs. Since Mao Zedong himself appeared to support a strict class line, these middle-class youths in Chen Village finally despaired of ever being appreciated or successful in China. The fault appeared to them to lie with the national polity rather than just local 'power-holders'. They had protested from within the political system during the Cultural Revolution, in the name of Mao, but gradually they shifted toward disaffection with the system itself. By 1974 the majority of Chen Village's urban-born Mao Study counsellors and Communist Youth League members had swum to Hong Kong.

THE 1970S: THE EROSION OF BELIEFS IN CLASS

Even though the nationwide favouritism shown to the good-class families had resulted in the disaffection of portions of the middle classes, the more 'Maoist' wing of the Party was willing to pay that price. Among other things, the 'Maoist' wing presumably hoped, in return, to gain stronger support from the good-class peasantry. But in Chen Village and probably most other villages, that support did not materialize. By the mid-1970s, in fact, the Chen peasants' faith in Mao Thought and the Party was dissolving.

136

This decline in enthusiasm was due in part to the erratic nature of policy changes dictated by central authorities. Repeatedly the peasants heard programmes and leaders fulsomely praised one day only to be condemned the next. Perhaps even more perturbing was the damage being done to Chen Village's economy by inflexible higher-level demands. The village was pressed in Loyalty campaigns to contribute extra grain to the state at sub-normal prices; to 'self-reliantly' grow crops such as wheat and cotton which were woefully unsuited to the climate; to forego vegetable farming and fill in fishponds (both of which had been highly profitable) in order to plant yet more grain. The Chen peasants watched in frustration as their incomes declined from one year to the next.

In such circumstances, they were no longer so willing to accept the roles assigned to them by the Party's class teachings. When the Party bureaucracy demanded that they provide extra Loyalty grain or cut back on private plots, these 'requests' invariably alluded to the innate political nobility of the poor and lower-middle peasants and their mission to achieve a higher level of socialism. The peasants did not want that type of nobility; many were becoming increasingly uneasy with the way class teachings were being utilized to justify actions which went against their interests.

Moreover, the younger generation in Chen Village was growing weary of the Party's rhetoric concerning the duty of poor and lower-middle peasants to be grateful for their deliverance from feudal tyranny. They had not themselves experienced the sufferings of the pre-Liberation era. Their concern was whether the Party was accomplishing anything for them in the present, not the past. At the 'recall bitterness sessions' of the mid-1970s:

hearing these stories was, for these youths, like watching an unreal movie. They joked about it, smirked and laughed at the old people telling these tales ... Most of them didn't believe in it. They'd never experienced it personally and felt it couldn't have been *that* bad. They felt people shouldn't always be looking back like that, shouldn't always compare the old and new society, should not use the past to measure the present.

The peasants' patience, young and old alike, was strained yet further when, in the interminable political meetings, ambitious young activists rose to proclaim the depth of their 'class hatred'. In the local view, such declarations had become hypocritical: 'All this talk about class struggle just seemed formalistic', an emigrant observed in 1978. 'If the Party didn't keep rekindling the fire, the peasants wouldn't do it ... Everyone brought things to do at the meetings, and the women sewed and knitted. They've become numbed.'

One of the central premises for perpetuating class discrimination had been that attitudes are inherited. By the mid-1970s, however, many young people were having private doubts on this score, too. How tainted, after all, could the sons, grandsons, and even great-grandsons of the four-bad elements really be? As some of these good-class peasants became sceptical of Party teachings they began to ignore some of the social barriers that had been imposed against the bad classes. A rich-peasant son commented in 1978: 'In general the younger poor and lower-middle peasants nowadays don't think we should be treated like this, that we should be stepped on like this. Some of them began to talk with us.'

This new attitude toward class discrimination may well have been reinforced by the fact that the benefits to be gained from the class line were no longer substantial. The poor and lower-middle peasants, after all, comprised 80–85 per cent of the village population. At best, the class line had provided them with only a modest edge, and by the late 1970s, even that edge had diminished. To the young people's irritation, the best jobs increasingly were going to the relatives of village leaders; in practice, the 'back door' of cadre privilege had begun displacing the class line. And by the mid-1970s the demographic imbalance between the sexes was receding. Only the weakest, poorest, and least capable of the young men had to worry seriously that they might not be able to find a suitable spouse. With or without the class line, in short, the life of the average good-class peasant would remain basically the same.

It should not, however, be assumed that the system of class discrimination no longer had any supporters in Chen Village. Some members of the older generation still clung to the feelings of the previous decades. But generally the beliefs were eroding. By the mid-1970s increasing numbers of the villagers were willing to see the system of class labels overturned.

POST-MAO: THE DESTRUCTION OF CLASS BARRIERS

Following Mao's death in 1976 his political successors moved to abandon the Party's policies of class discrimination. They evidently were aware that the old system no longer constituted an effective means of appealing to the majority of peasants. But more than this, the new leadership believed China needed a new era of social stability and economic progress, grounded in a new set of political premises. They wanted to end the sense of conflict which 'class struggle' purposely had induced and the growing political disaffection among those who had lost out.

In particular, Party officials wanted to defuse the resentments of China's middle-class constituencies. Their concern here obviously included the middle peasants and the sent-down youths. But above all, the leadership needed to win back the support of the urban intelligentsia and the middle-class technocrats who had been alienated by the intense class policies of the 1960s and 1970s. The success of the Four Modernizations campaign depended upon regaining their confidence.

Thus, for reasons partly tied to a new rural political strategy but partly also to the new drive to modernize China, Beijing made a series of sweeping announcements in late 1978 and 1979. To symbolize an end to class struggle throughout the nation, it was declared that most of China's four-bad elements, including the great majority of the old landlords, had 'remoulded' themselves over the past three decades. Though their class-origin labels would remain in dossiers, the Party central committee directed that their 'hats' – the official stigmata – be permanently removed.[24]

Already weakened, beliefs in the immutability of class labels collapsed in Chen Village in the wake of these pronouncements. Some of the older peasants were displeased initially, but their opposition soon subsided. Much as if rigid discrimination had never existed, the bad-class households eased back into the village's social and political life. For example, within two years one of the production teams elected a former rich peasant to serve as its team head, while a second team elected the son of the ex-guerrilla 'rotten element' to serve as head. Remarkably, interviews in early 1982 revealed that class origins were no longer taken much into account even in marriage decisions. Bad-class youths could now obtain brides on almost equal terms with the young men of good-class backgrounds.

In short, in a period of less than three years, a structure of discrimination based on class labels had simply disappeared, with scarcely a trace remaining. Interviews in 1982 regarding other villages in Guangdong suggest the same rapid disappearance of class distinctions. I would suspect that this pattern has been widespread throughout rural China – for reasons basically similar to those of Chen Village. From Chinese media reports it is clear that in the 1970s much of the Chinese countryside had experienced similar troubles and bureaucratic impositions, with a corresponding erosion of faith in Party policies.

In earlier decades, the men who currently run China had been firm adherents of the rural class policies. The reasons are apparent given the historical circumstances. The Party had been unable to live up to its economic promises of the collectivization 'high tide' and Great Leap Forward; throughout the 1960s and 1970s most of the countryside remained impoverished. In lieu of prosperity, the Party could provide the majority of good-class peasants with marginal advantages (both material and non-material) offered by the class line. These gave the peasants the satisfaction of an honoured status; the belief that they were bearers of a noble mission; and the feeling that they were innately superior to the scapegoats in bad-class households.

When these beliefs, along with their faith in the Party, began crumbling in the 1970s, a new means for appealing to the peasantry became necessary. By the late 1970s, national leaders wagered that peasant loyalties could be retained by introducing new material gratifications which would supplant the earlier symbolic rewards. It was clearly felt that a programme of economic liberalization (with expanded free markets, larger private plots, and better prices for agricultural produce) would bring noticeable improvements in the peasantry's standard of living. Full food bins would render obsolete some of the political functions which the class system had served.

In Chen Village, that is exactly what happened. In 1980 the communities near Hong Kong were allowed to sell food directly to buyers from the colony's booming markets. At the same time, under a new government programme which, in effect, decollectivized agriculture, the fields surrounding Chen Village were parcelled out to individual households to be tended – independently – as family enterprises. The peasants quickly reconverted rice paddies into lucrative vegetable plots and commercial fishponds. Incomes rose several fold in just two years. By 1982 a household's success at its private endeavours had become a major source of its status. As an emigrant from Chen Village commented in 1982: 'It's not class origin which counts any more; what counts now is making money.'

However, only a small minority of Chinese villages enjoy access to a high-priced urban market like Hong Kong's. It remains an open question whether, for much of China, the new programme of dividing the land into family holdings will have the desired effect of boosting productivity and living standards over the long term. If not, the Party leadership will be under pressure to devise new means to enlist peasant backing. In the past, the Party had appealed for peasant support by promoting rigid class distinctions and by mobilizing attacks upon 'class enemies'. But it is improbable that leaders will want to turn back to such techniques: for it has become questionable whether such a strategy, in any guise, would work again.

7

BOURGEOIS RADICALISM IN THE 'NEW CLASS' OF SHANGHAI, 1949–1969

Lynn T. White III

Shanghai has been the largest centre of China's bourgeoisie, but it has also been the centre for China's radicals. The home of coiffures and English is also the home of the Gang of Four. This paradox would be less intriguing if the two syndromes could be identified with different, opposing urban groups. This cannot be done, because radical leaders have come largely from the same social backgrounds that provide the leaders whom radicals castigate. Although the labels 'capitalist' and 'proletarian' have often been applied in China as if they pertained to coherent political groups, it will not be hard to find evidence that the actual situation is more complex.[1] Shanghai's emergent 'middle class' has produced the smug and the visionary together. Its conflicting parts have inspired two different kinds of politics.

An attempt to explain this dilemma requires a preliminary excursion into definitions. Unless we know what a 'class' is, the task of assigning predicates to various classes will prove difficult. Sociologists disagree whether there are ordinarily two or a larger number of classes in a country, whether other social groupings are just as important, whether classes become major actors in world history, and whether the existence of a class can be determined objectively in the absence of a 'class consciousness'. Despite such disagreements, there is surprising consensus on the main elements in the definition of class. Thinkers as diverse as Max Weber and Karl Marx would agree that 'classes' are groups of people who share the same opportunities in life because of the roles they fulfil in production.[2]

OFFICIAL LABELS AND NEW MANAGERS

Concocting a definition is easier than applying one. In China, 'classes' have been less important as subjects of academic definition than as brands in official policy. The government in the early 1950s assigned a social class label to everyone. The classification of households became an important public measure throughout the country, after the rural land reform and urban 'Five Anti' movements.[3] Similar policies had also been important in Communist rural base areas before 1949.[4]

In cities, class labels are recorded in 'household registration books' (*huji bu*), of which the authoritative copies are filed at local police stations. According to interviewees and an article in a Shanghai journal, household registers contain two entries that are relevant to class: 'family origin' (*jiating chushen*) and 'individual status' (*geren chengfen*).[5] The family origin of each household is set on the basis of regulations first issued in 1950,[6] and it describes the type of income source for the family in the three years before 1949. In urban Shanghai, most people were labelled either 'worker' or 'national capitalist', although some people with solely rural income sources were given labels from strata in the countryside, and a few households received the stigmatizing title 'bureaucratic capitalist'. Family origin was inherited by children from the heads of households in which they grew up (this almost always meant it was inherited patrilineally). There has been latent and open disagreement, during the first decades of the People's Republic, whether these class categories should have practical consequences, especially for children from 'bad' class households, born after 1949.

'Individual status' has also been recorded in the household registers separately for each adult of eighteen years or older. It can differ between household members – as 'family origin' cannot.

For many offspring of pre-1949 business families in a city like Shanghai, the use of these individual ratings reduced the effects of a 'bad' social classification. 'Individual status' indicated a person's contribution to New China. It ameliorated the labelling system for patriotic, talented children from politically unsavoury backgrounds.

The individual status labels, as they developed over time, were somewhat ad lib. They could include titles such as 'worker', 'teacher', 'cadre', 'education worker', 'intellectual', or 'dockhand' – the list of possibilities was not always bounded and so became diverse on the record books. Furthermore, as a Shanghai publication of 1956 explained:

Individual status can be revised. This depends on social changes of the economic positions and sources of livelihood of household members. However, their family origin reflects their history; it is an objective historical fact and cannot be changed.[7]

Official classification creates self-conscious 'classes' and conflict groups, irrespective of whether classes in general must be conscious or conflicting. Government labelling may seem – at first – to preempt our task here of trying to determine a less policy-dependent list of such groups in Shanghai.

Another kind of analysis, however, would show in Shanghai the emergence of a 'new class', different from the older ones, comprising managers and Party bureaucrats. Milovan Djilas emphasizes the importance of such groups in Communist systems.[8] The 'new class' in Shanghai would include two types of members. The first type was recruited from the bourgeois management classes of the pre-Communist period; many pre-Liberation capitalists proved to be essential in serving Communist management goals. Their individual statuses (usually as 'workers' or 'cadres') have either dominated their 'bad' class designations; or in some cases, they have been able to change their class labels despite regulations discouraging such changes. A second kind of 'new class' member includes people who were born into proletarian or peasant families but are trained in Party schools to assume management positions. This latter group (like the former one) may wear blue tunics, but they are not blue collar. The managers-turned-'workers' and the workers-turned-managers do not, even together, begin to constitute a majority of people in Shanghai; but they are numerous and functionally crucial.

Much of Shanghai's politics, in the first two decades of revolution, reflects tensions among the parts of this newly emerging elite. Individuals in this group are of various origins and have espoused different and conflicting causes. Despite diversity, they have slowly formed a management class, in the sense that they control many tangible and intangible resources and have similar productive functions. But this class has not consistently been unified. The 'new class' overlaps with and includes older managerial groups that were deeply affected by – and often resented – official labelling.

LATENT AND OBVIOUS TENSIONS: MORE BASES FOR CLASSIFICATION

To explore this highly political subject, it may be necessary to look at struggles. A class becomes easiest to recognize in contest situations, in expressions of latent tension or in actual conflicts – although a class is something bigger than a short-term political faction. It should involve a substantial sector of society, with a broadly definable economic function, not an evanescent group with just a few members. Many societies in the present world show that severe stratification can persist for decades without much overt conflict. This may even be the typical case in developing cities, such as Shanghai, where the configuration of classes is slowly changing. A French sociologist, François Bourricauld, describes Peru's cities as places where social stratification has not led to political explosion, because resentment of class repression has not been extensively communicated within or between classes. Violence from the poor has been sporadic, scattered, 'acted out', and non-cumulative.[9] Lima's urban poor are not Lima's urban radicals; the political left is managed by the same groups, generally, that manage the political right. American researchers, such as Wayne Cornelius and Joan Nelson, have shown that the urban poor, when they are recently immigrated to cities from rural places, do not quickly oppose governments – which therefore enjoy a spell of time to assimilate the offspring of urban immigrants in national systems of politics.[10] Albert Hirschman argues that disadvantaged social groups will for a long time tolerate other groups' obvious progress, as a good omen of modern change in which they hope to participate later.[11]

Stratification is conventionally defined as inequality that persists over time, from generation to generation. Especially in situations of quick, forceful, government-led change, a decrease of stratification does not necessarily mean a decrease of inequality – decreasing stratification may just mean that certain new groups replace old ones in privileged statuses. This very political process may correlate with a reduction of inequality between households, but it does not always involve less inequality. Comprehensive data on this topic from Shanghai are unavailable, but the city has apparently experienced both a decrease of inequality and a decrease of stratification during the decades since mid-century. In some periods such as 1952–6, high turbulence in stratification patterns has been more apparent than the reduction of overall inequality.[12] Stratification changes in Shanghai have been caused by conflict in political campaigns. Changes have also been caused by personnel-training and infrastructure-building efforts of the Party in non-campaign periods (which have received less study). Any degree of equality for income, power, or other goods is generally a result of slow social processes, the effect of many policy intentions and their unintended consequences over long durations of time.

Political conflict between factional groups smaller than classes has engaged large amounts of comparative political science literature, including many fine works about China;[13] but less political analysis has been made of long-term relations between classes. One conclusion from the literature on high leadership is that the heads of radical movements, able to use violence to politicize social strata in either rural or urban contexts, have often been city-educated and from the pre-1949 urban or rural management classes. In many developing countries – not just socialist ones, and not just in China – the offspring of middle-class families receive schooling to become aware of the relevance of political change in their nations to their own personal fates. They have, when young, freedom to read widely about politics, a freedom that few real workers and peasants enjoy. The management classes have provided most of the cadres for governments, would-be governments, and anarchist oppositions. They staff the apparatus for either regimes or revolutions. They lead either in obfuscating class tensions or in bringing such tensions to conflict.

This paper will retrace the development of Shanghai's management class chronologically, to highlight varying conditions in periods when class boundaries were permeable or rigid, when class conflict was unimportant or important. The main message here concerns the rise of a new class through the combination of parts of old ones – but the process was a bumpy one. The change cannot be analysed without periodization; no study of a single time, or only of campaign times, could cover the subject of class reformation. The end of this essay will attempt to generalize about the conditions of such change, to indicate the roles in cultural and economic development that the managers of Shanghai have played, and to see the causes of both the radical and gradualist forms of management-class leadership in Shanghai.

BEFORE 1952: THE BOURGEOIS STAFFING OF THE COMMUNIST MOVEMENT IN SHANGHAI

The importance of Shanghai's management class in political movements did not begin recently. A few early twentieth-century examples deserve special mention: Mark Elvin has studied the growth of a commercial/official 'gentry democracy' in Shanghai at the end of the last dynasty.[14] Mary Rankin has traced the rise of revolutionaries in East China, mainly in opposition to this gentry, before 1911.[15] During the intellectual ferment of the May 4th Movement, and the surge of nationalism among many urban strata in the 1920s, a nascent Chinese Communist movement recruited most of its leaders among students whose families were not poor. The Kuomintang elite was based in similar groups. As Kau Ying-mao has shown, the CCP (Chinese Communist Party) is unique in having been forced to adapt its organizational skills, learned first in cities, for survival during its later career in the bush, among peasants.[16] The Communist elite remained surprisingly coherent for three or four decades after 1930.[17] Its mass support lay in the peasantry but its leaders came largely from middle-class and intellectual backgrounds, and virtually all had long urban experience. By 1932, CCP contact with the proletariat had declined so sharply that 'Red' trade unions in cities included no more than a thousand of China's three million industrial workers.[18]

In the war period, from 1937 to 1945, Shanghai's Communist organizations had more luck in recruiting students from bourgeois backgrounds than in recruiting workers. By mid-1946, the journal *Qunchong* (Masses), whose readership and editors were mainly middle class, criticized the KMT (Kuomintang) for a law under which 'a policeman can at any time go into any private home or shop in the district for regular or irregular visits'.[19] Policemen could demand bribes from bourgeois shopkeepers so that 'all the legal businesses in Shanghai are objects of their extortion'. The Shanghai CCP recruited many middle-class students and entrepreneurs to work against the Kuomintang.[20]

In May 1947, the local KMT police gave orders to close down three liberal newspapers, the *Wenhui bao*, *Xinmin bao*, and *Lianhe ribao*.[21] In the same month, 5,000 students organized a 'hunger parade', which was reported in remaining bourgeois publications.[22] The KMT summarily expelled hundreds of students from Shanghai middle schools, and it raised tuition fees for the rest. The students, mostly bourgeois, organized a campaign to 'purchase a large quantity of national products from famous patriotic manufacturers' at low prices, and then resell them, retaining the profits for tuition. More than 1,000 'teams of salesmen' from seventy schools joined this movement, which shows the closeness between the radical and bourgeois oppositions to the KMT.[23]

From pre-1949 Shanghai textile manufacturers, the KMT Government occasionally commandeered factory output at low, state-fixed prices for army uniforms. Many bourgeois supported the KMT, but some opposed it. After 'liberation', important members of the Communist underground turned out to be capitalists. The head of the Activities Brigade of the Shanghai Office of the KMT Central Bureau, who had been very assiduous in suppressing some anti-KMT democrats, revealed that he had been a CCP secret agent. He had done his job so as to maximize bourgeois resentment against the KMT, without harming crucial CCP activities.[24] The head of a large Shanghai life insurance company and other businessmen also made public their Communist Party memberships at this time.[25]

Cooperation between certain capitalists and the Party was also encouraged by circumstances after the Red Army marched into Shanghai. The KMT naval blockade caused marketing and supply problems that forced many capitalists to seek nationalization more quickly than the Communists alone could have arranged. In some factories, 'associations of workers and capitalists' negotiated mutual reductions of wages and salaries.[26] Assets were confiscated from seven categories of entrepreneurs, who had been 'war criminals, collaborators, bureaucratic capitalists, bandits, [KMT] secret agents, despots, or counterrevolutionaries'. The vast majority of managers, however, were not in any of these miscreant groups.

The Korean War provided a patriotic, non-class basis for the new government to claim greater loyalty from all classes. In this context, some of the most virulent *anti*-Communist organizations were impeccably proletarian (especially secret societies associated with the construction and transport industries). Government purchases associated with the war brought greater prosperity as early as 1951. A few wartime *nouveaux riches* sprang up in Shanghai; and Mayor Chen Yi spoke favourably of 'smuggling for the revolution', as capitalists brought needed raw materials from overseas through the blockade.[27] The class situation was somewhat flexible, especially until 1952, when the 'democratic reform movement' (*minzhu gaige yundong*) was completed so that all legally resident households in the city had social class labels.

Because of the foreign war, and because of CCP statements about the need for patriotic capitalists to run their businesses productively, the degree of compliance with class registration was fairly high. As an ex-cadre interviewee said, 'Even if one could hide bourgeois class status in the beginning, the fact would eventually be discovered through rechecking that took place in the later stages of this movement, or in other different movements.'[28] The Korean War created a mixed atmosphere of political tension and economic expansion, whose results ranged from an increase in the officiousness of neighbourhood organizations[29] to the 'Five Anti' campaign that put many medium-sized businesses under real or nominal government purview. There is no need here to repeat John Gardner's description of the Five Anti movement in Shanghai.[30] This campaign made the bourgeoisie conscious of the power that the Communist Party could mobilize among workers. The Party could terrify the managers of this complex urban economy long before the Party could manage it directly. When capitalists saw their only choice – cooperation with the new government that could threaten them sporadically without being able fully to control them – their attitudes toward the Party became more sagacious. Their own class was dividing, but their talents were still needed. Workers recently trained in Party schools began to join many of them in similar economic functions.

1952–6: MOBILITY IN OFFICIAL AND ACTUAL CLASSES

Chinese property ownership was restructured in a three-stage process. From 1949, a land reform disorganized the previously dominant rural classes; and in cities, a similar process climaxed with the Five Anti movement.

The next period, from mid-1952 to early 1956, was longer and more relaxed for most citizens. The economy boomed, and in Shanghai the gross value of industrial output grew 17 per cent annually (in 1952 prices).[31] For managers of some large businesses, 'joint public–private management' became real; but for the more numerous heads of small and medium-sized private firms, this was a period of relative freedom. The planners trained a new cadre and strengthened Party discipline; they only gradually collected accounting personnel to keep track of smaller economic units. This was a time of high social mobility; new cadres quickly assumed property-control functions alongside old ones. Many individuals from 'bourgeois' families took jobs as workers, not only at low levels but also as technicians and foremen. Some 'workers' took managerial roles. In handicraft industries, new entrepreneurs from various family backgrounds could set up a new business and hire a few workers, to participate in the economic boom. A new middle class, temporary but of a traditional sort, emerged along with a new middle class of a socialist sort, even before the old middle class was fully coopted or destroyed. The proletariat, now larger, included people from 'capitalist' families. This was a time of class creation and rearrangement.[32]

The third stage of ownership change, 1956–8, was socially just as tumultuous, and administratively even more so. From the Transition to Socialism of 1956 to the Antirightist Campaign of late 1957, cadres were sent to lower-level offices – a change that was the organizational basis for the Great Leap Forward of 1958. This sharp structural change was inspired locally by a precipitous drop in the growth of Shanghai's industrial output (measured as above) in 1956–7 to only 5 per cent. The Transition to Socialism disrupted supply patterns and authority patterns in many small units. Its aim was to use more previous managers for the new order, and it intensified a process that had been proceeding more gradually since 1952.

In other words, the 1952–6 era was framed by periods of even more extensive campaign. During the middle era, some private firms in selected industries came under joint or state management, but the rate of official change was not fast. Even by the end of 1953, only forty-odd 'joint' factories existed in Shanghai, all of which were large. They retained capitalist managers, who cooperated with Party overseers. A year later, the number had increased to 180; and by the first half of 1955, the 225 joint factories accounted for less than a third of industrial output value in the city's private and semi-private sectors.[33]

The Party had to rely on industrial and commercial guilds of a traditional sort, to administer these changes. It had counted on entrepreneurs' federations at the very beginning of the Five Anti campaign,[34] but activist cadres had quickly discovered that intensification of the movement required more direct structures to mobilize worker support for campaigns. From mid-1952, the renewed emphasis on production meant a return to the guild framework. A mixture of trade union leaders and previous managers took charge in many sizeable firms.

In smaller firms, household heads often remained important, even when these shops became nominal branches of larger trading corporations.[35] The Party's *Liberation Daily* cautioned proletarians against assuming that the authority of previous managers was illegitimate. In an editorial on 'Strengthening Leadership over Workers' Political Education', the newspaper warned: 'Education must not deviate from reality and lead to excessive expectations.' It averred that 'blind adventurist advances' would lead to disregard for 'subjective and objective conditions' and to shoddy production.[36] Running an economy required managers not so contrite that they lacked authority.

The Party's policy was to let old managers administer most of the urban economy, but at the same time to train socialist cadres who could assume roles in strategic industries. The number of worker-origin students shot up; the number of capitalist-origin ones also rose. Individuals' improvements of their class designations made an exact comparison between these groups impossible; but already by mid-1952, the university-level residents of Shanghai were distributed by individual statuses as shown in Table 1. The largest category in this table may well include many people of capitalist origin, employed by corporations that they did not own. The Party's need for new cadres is attested by the fact that for every three Shanghai residents of a 'university-level cultural standard', another was being trained in 1952. The editorial containing these statistics implied that some members of the Five Anti work teams were recorded with a 'university-level cultural standard', even if they had not been long at universities. Some of these were middle-school students who participated in the Five Anti movement and were thus given quasi-

LYNN T. WHITE III

Table 1. *University-level Shanghai residents, 1952*

	Number	Percentage
'Members of labour unions or of the working class'	53,000	56
Studying in universities, 1952	23,000	24
'Petit bourgeois in free professions'	10,000	11
'Commercial and industrial elements'	8,000	9
TOTAL	94,000	100

Source: Computed from *Da gong bao* (L'Impartial), Shanghai, editorial of University graduates and current students are all included above; and others may also be included, as the text notes.

diplomas because the Party needed them in offices rather than in classrooms. The editorial was explicit that, 'Certain capitalist and management representatives have taken direct part in the struggle.'

School admissions during 1952 involved affirmative action for the children of workers and peasants. In 'factory areas', secondary schools were able to recruit large numbers of offspring from proletarian families, so that previous stratification in the school system decreased.[37] To further this policy, the Party conducted a minor campaign in late 1952, sending teachers from Shanghai schools into factories to urge that worker-parents prepare their children for education.[38] Even in late 1952, however, Shanghai had three times as many private as public primary schools,[39] and these tended to admit many non-proletarians who did well on the entrance exams.

As the Party was educating usable persons from all classes, forming a new composite class for the management of socialist Shanghai, debate raged among leaders at high levels on the speed with which the Party should displace helpful but non-Communist urbanites from management roles. The winter of 1953–4 was apparently a period of intense discussion at the national level on steps to be taken in the socialist transformation. The policy substance of this dispute received less publicity than the question of whether regional or central authorities should have power to decide it. The consequent purge involved Shanghai's ex-First Party Secretary Rao Shushi. Rao had organized the most intense period of the Five Anti movement against capitalists. His associate and fellow-purgee in Manchuria, Gao Gang, was accused of having:

152

invented the utterly absurd theory that the Party consisted of two parties –
one, the so-called 'party of the revolutionary bases and the Army' and the
other, the so-called 'party of the white areas'.[40]

Their purge was clearly a victory for moderates on this issue, especially
Liu Shaoqi and Zhou Enlai. Socialist personnel continued to be
trained from all classes after Rao lost power.

Limits to the policy of accommodation were shown, however,
by the purge of Pan Hannian and Yang Fan in March and April
1955. Pan had been a Shanghai CCP underground agent during
the anti-Japanese War, adept in shuttle diplomacy between Yenan
and Shanghai. Pan had maintained important connections with
bourgeois leftists, especially with a radical literary front named the
'Ant Society' (*Mayi She*).[41] He was Shanghai's first Communist
Deputy Mayor, in charge of security work. Yang Fan, Director
of the Public Security Bureau, was his subordinate. In the middle
of 1955, Peking leader Peng Zhen announced that Pan had been
'arrested and judged at the request of the Head of the Supreme
People's Procuracy ... because proof has emerged that he was
engaged in counterrevolutionary activities'.[42] Pan had been highly
respected among other cadres for his skills in the 'white areas', and
he seems to have been purged for too much sympathy with the
plight of patriotic capitalists. Yang Fan was accused of having moved
too slowly on efforts to hunt down anti-regime bourgeois critics
soon after 1949.[43] Many in Shanghai were surprised, because Pan
had been considered the perfect choice to head Shanghai's security
work after Liberation.[44] Some businessmen believed that Pan would
become Mayor.[45] The Party was not of one mind concerning the
best speed to consolidate its managerial cadre position in Shanghai,
or concerning the extent to which previous managers could be
excluded from it.

The fact that many members of the old ruling class were needed to
run the new society – and that ex-worker cadres replacing them were
often attracted to bourgeois ways – deeply disturbed some Communists. A drama, *On Guard Beneath the Neon Lights*, praised the 'Good
Eighth Company of Nanking Road', which led moral resistance to
cultural 'sugar-coated bullets' in downtown Shanghai.[46] Newspapers
regretted that,

During the stage of socialist revolution and socialist transformation, the

153

bourgeois class still exists; dissipation in life and indulgence in pleasures are still seen ... We are still surrounded on all sides by the petit bourgeoisie, and our Party members and cadres still keep in close contact with such classes.[47]

Reporters criticized the bad example of Luo Heng, a Communist in Shanghai's Yulin District, who fell prey to bourgeois influences and was purged.[48] When a light-bulb maker discovered in 1955 that the spiral on the mould of some metal bulb bases was too narrow, she concluded that:

The mould for the bulb was carved by counterrevolutionaries in order to damage production ... Working in a private factory, one must always keep watch against damage by the counterrevolutionaries and supervising capitalists, in order to improve production.[49]

Puritans in the Party did not know what to do with the diversifying management class – but there was also no way to do without it.

Community spirit could not be monopolized by proletarians. When 800 members of a trade union each demanded an enamel cup and a towel from their cotton mill, the factory Party secretary secretly suggested to the capitalist that he deny the request on grounds of cost. The manager did so – but workers took the problem all the way to the Municipal Bureau of Labour, which provided a forum for a 'struggle meeting'. After ten hours of harangue, the capitalist chose to cut his losses and reverse his decision – despite quick pleas from the official arbitrators, who now intervened, asking him to reconsider.[50] When repression helped development, Party leaders were chagrined that the old managing class caused the new one to take some responsibility for it.

The Party could not afford to alienate most bourgeois. If mid-1955 was a period of pressure against some liberal styles, it was also a time to honour capitalists who seemed loyal. Previous members of the local Kuomintang formed a 'Revolutionary Committee of the KMT' in Shanghai.[51] The 'Democratic Women's Federation', Shanghai's closest equivalent to a Junior League in 1955, strengthened its 'ideological work among democratic sisters' from capitalist households.[52]

Socialist transformation implied that capitalists might be allowed to remove their stigma by joining unions. When a group of Shanghai's most prominent industrialists, including Rong Yiren, Sheng Peihua, and Hu Juewen, visited the Shanghai Federation of Trade Unions, they expressed a wish to become members.[53] Although proletarian stalwarts saw political disadvantages in such obvious cooperation between classes, many talented youths from bourgeois families were admitted to the Democratic Youth League at this time.[54]

1956–8: CHALLENGE AND LEGITIMACY FOR THE NEW MIDDLE CLASS

The Transition to Socialism began an era for both the old and new management strata. The event was festive, celebrated on January 20, 1956, when 'a long line of shining motor cars' with capitalists inside and portraits of Chairman Mao outside, rolled through Shanghai. The limousines were decorated with 'double happiness' traditional Chinese wedding symbols, and indeed two crucial leadership groups were then married.[55]

For fifteen months thereafter, capitalists were more able to criticize Party cadres than ever since. Socialist planners still needed their talents. As a Communist deputy mayor of Shanghai admitted in late 1956, 'Public representatives are still absent in many enterprises.'[56] Almost half of all big firms, even large department stores serving whole urban districts, were managed by 'private representatives'. Only a quarter of 'large' firms were managed by cadres sent from higher organs.[57] More political schools were established, to instill loyalty in capitalists who might become socialist. The Women's Federation sent bourgeois wives to a 'political night university'.[58] Their offspring in middle schools were given 'current affairs policy lessons'.[59]

The military draft law of 1956 was not passed because the People's Liberation Army was short of manpower, but because the Army wanted an option on skilled, urban youth. Disproportionate numbers of the conscripts were almost surely ex-bourgeois.[60]

Even the Communist Party took more reformed capitalists as members at this time. National statistics announced by Deng Xiaoping imply that from 1956 to 1957, the Party membership of workers and peasants increased 16 per cent and 15 per cent respectively – but the number of 'intellectuals' who were neither workers nor peasants increased 50 per cent.[61] This 'intellectual' group (which may have been largely ex-capitalist, because anyone who

155

could justify a 'worker' or 'peasant' designation would be classified under those better titles) comprised only a seventh of the Party's membership in 1957; but it was disproportionately urban and politically important.

The Party admission process at this time was more lax than might be expected. Any basic-level Party secretary could provide an application form to an individual expressing interest in membership. At least in Shanghai, the applicant's social background was not always crucial to success in seeking Party membership, according to interview reports. Workers had a first-face advantage over offspring of capitalist families, but this advantage was counterbalanced by the generally higher 'cultural level' of bourgeois applicants.[62]

On January 14–20, 1956, the Central Committee held a 'Conference on the Question of Intellectuals'; and on May 2, Mao delivered his famous unpublished 'Hundred Flowers' speech in its first and most liberal version. By July, the Shanghai Democratic League was 'actively admitting new members'.[63] A prominent bourgeois journalist named Jin Zhonghua (who was soon to be a deputy mayor and was sometimes rumoured to be a secret Party member) nonetheless made a speech in July indicating that, 'Consultative work is not going well.' He said the Shanghai Government was insufficiently aware of how people – he clearly meant ex-bourgeois people – felt about the Transition to Socialism.[64] Jin suggested that the multi-class patriotic enthusiasm of the Korean War and immediately subsequent years had subsided.

The Hundred Flowers movement was an attempt by a small, new ruling class, in just a few cities including Shanghai, to muster help for the post-Transition economic order from a relatively large, older management class. At first, no flowers bloomed. To enliven the campaign, the Politburo decided in December 1956 to encourage criticism of the Party. The First Secretary of the Shanghai Party Committee, Ke Qingshi, gave a talk on January 9 about 'resolving contradictions in socialist society by persuasion'. Mao gave yet another, similar speech on February 27. In mid-April, Ke invited 'intellectuals of various circles in Shanghai' to special symposia, where Party spokesmen assured participants that, 'At present the class struggle has been basically concluded, and the major questions are those within the ranks of the people.' Ex-capitalists still asked, whether it was safe to speak freely. Mao's address was played by tape recorder to them, but the first mumblings against the new officialdom were cautious.[65] Zhou Enlai himself came to give a pep talk for criticism to 14,000 people gathered in Shanghai's Culture Square on April 29.[66]

A private-side manager in a rubber shoe factory, who was pressed to make some complaint, ventured to suggest that the workers were no longer cutting pieces for outer and inner layers of the shoes to fit together. This was not too brash. Another manager in the same factory declared that austerity movements had prevented the use of wrappers for the shoes: 'They can be damaged very easily. When they are placed in shopwindows, they are exposed to the sun, and this affects the quality of the shoes.'[67] These assertions were published as late as May 4 – a date when something bolder might have been in order.

The topic of discussion at other meetings was more apropos: whether all kinds of ideas should be given free rein. 'A majority in these discussions said this was right.'[68] Some capitalists remained reticent: 'We belong to a class that has to be transformed.'[69] Then, quickly in early and mid-May, the rhetoric became more blunt. One critic called Party members 'monsters and freaks' (*niugui sheshen*). A doctor said he had 'an office but no power' (*youzhi wuquan*).[70] Schoolteachers, scientists, managers, deputy mayors, publishers, car wreckers, funeral directors, educational leaders, humorists, women's cadres – most of them bourgeois – hastily bloomed with criticisms that were particular or general, cautious or reckless, polite or rude, all about the Party's new managing class and its works.[71]

Many critics cited Marx and Engels (two radical theorists from bourgeois family backgrounds). The assistant manager of a Shanghai cotton mill said, 'The economic system of socialism can grow quickly only when it is built on a highly developed capitalist economy.'[72] A Fudan University professor captured the nervousness of these proceedings when he later described himself as a 'Don Quixote on the ideological front'.[73] This must be a general definition of a radical visionary. The bases of the criticisms were no more stable than the political positions of the largely ex-capitalist critics.

The Antirightist movement was formally a continuation of the blooming. It was conducted, at first, in the same forums; the most obvious change was that different people were now speaking. Some managerial workers had always been present at the meetings, and now they defended themselves. Particular scorn was heaped on their own class brethren who had joined in criticism of the Party.[74]

Even before September, when First Secretary Ke delivered a 'summary report' to the Shanghai People's Congress, many of the Party's critics were sent for 'reform through labour'. Ex-bourgeois people were induced to volunteer for assignments at smaller offices, in and around the city. Party members who had been criticized (and many who had not) were sent to lower-level, more dispersed, decentralized agencies by the end of the year. All of Shanghai's leaderships were physically scattered to small offices at this time. The result was the administrative infrastructure for the Great Leap Forward.

No campaign, not even the Antirightist movement, could build personnel resources in the sure way that inter-campaign periods did. Secretary Ke by December 1957 was openly trying to mend fences with ex-capitalists who might still help. As he said on December 25:

The great majority of the bourgeoisie and the capitalist intellectuals may accept socialist transformation and the leadership of the proletariat. We should trust the majority of them ... and try to win as many of them as possible to the left, so as to expand the forces of the left.[75]

An editorial of the time put the Party's question neatly: 'Can the left-wing bourgeois intellectuals measure up to the standards of the working class?' These standards were enumerated in three categories: support for the regime, a Marxist outlook, and technical skills. The official conclusion was: 'Recent revolutionary movements show that the left wing of the intellectuals measures up to the criteria of the working-class intellectuals.'[76] But in late 1957, this was a prescription for the future, not a description of the recent past when ex-capitalists had suffered badly.

By the early spring of 1958, as many as 10,000 'democratic persons' held a rally in Culture Square. The leaders of one democratic party promised that at least 35 per cent of its members would become 'genuine intellectuals of the working class'. In a parade at the rally, members of another party pinned to their chests 'red hearts made of cardboard, symbolizing their determination to be loyal'.[77] With economic decentralization, it was in the interests of the leading middle strata, despite their recent conflicts, to claim unity. The pretence might eventually become a reality, if the tensions could be held in check by a common commitment to quick social progress.

1958–62: COOPTION OF SHANGHAI'S BOURGEOISIE

In Shanghai, the Great Leap Forward was an outgrowth of economic and political decisions that had been taken in 1956. It would be unrealistic to say that the urban Leap began in 1958. Some large industrial projects began production in that year; but these were planned earlier and had been 'in the pipeline' for more than a few months. This movement was not, in cities, a completely new policy initiative.

Its effects on relations between classes in Shanghai were different from those of the Five Anti campaign, the Transition to Socialism, or the Cultural Revolution.[78] Culturally, the Leap in Shanghai was not anti-bourgeois. It involved 'self-reform' for ex-capitalists. Deputy Mayor Jin Zhonghua became editor of the *Wenhui bao*, a prominent newspaper published explicitly for bourgeois readers whose energies were now required for progress. Religion was not particularly suppressed at this time; maybe because the resurrection is a leap too, Easter masses were held in 1958. The immediately following years also saw more official efforts to reform religious practice than to stamp it out quickly.[79] In February 1959, the annual spring sales advertised 'Hawaiian electric guitars' and perfumed bedsheets.[80]

Ambitious quotas put pressure on all kinds of managers, as investments after the Transition to Socialism came on line and politicians called for quicker growth. Shanghai's industrial investment in 1958 was claimed to be 250 per cent of the 1957 amount.[81] Heavy industrial production expanded 3.6 times faster than light industrial production, by value, between 1957 and 1958. New economic organizations were established, and 'socialist institutes' were established in Shanghai's suburbs, to instill the values of 'military organization, militant action, and collective life' in short courses for bureaucrats.[82] These schools were founded as much to educate ex-proletarian bureaucrats as to educate ex-bourgeois ones. Leap ideals were supposed to lay a claim on everybody, without discrimination by class. During the autumn harvest of

1958, a 'labour army' of 120,000 people marched on foot from Shanghai to nearby communes, to help bring in the crops. There would not have been time to check all of the participants' class backgrounds, even if that had been part of the idea.[83]

The economic pinch, caused by Great Leap rural disorganization, led to urban shortages of food and raw materials. This disaster was at first unselective among classes. But scapegoats were needed. The head of the Shanghai Federation of Trade Unions at the end of 1959 spoke about the need to keep up both production and the struggle against rightists.[84] New foremen were recruited largely from trade unions, which contained proletarians as well as ex-bourgeois workers. Three-quarters of the management for the new Shanghai No. 5 Steel Plant were promoted 'from the ranks of new workers'.[85]

The whole 1956–62 era was typified, for many members of the new class in Shanghai, by an unprecedented number of meetings. At first, in 1956, a retained manager might be invited to join a political party (probably a democratic one), for the sake of his job and unit. In 1957, there were meetings to hear criticisms, then meetings to hear criticisms of the critics. Later that year, the Anti-rightist campaign involved further meetings, often organized by the Chinese People's Political Consultative Conference. Marxist study meetings were mandatory for 'rightists' or 'volunteers' who had been sent for work in new units. By 1961, 'meetings of immortals' discussed political topics in professional disguises.[86] This menu of meetings was for high-level members of the previous and new management strata.[87] Formal conclaves between members of the two large sectors of Shanghai's main class were very frequent, in this period of their slow union.[88]

As the recession ended, a cause for division between the old and new parts of the middle class ended with it. A few rich, old families fared well even during the depression, because of their international importance and the Party's hope for a good press at its worst time. This tiny stratum was described by a Hong Kong newspaper:

They drive in 1961 Buicks and Chinese-made Tungfeng cars, wear well-cut British suits, smoke British 'State' brand cigarettes (much favoured by Mao Tse-tung himself), and allow their wives expensive coiffures.[89]

160

In a museum or sent down to a farm, the bourgeois class had lost its separate political punch – even though many of its members had joined a new ruling class. By early 1963, struggle between real proletarians and real bourgeois had become a matter of history. With the return of prosperity, new neon lights were seen on Nanking Road. A bright advertisement summed up what had happened by depicting 'One Hundred Flowers Blooming and Contending'.[90] A struggle fit for a gay sign: the symbols were still important, but the meanings had all changed.[91]

1963–6: TWO FUNCTIONS OF THE MANAGEMENT CLASS

Shanghai's leading class was now mainly unified, but its leaders evinced a division of basic interests that may be common for management classes: most of its members were concerned with plans for economic modernization. A few others, however, were more concerned with the loss of political will that accompanies the rise of modern bureaucracies. Neither of these is at all unique to China. Management classes in many countries face them, and often divide politically because different groups within them emphasize either the economic–technical issues or the political–cultural ones. A society that produces a Kubitschek will produce a Quadros; a McKinley implies a Bryan. Even when the social constituencies of such leaders are multi-class, the leaders at the top are generally of middle-class origin.[92] Modernization, however it is undertaken, may involve two basic problems that these two kinds of middle-class leaders face.

Shanghai's economy at the end of 1962 was reviving rapidly,[93] and its culture thus became more cosmopolitan. The city's factories were making more than sixty types of cosmetics, including a 'cream for the peasants'.[94] Motion pictures from France, Italy, West Germany, Britain, and Hong Kong were screened.[95] Nativist reactions against these trends, and an effort by part of the newly forming mixed elite to use these reactions to shape its formation, should not have been surprising.

In the spring of 1963, Mayor Ke appointed a little-known journalist named Zhang Chunqiao (later one of the 'Gang of Four'), to head the Municipal Party Propaganda Department.[96] Zhang's origins were urban and intellectual; he was apparently never a peasant or a factory worker.[97] Yao Wenyuan, a protégé of Zhang, was also of petit bourgeois background. His father, Yao Pengzi, authored many articles and several books, and the younger Yao graduated from Fudan University in 1949. His métier was polemic journalism, and for two decades he wielded the sharpest pen in China. All of Yao's writings copiously use the vocabulary of anti-capitalist class struggle to castigate the moral degradation that he saw in Shanghai's new class.[98] As early as 1957 Yao had special venom for bourgeois sentiments within the Party:

See how many poisonous worms, pulled out in antirightist struggles, are from literary circles! Not only do we now see these rightists defrocked, because they can no longer use their disguises such as 'old author', 'revolutionary writer', 'reformer', 'professor', or 'director.' We now also find that there are anti-Party elements among such famous young authors as are cherished, promoted, and at all times taken to be important by the Party.[99]

Yao demanded affirmative action in publication for writers from proletarian backgrounds. As one of them put it, 'Give us time to make friends, to study, and to think about problems.'[100] But if they were talented, the Party needed them for economic work. A worker-accountant-writer said that he was given too many 'sudden attack' chores in his office, and he had no time.[101] Zhang defended special fees for worker-writers, despite his admission that: 'The masses in organs, enterprises, and factories, where the young authors work, have little understanding for them.'[102] Most workers did not even understand China's greatest modern writer, Lu Xun, although he was their friend.[103]

Some workers, however, had become middle class. Shanghai still had more officially labelled 'capitalists' than any other place in China,[104] but they were joined in management by 'proletarians' especially in large plants (from which statistics are available). By the mid-1960s at the Shanghai Machine Tool Factory, 37 per cent of the technicians were proletarian. In a sample of large model factories, not all in Shanghai, 40 per cent of the managers and 31 per cent of the Party secretaries were of worker origin. Another 33 per cent of the managers, and 45 per cent of the Party secretaries in these favoured factories, claimed to be of peasant origin.[105] (Retired soldiers often obtained auxiliary jobs alongside promoted workers and socialized capitalists, and many ex-soldiers were from peasant families.) There was considerable harmony among the economic decision makers in this compound new class. For some time, they conducted progress as usual, despite potential opposition from radicals in propaganda departments.

High members of the new leading class enjoyed perquisites. For example, there were two main cadres' clubs in Shanghai. The Culture Club (Wenhua Julebu) in Shanghai Mansion was open only to a small minority of the very highest officials. The other, for a larger number, was located in the Peace Hotel.[106] Between 1963 and 1966, life in Shanghai became more comfortable for functionaries and their families, and the evolution of status groups was definitely influenced by the habits of overseas Chinese.[107] According to some reports of some old capitalists, Shanghai had a resurgence, and 'their solidarity was reminiscent of freemasonry'.[108]

At many meetings, all the topics were economic. Speeches proudly drew attention to new investments, to the unprecedented prosperity of suburban agriculture, to 'worker-activists' (which at this time meant fast producers), and to likely future growth rates. At some sessions, politics were scarcely mentioned.[109] A large group of engineers, technicians, and high-level mechanics had become essential in Shanghai factories, and they knew it.[110] Their relation to capital was not expressed in legalistic property terms – but, in fact, they controlled it exactly as if they owned it.

Below them was a stratum of unionized workers in large plants, mostly of proletarian origin but now including many ex-bourgeois, whose perquisites ranged from health and pension plans to summer swimming pools and permanent legal residence in Shanghai. These unionized workers had a considerable stake in the established order. Still further down the scale were non-unionized contract workers, whose jobs depended on the continuation of urban prosperity and the pleasure of the managers.[111] Some of these labourers were seasonal, available in Shanghai under the 'both worker and peasant' (*yi gong yi nong*) plan that was approved in many official speeches of the period. Others were middle-school graduates who declined to accept job assignments in rural areas; they hoped for permanent work in Shanghai. The contract proletariat and the unionized proletariat had few interests in common, although the official ideology fudged distinctions between them. It is probable that members of both groups hoped, in a time of generally increasing prosperity, that they might soon advance into the management class;[112] and official statements encouraged such hopes, although official policies did not actualize them.

Tolerance for inequalities in development, as Albert Hirschman has suggested, may last for a while but not indefinitely. Chinese bureaucrats were thus urged to forgo usual management perquisites, to 'rid themselves of bourgeois ideas' and 'preserve their features as workers'.[113] When technical innovations were made by managers who happened to be from worker families, the newspapers reported their class origins enthusiastically;[114] but many such reforms were reported without notes concerning the innovators' backgrounds, and in this movement many ex-bourgeois contributed.[115]

The Socialist Education campaign propagandized fears that China's development might be sapped by regressive class forces, even after the previous ruling classes had been absorbed. The newspaper *Branch Life* (*Zhibu shenghuo*) under Zhang Chunqiao ceaselessly preached proletarian fraternity. A 'half-illiterate worker', writing in it, 'tried [his] best to help reform the brothers and sisters of our class, so that we may advance together'.[116] Zhang's arts clubs, youth clubs, and libraries organized lectures on the history of the lower classes.[117] The Army sponsored 'national defence athletic training', radio clubs, navigation clubs, and shooting clubs.[118] For a while, a 'brotherhood troop' (*zidi bing*) of worker-dramatists staged didactic skits for anyone passing through the waiting room of the Shanghai North Railroad Station.[119]

In the summer of 1964, more than 300,000 Shanghai factory militiamen were invited to camps in the suburbs for training and propaganda.[120] Their units later assumed patrol duty in public places.[121] Some factory and union cadres, who were militia officers, went to 'winter military camps' (*dongji junshi yeying*), where they must have formed acquaintance networks that created a new kind of city-wide armed force.[122]

Class struggle was the motto of these organizations; but some of their members were ex-bourgeois; and some publications from Peking, at least, gave assurances that family background was less important than individual achievement.[123] Even in Shanghai, the leaders of a lane meeting might assure residents that 'class struggle' was mainly a means to deal with disputes, so that a 'unity of revolutionary principles' could be maintained.[124] The 1964 press intimated disagreement among managers whether socialist education still concerned real class struggle, or only dubious moral habits. People at teahouses were urged not to 'chat with one another about bourgeois things, such as good food and luxuries'.[125] Feudal stories and witty talk were criticized.[126] In the end, the reformers had to admit, 'We struggled to dissuade such conversations in vain.'[127]

At the beginning of 1965, after a National Work Conference convened by Mao, the Socialist Education movement sharply intensified. For example, a 'Four Clean' work team of thirty cadres went to the Shanghai Tobacco Company, temporarily taking over the offices of the manager (an ex-capitalist in semi-retirement), the deputy manager (in charge of operations), and the Party secretary. The team sent down detailed orders, but it did not mobilize worker support extensively within the factory and 'did not affect a great many people directly'.[128] The team investigated the personal and family histories of managers, including Party members; but most were not removed at this time, unless the team uncovered gross misdeeds. At the Shanghai Public Utilities Bureau, three high cadres who had claimed to be of 'poor peasant' origins were proved to come from landlord families. Three more were embezzlers. Another three had unreported relatives on Taiwan. Most had committed peccadilloes only; forty-five were accused of private bargaining or spreading rumours. Such minor sins were recorded but did not yet lead to punishment. As a result of the investigation at this Bureau, six persons were expelled from the Party and four activists were accepted for membership.[129] As a portion of total employment, few criminals were found – even though many managers must have been disquieted by so much research into family histories. A report on another factory indicates that only three people lost their jobs, out of a full staff of 4,200. Most of Shanghai's mixed elite found difficulty with this campaign's implication that it should be removed from power.

New, proletarian-origin cadres may have seen a chance for further career advancement in the work teams' radical approach. The worker-managers were overwhelmingly led, however, in both large and small units by non-proletarians (Mao, Zhang, and Yao are only some famous examples). Such leaders apparently resented their own origins but hoped to save themselves through Communist faith, through a radical will to acquire a new identity. They did not lack the entrepreneurial ambition so often associated with the bourgeoisie (especially in Shanghai), but they found a way to apply that spirit under socialist conditions.[130]

Continuing public ambiguity surrounded the question of whether persons of bourgeois origin should be considered to have a bloodstain on their records. Some theoreticians in early 1965 argued that capitalists depend on their own personal labour when they begin to build their fortunes, even if they depend on exploitation thereafter – so their situation after the exploitation ends must make them workers again. Opposing theoreticians, however, held that the capitalists' intention all along was to establish a system under which they would not have to be workers, so that they should receive no social credit for their early labour. Some participants at 1965 forums even said that 'only labour which produces material goods is productive labour', and that the capitalist's labour brings him surplus value which is not properly his own. Labour power, in this view, is a special productive factor that 'needs no further processing' to increase its worth, since it is the very measure of worth. However consistent this view may be with a labour theory of value, it implies that management cannot be priced in the same coin as labour which produces commodities. Other participants at these 1965 meetings replied that now, in socialist society, no capitalist can hope to establish such exploitation, so that Communist management is indeed labour. But these discussions did not lay to rest the views of those who felt that proletarian-background managers were inherently better than capitalist-background ones. The problem was not academic: an ex-bourgeois who could be socialist might claim a promotion, or might object to the proletarian discrimination that since 1963 had sent bourgeois-family offspring (more than proletarian ones) to rural jobs after graduation from school.

1966–9: THE CULTURAL REVOLUTION

In early 1966, clubs of students formed in Shanghai universities and middle schools on the basis of common descent from parents in the 'five red categories' (*hong wu lei*: workers, poor and lower-middle peasants, revolutionary cadres, revolutionary soldiers, and revolutionary martyrs). This proletarian – conservative movement began in schools, and it may be partly understood in terms of the social dynamics that create youth gangs in many countries. If 'five red' parents, who were often recently promoted proletarians or ex-soldiers in factories, had first established such groups in adult institutions, the disruptive effect on production would have brought quick criticism. It is clear nonetheless that many groups in the Party and public security forces, including many ex-peasant army men who had been demobilized to Shanghai for political work after 1949, had a family interest in this movement. There is evidence that some high Party leaders, including Liu Shaoqi, Tao Zhu, Tan Zhenlin, and Li Xuefeng, at least discreetly agreed with this pure-proletarian initiative.[131]

The emphasis that they drew from the need for 'proletarian dictatorship' was a stress on law and order, on the stable preservation of workers' past gains in the management class. In political action terms, this conclusion was diametrically opposite to the position of leaders such as Mao, Zhang, and Yao, who had to favour change that would allow anyone to prove radical, revolutionary virtue.[132] Personal class background did not tightly predetermine a leader's position in the Cultural Revolution. It nonetheless is clear that the new class, in Shanghai and nationally, was hotly debating the relevance of family origin to its membership in 1966.

This is not the place to retell the whole story of the Cultural Revolution in Shanghai.[133] The creation of 'five red' clubs in many kinds of institutions did not threaten the Shanghai Party apparatus, so long as police remained available to assure such energies would be channelled into a campaign-as-usual. The crucial event, which made the Cultural Revolution different, was the effect on political police of the 'Sixteen Points', resolved by the Eleventh Plenum of the Eighth Central Committee in August 1966: 'Trust the masses, rely on them, and respect their initiative. Cast out fear. Don't be afraid of disturbances.'[134] Public security cadres were ordered to cease their previous work in political groups.

This decision was 'ardently hailed' in Shanghai.[135] Many kinds of interests could now organize. In the ex-French Concession part of the city (which has some of the most pleasant, and very capitalist, residential areas in all China), there was literally dancing in the streets. An evening newspaper reported that thousands of people attended a forum to talk about their joy that, 'all the demons with oxheads and embodied serpent-ghosts' would now be criticized and swept aside.[136]

The August Plenum climaxed a local trend. Partly because rising prosperity had decreased the efficiency of urban control systems in the mid-1960s,[137] and partly because political expression by ex-bourgeois people could no longer be mustered by Hundred Flowers slogans, the direct cooption of ex-capitalists into Shanghai politics had been somewhat increased since 1965. In that year, 30,000 people joined the local Party; and 200,000 joined the local Communist Youth League. They were assured that: 'As to family background, class status, and social relations, we must carry out the Party's class policy of stressing performance.'[138] On the other hand, 400,000 young workers in Shanghai were also designated 'tiger cubs' for the technical innovations they had conceived.[139] Ex-bourgeois radicalism was represented not only in some branches of officialdom (Zhang's CCP Propaganda Department, for example) but also by a very non-official, tiny group of intellectuals who espoused a 'new tide of thought' (xin sichao). This small anarchist-liberal stream, which is classic in the coffeehouses of developing cities, denounced all 'powerholders' as 'privileged persons who ignore the masses'; it called for direct popular representation, for a 'continuous redistribution of wealth', and for 'genuine socialization' (zhenzheng gongyou hua).[140] Finally, low-level members of the Party itself were now also free of usual police restraints. Many were indignant when Red Guards (hongwei bing, some of whom were ex-bourgeois) attacked local Party offices.[141]

The Scarlet Guards (chiwei dui) of the proletarian trade unions conflicted both with student groups and with contract workers. Although most Scarlet Guard leaders in Shanghai were almost surely Party members,[142] they differed strongly with high Party officials in many issues. (In this, they were like the largely ex-bourgeois Red Guards, with whom they differed even more strongly.) Paralysation of the police meant that Shanghai's mixed elite came apart at the seams. In a general free-for-all, workers pressed for higher wages, household registration controls collapsed, and many sent-down youths returned to their homes in Shanghai. In armed institutions, residential institutions, education institutions, and labour-recruitment institutions the bases of authority were severely eroded.[143]

The Army and Zhang Chunqiao, with the eventual blessings of Mao, spent the next two years trying to restore order. These efforts have been treated elsewhere generally,[144] but not in terms of the 1967–9 variations in the class content of Zhang's policies. At first, his Shanghai Commune promised a new deal for contract workers. Zhang's newspapers declared that 'Temporary (*linshi*) labour and outside-contract (*waibao*) labour are remnants of the capitalist system.'[145] A tabloid asserted that,

The purpose of hiring temporary workers and contract workers is to make maximum profits with minimum investment. This implied exploitation and ... dissipates the revolutionary spirit of temporary and contract workers. Their concern all the time is only to safeguard their personal livelihoods.[146]

Re-enfranchisement was promised by a manifesto from seventeen of Zhang's organizations that: 'Temporary workers, contract workers, workers on rotation, and workers on outside contracts are revolutionary and loyal to the Party and nation.'[147] Although Zhang took steps to confiscate the assets and freeze the bank accounts of certain contract-labour political groups that sprang up in late 1966,[148] he was clearly also trying then to recruit the contract proletariat's political support.

Similar outreach attempts were made toward workers of capitalist family origins in early 1967. They were Zhang's natural allies at this time, because the main threat to his nascent government was of long-time worker pedigree, led by Geng Jinzhang and Chen Hongkang. The epithets with which some true-blue proletarians regaled Zhang's main local assistant, Wang Hongwen, included some of the nastiest vocabulary in the political lexicon: reformism, eclecticism, small-circleism, and sectarianism.[149] Each of these was justified, from the viewpoint of veteran workers; but Zhang had the Army on his side, and he simply arrested workers with 'born red' ideas.[150] As Zhang's newspapers vowed clearly at this time: 'It is necessary to eradicate the blood pedigree theory (*xuetong lun*).'[151]

The pure-proletarian movement collapsed, because it relied on the support of demobilized soldiers who were ordered by local Army units under Zhang's influence to dissolve themselves.[152] Also, Shanghai was still a largely bourgeois city. Geng's rampant proletarianism went against the ambitions of many – who thus supported the main alternative, Zhang Chunqiao. Partly because of Shanghai's economic slowdown,[153] Zhang's Revolutionary Committee made major efforts from February to recruit the support of both ex-bourgeois and old cadres. In particular, cadres who had passed safely through the Four Clean movement were not to be struggled further.[154] Old proletarians were told to accept ex-bourgeois leaders, and to 'eliminate ideological obstacles in the way' of cadres' rehabilitation.[155] Previous 'reactionaries' were accused of having 'persuaded those with poor or proletarian family backgrounds that they were the only true revolutionaries'. They had mistakenly encouraged workers 'to exclude children whose parents were members of the former exploiting classes'.[156]

Zhang's opponents accused him of spreading the doctrine of the extinction of classes. Handbills bitterly indicted Zhang of betrayal to the proletariat.[157] In the face of such attacks, Zhang needed the police. By March, they were resuscitated; but arrests were not always easy to carry out, because worker militias were tough, armed, and locally organized. The police in one case meekly announced that: 'The violators will be prosecuted. It is hoped that revolutionaries will help in the suppression of this organization.'[158]

The old-workers' organizations were strong, and their 'bullies' could sometimes inflict considerable violence on students occupying municipal offices.[159] Since Zhang's major mandate from Peking was to restore order, it now behoved him (despite his own family background) to make an accommodation with old-worker power at low levels in Shanghai. By the mid-summer of 1967 (after the Wuhan Incident had suggested that bourgeois radicalism should have limits, even during a Great Proletarian Cultural Revolution), Zhang shifted direction. 'Factionalism' was now identified as a 'petit bourgeois' phenomenon. Political groups from different social strata were told to keep out of each other's hair:

It is hoped that students will not interfere with the struggle in factories, mines and enterprises. Workers will not interfere with the struggle of the students. People from other places will not interfere with the struggle in Shanghai.[160]

By late summer, Zhang was saying clearly that workers should be supreme. A tabloid quoted him in a typically relaxed conversation: 'The leadership status of the working class must be definitely established.' Zhang advised his listeners: 'Do not be led by the nose by students!'[161] By December 1967, Zhang's newspapers decried all attempts 'to turn trade unions into "trade unions of the entire people" that do not distinguish between classes'.[162] At least in some factories, proletarian-born workers fared very well under this regime.[163]

Temporary and contract workers were excluded, once again by 1968, from the respected proletariat:

None of them shall be switched into the status of permanent workers; they must not form independent organizations and must not exchange experiences, establish ties with one another, or organize visits of personnel to higher levels.[164]

Zhang's old-worker allies also criticized the Party Constitution, especially its provision that: 'Any Chinese who engages in labour and does not exploit other people's labour ... may be a member of the Party.' According to them, this clause obliterated the proletarian character of the Party, making it a 'party of production'[165] or a 'party of citizens'. This hard line was inseparable from the Shanghai Government's 1968 policy to have an unprecedently large rustication of middle-school youths. Zhang knew that he was heartily disliked by these students (who were still disproportionately from ex-bourgeois family backgrounds). He admitted that:

Several hundred thousand middle-school graduates at present have not been handled well. The enemies will take an opportunity to provoke them. There are also the temporary workers. The enemies often adopt indirect methods, and they may launch an attack on us.[166]

One of Zhang's local newspapers was equally candid that spring, when it called for 'uniting with people who have conservative ideas' in order to 'carry out an exact struggle with conservative authorities'.[167] The distinction was a very fine one, but it allowed approaches to further constituencies, and Zhang needed all the support he could get. As the movement to restore the Party proceeded in 1968, an effort to recruit competent personnel from various classes was also restored. A new 'leap forward' had been announced in the economic sphere,[168] and some no doubt hoped it would be as blind to classes as its predecessor of the same name. They were not disappointed. By late June, the local Party newspaper was suggesting that: 'Persons with general historical problems should be distinguished strictly from renegades, secret enemy agents, landlords, rich peasants, counterrevolutionaries, bad elements, and rightists.'[169] The list did not include 'bourgeois'. As Party units were restored in Shanghai, the main targets of new attacks were people who had been members of the KMT before 1949, at specified high ranks in that organization.[170] This policy hurt a few old capitalists; but in the context of 1968–9, it was pure symbolism – and it served to exonerate far larger numbers of young people from ex-bourgeois families, who had been children in 1949.

The final acme of Zhang's constituency policy came in mid-1968. He simultaneously authorized two kinds of investigation teams, assigned to accomplish diametrically opposite functions among different kinds of people, all in the name of orderly development. No finer monument of bourgeois opportunism has even been conceived:[171] 'Class Clearance Troops' (qingli jieji duiwu) were sent to legitimize the existing leaderships in the great majority of Shanghai's organizations, in which ex-bourgeois support was still essential. These investigators espoused the following slogans: 'Remnants of the Kuomintang must be distinguished from those who have problems in their political histories.' 'Bad people doing bad things must be distinguished from good people doing bad things.'[172] And, 'The bourgeois right wing must be distinguished from ordinary bourgeois elements.'[173] But to some other organizations, where local leaders from worker families dominated, Zhang sent 'Rebel Purification Teams' (zhengdun zaofan dui). These dealt with the 'contradiction between proletarians and bourgeois', in groups where that was expedient. After so much strife within Shanghai's new class, the restoration of order required more cleverness than principle. Zhang acted accordingly.

The rise of gross real value of industrial output in Shanghai from 1966 to 1969 was only 3 per cent per annum; but the increase during the 1968–9 year alone was 15 per cent.[174] Slowly, a leading class similar to the 1963–6 management was reconstituted. The Shanghai Government directed that: 'In places where Party members and non-Party rebels are more or less hostile to each other in feeling, ... open-door campaigns should be carried out.'[175] Tensions between new-class members of different backgrounds still existed; but after the experience of the Cultural Revolution, few in Shanghai were inclined to use them for advancement. In other words, the socialist management class was now stable.

172

CONCLUSION: DIVISION AND UNITY IN THE JOB OF THE
LEADING CLASS

This essay began with a dilemma: the apparent conflict between Shanghai's radicalism and its largely bourgeois culture. By now, the reason why such things go together should be clear. This metropolis is typical of cities in developing countries; it is led by a class adept at 'managing' two different problems that occur in quick-changing places. On one hand, the city is a centre of economic leadership; it has all the bureaucratic culture of office, the progressivist spirit of Rotary Clubs. On the other hand, it is also a place where people have the leisure to politick about larger questions of human organization and personality, and about future reforms in them. Material growth is organized by the same class that organizes political will to steer the modern process toward some vision of social good.

That class has gone through several stages of weakness and consolidation. Its members have shifted between its two main poles of concern more readily than is conveyed by the vocabulary of revolution in sources from Shanghai. The language of the city (and the usual aversion of politicians to mention the needs of their own careers) have obscured the extent to which cadres of different family origins came to cooperate in periods of increasing urban prosperity, such as 1953–5, 1958, 1963–6, or the era after the death of Mao. Such cooperation has often been assailed, and its good reasons have been neglected.

Radical and developmental strands in Shanghai's management-class politics are both endemic to all recent periods there. Radicalism became prominent whenever visionary groups could tap the frustrations of old strata to press for political change. It is easy to claim, for periods such as 1951–2, 1956–8, or 1966–9, that a political decision (usually from Peking) initiated a campaign to encourage radicalism. Of course this is true; the long periods of training new cadres have been punctuated by campaigns, which through intimidation and other encouragements have induced ex-bourgeois managers to help the Party. A more thoroughgoing analysis, however, would look beyond these administrative directives, to ask how a mandate for radicalization can find local support.

For example, the Five Anti movement, which was the crucial

173

event for urban stratification in the early People's Republic, was based on high Party decisions; but the Korean War climate was prerequisite to the government's claim for so much compliance from the urban bourgeoisie. The Transition to Socialism was also, in immediate terms, the result of a directive-from-on-high. But that campaign could not have been contemplated, unless the Party by then had trained some loyal accountants, unless the capitalists in previous campaigns had become generally resigned to their fate as socialist managers, and unless they had been attracted by 1956 promises of a more liberal regime in which to work. Quick campaigns and slow training of worker-businessmen together made the meaning of joint management. The Great Leap Forward (as conventionally dated, from 1958) was one of the educational, infrastructure-building eras in Shanghai; in terms of class relations, it was not one of the city's radical periods, and it became an urban campaign partly because of rural shortages. By 1963–6, the developmental and radical strains in Shanghai's management class were both evident; the new class only seemed to dominate its older parts. Initiatives from Peking, especially from Mao in 1966, garnered the support of ex-bourgeois who feared dropping out of the leading class. In sum, radical trends became salient, when shadow elites that could demand inclusion in the new class were excluded from it. Slower change and management-class consolidation was the rule at other times.

The different sectors of Shanghai's management class have grown to depend on each other. They have conflicted too, but not on a big scale for more than a decade. Shanghai's new class is now consolidated. Neither the commitment to economic growth nor the commitment to social fairness has ever been completely forsworn by any part of this class. The two aspects of its job have always been admitted; they are separable from each other only analytically. The language of class struggle obscured their unity for a long time, even as it provided ways to talk about them. Members of Shanghai's leading class have put effort and worry into finding proper roads to the future. That care is their main claim to our attention.

8

MARRIAGE CHOICE AND STATUS GROUPS IN CONTEMPORARY CHINA

Elisabeth Croll

In the anthropological study of complex societies, marriage choice and the establishment of affinal alliances have been related to problems of stratification and socio-economic differentiation. Of all the forms of association and social intimacy that express social equality, courtship and marriage have been singled out as one of the most significant of indices.[1] Equally, marriage prohibitions and restrictions with their correlating rules of avoidance and accessibility have proved to be effective means of maintaining social distance between status groups.[2] Social scientists have thus created two poles of theoretical construction according to the degree of restrictions bounding the field of eligible marriage partners. They have distinguished between closed marriage systems which prescribe that spouses be chosen from one or more designated socio-economic categories of persons and open marriage systems in which the only group of persons unequivocally proscribed as marriage partners are those to whom the incest taboo was extended.[3] However, in many societies, anthropological studies of what are commonly conceived to be open marriage systems suggest that marriage choice usually remains structured by such factors as social class, ethnic origin, religion and education with a strong endogamous or preferential in-group trend characterising some status groups. The growing literature on mate selection in North America, for instance, suggests a preponderance of homogamy, or assortative mating, in which persons choose spouses of similar characteristics, over heterogamy. Wide disparities in the status of marriage partners were found to be infrequent.[4] The role of marital choice in accentuating or confirming patterns of stratification have led anthropologists to hypothesise that to encourage 'random mating' or at least preferential out-marriage could mean a radical change in the existing social structure.[5] In China reforms in the institution of marriage over the past three decades have both consistently and continuously been linked to strategies for reducing systems of stratification. The government of the People's Republic of China has attempted to substitute an open marriage system characterised by free-choice marriage for the traditional marriage system where choice was almost uniquely structured by kin prohibitions[6] and socio-economic homogamy.[7] The free choice of marriage partner was both to contribute to and reflect a reduction in social stratification.[8]

'FREE-CHOICE' MARRIAGE

The Marriage Law of 1950 removed most previous restrictions from the marriage system in order to establish a broad field of eligible mates[9] and increase the range of choice for each individual.

Article 5 of the Marriage Law reduced the number of kin prohibitions,[10] and subsequent marriage campaigns not only left preferential marriage partners socially undefined, but specifically rejected socio-economic criteria as a factor governing choice of marriage partner. 'Freedom of choice' meant not only that an individual might voluntarily marry according to his or her own choice and without unreasonable interference from others, but also that this choice was not to be bound by race, social status, occupation or property.[11] Instead, desirable or preferential mates were defined according to their levels of political consciousness. The ideal marriage partner was one who was 'politically compatible' and 'in ideological agreement', *zhitong daohe*.[12] What this new criterion in selecting a spouse meant in practice was spelt out in a number of educational materials published after the promulgation of the Marriage Law. As one article said: 'In choosing a life partner, the fundamental thing is to have a common interest in politics as well as in ideology.' It went on to say that it is the quality of political thinking and attitudes towards labour that are important.[13] A booklet written to advise on these matters stated that the most important condition is the character of the person; finding out whether he/she shares the same political standpoint, ideological views, class sentiments and revolutionary ideals. Therefore there is a need to understand clearly the person's political viewpoint, attitude towards work, style of life and quality of thinking.[14]

The preface to a booklet also published in 1964 and entitled *Between Husband and Wife* again stressed that the individual parties to the marriage contract should 'respect and love each other' and that common levels of political consciousness should provide the exclusive basis of their relationship. 'In a socialist society', it said,[15]

love between a husband and wife is built on common political thinking and on the foundation of struggling together for the revolutionary cause. The relationship between husband and wife is first of all comradeship and the feelings between them are revolutionary. By revolutionary is meant that politically he should take her as a new comrade-in-arms, in production as well as in work, he should take her as a class sister and labour together, at home he should regard her as a life companion, besides that a couple should respect and love each other, help each other, and encourage each other so as to achieve progress together.

All the recommendations had a common emphasis on the partner's *lichang* (standpoint), *shijie guan* (literally 'world outlook') or political attitudes defined in the broadest possible sense and made no reference to socio-economic criteria. In the new campaigns in support of free-choice marriage of the past five years, there is a change of emphasis in that the literature more specifically admits to and rejects the influence of socio-economic criteria on choice of marriage partner. Current articles draw attention to the general role of money, occupational and family status and social connections in determining present-day marriage choice, and criticise the persistence of these materialist criteria.

Since 1950 the promotion of free-choice marriage has been elaborated and publicised in all forms of educational materials which have been popularised by government personnel, the Youth League, the Women's Federation and other mass organisations. All aspects of the media and the arts have been marshalled in its support and they have constantly advocated and given maximum publicity to heterogamous marriages between say professional and manual workers or urban-educated brides and peasant grooms. The ideologically prescribed field of eligible mates, disregarding as it did most previous kin prohibitions and socio-economic restrictions and divisions in society, theoretically established an open marriage system, a broad field of eligible mates and a wide choice of mates for each person. As one article pointed out: 'now there is sweet grass everywhere' for all young persons.[16] The modification of the procedures and symbols of marriage has composed an important means by which the State has intervened to reduce the social distance between status groups and progressively to abolish them altogether. This paper examines the criteria on which mate selection is now based in contemporary China before assessing its contribution to reducing systems of stratification.

A study of mate choice in contemporary Chinese society suggests that although the new law and educational campaigns were designed to establish a broad field of eligible mates and encourage random mating, choice of spouse has continued to be structured by certain political and socio-economic dimensions of preference. The location of preferential spouses results from the operation of two separate and competing status systems, one political and the other socio-economic.

THE POLITICAL STATUS SYSTEM

Although the new ideology defined preferential marriage partners according to their levels of political consciousness, in practical terms political status has usually been defined by the degree of formal recognition or the honours conferred upon an individual by the government or the Communist Party. On this basis it is possible to identify a gradient of approval and disapproval based upon the differential distribution of political status with members of the Communist Party and Youth League forming a clearly bounded category of preferential mates. In the many life-histories, letters and media reports published in the last three decades, young people have constantly commented on the attractions of those in positions of high political status. One young girl thought that what had initially impressed her about her husband was that 'he had participated in the revolution since 1939 and was a member of the Communist Party'.[17] Another girl could not believe her luck when she met an attractive young man who 'laboured well, worked well, was honest and was a Communist League member to boot'.[18] Those who had achieved positions of political power and acquired public awards found themselves to be the object of some competition. One young bachelor in his mid-twenties who was an official in village government and a leader of the local militia was described as the 'object of purposeful attention from all the young unmarried women of the villages for 10 li around'.[19] Another, who had been elected a 'five good commune member' many times over, had attracted the attention of the local girls, some of whom had 'come forward of their own accord and offered to marry him'.[20] A survey of marriage patterns in the mid-1950s had suggested to one commentator in the youth magazine that the cases of girls marrying cadres in order to gain Party membership for themselves and win support of the leadership were unfortunately many.[21] More recently too, girls have been criticised for seeking political status through marriage, and cases of ambitious young men seeking out girls whose fathers were in a position to secure a good future for their sons-in-law have also been reported.[22]

The competition for cadres, Party members and others similarly categorised has been known to have aroused some envy and resentment among those not similarly endowed. A discussion of the problem of mate selection in Hunan province in 1957 revealed that many young men were rather resentful of the way in which young women were attracted to cadres rather than to fellow peasants and labourers.[23] On another occasion young people complained that the desire to maximise political status through marriage was so high as to cause membership of the Youth League or Party to be almost a pre-requisite to a 'good match'. In *Shaanxi ribao* it was reported that some young people who were 'disappointed in love' blamed the leadership for not promoting them, or the Party and Youth League for not accepting them as members. They complained that without either attribute they were 'just nonentities', 'unable to get someone to love them'.[24] It was also not unknown for prudent young men to exaggerate their political credentials. In extreme cases the fraudulence was brought to light during subsequent court proceedings. One case of 'marriage by fraud' was brought to court in 1957. A young man was accused of fabricating a personal history of colourful participation in the revolution and posing as a member of the Communist Party in order to win his mate. The woman admitted during the court hearing that she had been attracted to him because he seemed to be 'a hero of the revolution'.[25] More recently in 1979 a number of cases have been reported in which girls wishing to secure advantages and good fortune had fallen prey to young men who posed as government cadres or as children of high ranking cadres. One report cited the case where a young woman worker had chosen a young man who falsely claimed to be a Communist Party member since he was aged eighteen years. He had also boasted that his family was wealthy and had good social and political connections: his father was working abroad, his second uncle was deputy chief of the People's Liberation Army General Staff and his third uncle was an Air Force deputy commander.[26]

If political status, expressed in terms of occupation, award or membership of exclusive political associations, formed a clearly bounded category of preferential mates at the positive pole of the gradient of approval, those who were said to be of 'exploiting class origins' could be said to form the negative pole of the gradient. Below the most preferred category of those rewarded positively and individually, political status seems to have been allocated collectively according to social class origins.[27] Landlords, rich peasants and urban capitalists were generally categorised as the 'former exploiting classes', and poor and lower middle peasants and urban workers were said to be of 'good' as opposed to 'bad' class origins. Initially, during land reform there were certain rules banning inter-marriage between the two groups. In 1952 *Nanfang ribao* stated that marriage between those of peasant and landlord family background could not be tolerated, for it was not unknown for landlords to marry off their daughters to poor peasants in order to establish alliances, blur class lines and so soften the conflict.[28] Many local Party and Youth League organisations still seem to have imposed these rules in the mid-1950s, but they were criticised in the media for so doing. Since this time, and especially on the eve of and during the Cultural Revolution, the government has stressed that levels of political consciousness are not supposed to be predetermined by social class or ascriptive criteria and that class origins should not therefore affect or influence the choice of marriage partner. Rather, just as for other social categories, individual levels of political consciousness should form the criteria for those of exploiting class origins. One piece of advice stated clearly that there was a distinction to be made between members of the exploiting class and those born of the exploiting classes, and that young people, in considering whether they should fall in love and marry those of exploiting class origins, should appraise them according to their own behaviour and not their family background.

As long as those young people wanted progress, were willing to participate in politics, committed to the goals of the new society, then it is all right to fall in love and marry them.[29]

Although at the same time, the government has also suggested that compatibility in marriage was often much more difficult to achieve with members of the exploiting classes because they had frequently unconsciously and collectively inherited old family attitudes and opinions deriving from Confucian and capitalist ideologies.[30] This put the onus on the young people of exploiting class origin to constantly prove their revolutionary character or level of political consciousness in order to make a 'good' marriage. However, in practice it seems as if class origins have continued to influence or determine a person's 'future' and therefore their marriage prospects.

An examination of letters and reports in the media suggests that levels of political consciousness soon came to be associated with certain social origins and that this correlation disadvantaged those of exploiting class origins in the marriage market. What those of 'good' class origins feared was a reduction in their own political status as a result of association or a marriage alliance with those of exploiting class origins. There were many letters written by sons and daughters with parents of the exploiting classes which expressed concern about the effect of their social origins on their political status, and hence their relations or alliances with members of other social classes.[31] An observer living in Henan province in 1970 noted that though working relations between those of 'good' and 'bad' social origins might be free and easy, there was very little inter-marriage between the two groups. The patrilocal nature of marriage meant that the problem of attracting mates was especially great for the young men from the exploiting classes who would take their wives into households that were to some extent taboo, and girls of poor and lower-middle and even rich peasant families were understandably reluctant to accept such a proposal. In one case he quoted, the proposed bride was calculated by a poor peasant household to be ideal in every way, but the question was 'should a red-flag poor peasant get allied in marriage with a former rich peasant family?'. The father of the boy decided that it was not only this particular match that had to be taken into account, but the

181

future of the entire family, and he therefore rejected the match.[32] In 1979 and 1980 dissension within two families resulting from a daughter's choice of a landlord's son and a counter-revolutionary's son as a future husband was only resolved by bitter court cases.[33]

There was a certain tension between collectively allocated class origins and individual levels of political consciousness in determining the acceptability of the individual as a potential spouse. Two correspondents writing to *Zhongguo Qingnian* and *Gongren ribao* in 1965 were specifically concerned with this problem. One letter was about the dilemma of a young Communist Party member who was attracted by a politically active girl who was a middle school graduate teaching in an elementary school. He wrote that there was one obstacle to their marriage: she was from a rich peasant family. According to some of their friends, this was a matter of real concern affecting his 'future', but according to others he need not be unduly concerned as long as her level of political consciousness was high. Confused by the contradictory attitudes, he had written to the magazine for reassurance that he had not so far committed any 'error' in his association with her that might affect his 'future prospects'. His letter ended with the question, 'did love and marriage with youths from families of the exploiting classes entail loss of class stand or political status?'[34] The other letter suggested that even where individuals exhibited high levels of political consciousness, this was frequently not enough to cancel out their class origins and raise their political status within their immediate reference groups. The fact that his girl was a member of the Youth League and had made considerable efforts to study politics did not soften the reaction of the boy's workmates when he informed them of his impending marriage. They told him that as a son of the family of the working classes, he would lose his 'class stand' by marrying a girl born of the family of the exploiting classes. The young man said that as a result he was very confused about the association of social origins and political consciousness in determining political status and he was also very anxious that he should not do anything to lose his own 'class stand'.[35] Indeed, it was the apparent association of exploiting class origins and low political status and its importance in choice of marriage partner which caused another young man to contract a hasty marriage before his own exploiting class origins could be discovered,[36] and a young high school teacher in Guangzhou born of the family of a former

Marriage choice and status groups

Professions		Poor and lower-middle peasants	
— ---------------------------------- +			
Exploiting class origins	Technicians	Factory workers	Politically rewarded

Figure 1 Choice of mate: political status gradient

landlord to hide his social origins from his future spouse.[37] In each instance the subsequent discovery of deception was said to be a factor contributing to the later breakdown of the marriage.

If the association of levels of political consciousness with class origins was responsible for placing those of exploiting class origins at the negative end of the gradient, the association of high levels of political consciousness with 'good' class origins placed workers and poor and lower middle peasants in the middle ranges of political status gradient directly below those who had been positively rewarded for their level of political consciousness. Although the government has pointed out that those of 'good' class origins did not automatically assume high levels of political consciousness, there had been a tendency for the constituents of the 'revolutionary vanguard' or 'real proletariat' to take their ideological probity for granted unless there was some specific reason for assuming its loss. Any hint of misdemeanour, reprimand or punishment from the political authorities, for instance, could have the effect of cancelling out 'good' class origins. In one village in Henan in 1970, it was reported that the father of a marriageable girl had been brought before the People's Court, and that, although in this case the matter had turned out well, it was said at the time that if it had not and he had been jailed, then this would have certainly affected the chances of his daughter in marriage.[38] It seems as if those of 'good' class origins had a definite advantage in the marriage market in that they began with a 'clean record', but to remain within the preferred category they had to have an unblemished political record.

Political status measured according to reward or by class origins is an important factor governing marriage choice, and under its considerable influence the traditional social status gradient has largely been reversed (see Figure 1).

The new criterion determined by levels of political consciousness was influential to the extent that the traditional status groupings of landlord, rich peasant and the urban wealthy have been replaced by

183

new status groups of government cadres and certain skilled urban workers as preferential spouses, but socio-economic characteristics have also remained important criteria in mate selection and in the definition of those characterised as preferential mates.

THE SOCIAL STATUS SYSTEM

The social status system refers to the distribution of social honour or the extent to which individuals and groups receive respect or esteem, *zunzhong* or *zongbai*. The distribution of social status is revealed in the attitudes and expectations of their immediate reference groups such as kin, neighbours, fellow-workers or friends. It is mainly allocated according to occupation with its corollaries of levels of education, income, life-styles and degree of mobility or 'future'. Traditionally, marriage was seen to be an opportunity to maximise the resources of the household or kin group through the negotiation of a suitable alliance, and there is evidence to suggest that both families and young persons have continued to view marriage as a means of social mobility. They seek a partner who in the eyes of the immediate reference group is considered to have 'future'. Some local saying such as 'Ask not if he is a member of the Party, ask not if he is a member of the Youth League, but ask only if he has money' or 'first, look over the house, second look over the person, third look to see if he can earn one hundred per cent' are said to indicate the criteria underlying mate selection in China in the 1960s.[39] In letters and life-histories, young people explicitly considered the occupation, the income, the likely standard of living and the extent of the family burden of future spouses.[40] A lengthy correspondence conducted in the pages of *Zhongguo funu* in 1963–4 on the subject of mate selection indicated that prospects for a 'good livelihood' after marriage remained an important dimension in assessing the suitability of a spouse. As one correspondent said, she hoped to choose a man who had a high income, a high position and who was young and smart.[41] Another congratulated herself on finding a good husband. His salary was not low and he had no heavy family burden thus making for a good livelihood.[42] Others in aspiring for a settled and comfortable life gave priority to young men who had a high position and earned much income.[43] In 1979–80 there have been a number of criticisms published of those who want their marriage partners to be well-matched in both social and economic status.[44]

184

Marriage choice and status groups

| Unskilled factory workers, service workers | | Skilled factory workers | |

- ------------------------------------- +

| Peasants | Low-graded government cadres | Technicians, high-grade government cadres, professionals |

Figure 2 Choice of mate: social status gradient

Those with skills and high wages included those in specialist occupations in factories or the government bureaucracy and professionals such as engineers, professors and doctors, technicians, scientists and jobs of skilled industrial work which were rated highly in terms of remuneration and welfare benefits. They made up the positive poles of the social status gradient (see Figure 2).

Those who were unskilled and received lower wages and less welfare benefits were not so attractive as potential marriage partners. A recent report in the newspapers suggests that young workers in co-operative factories whose wages are lower and where there are fewer welfare facilities find it more difficult to attract marriage partners. They cite the example of a young girl who was beaten by her parents because she wanted to marry a young co-operative factory worker and even after they were married, she was looked down upon by many of her acquaintances.[45] An investigation into the reason for the high number of single young persons in one urban neighbourhood suggested that the main cause was the high number employed in low-status, collective enterprises run by the neighbourhood.[46] Again a report in the newspaper from Fushan coal mining region noted that Communist Party officials there had recently been visiting girls' families as part of a campaign to improve the image of miners and reduce their difficulties in finding wives.[47]

In rural areas where socio-economic status is universally held to be low, preferential mates may be defined generally according to environmental factors which determine the wealth of the localities in which they live and specifically according to the ratio of wage earners to wage dependents which affects the resources of their individual households. Parents have been reluctant to marry their

185

daughters into mountainous areas because of the lack of good roads, fertile land and reliable sources of food.[48] In order to maximise opportunities for a favourable marriage alliance within a region, the accumulation of household status symbols was reported to characterise the period immediately prior to negotiations. In the village of Upper Felicity in Henan the rapid purchase of a transistor radio, sewing machine, cycle or clock was said to be a sure sign that a family was embarking on marriage negotiations.[49] In the last two years there have been frequent complaints in the media that arranged or venal marriages and the extraction of goods, cash and services have been used by families to accrue wealth and socio-economic status and that these marriages were especially common in areas of low production and living standards.[50]

PREFERRED CATEGORIES OF SPOUSES

Not surprisingly the preferential mate was one who combined both socio-economic and political status, and it was this combination which was much sought after. As one girl in the midst of choosing a mate and faced by a constant discrepancy in political and social status was heard to utter: 'Wouldn't it be wonderful if I could find a suitor whose thought was good and who earns more money.'[51] Another girl, aiming to find a husband who had a high salary, a high position and who was young and smart fell in love with the deputy chief of a section at her place of work who was also a member of the Communist Party. She had some criticisms of him as a person, but on the whole she concluded that 'it would be nice to have a husband like him ... I felt that he would be a good husband in whom I could take pride in the presence of other people'. Her neighbours and friends also advised her to 'stick with him'.[52] Indeed so popular was the concept of the ideal mate as one who maximised both political and socio-economic status that by the 1960s it had been incorporated into the new ideology of free-choice marriage and modified the exclusive political criteria previously recommended in the educational materials. In answer to the question of what kind of marriage partner is most satisfactory in prospects, one booklet advised that political study, standing, ideological views, class sentiments and revolutionary ideals remain the first criteria in choosing a mate, but that economic situation and cultural levels should also be taken into consideration. 'In love and in looking for a partner,' it said, considering the other's profession, whether he works well, how much his income is the spaciousness of his home, and whether he is good looking – these cannot be considered wrong. The mistake lies in only considering these secondary issues.[53]

There were several categories which were most likely to meet these joint criteria and they are those which are located at points of congruence and concurrence on both gradients of status. They are high ranking government cadres, army officers and skilled factory workers who all have both political and socio-economic status. Several reports in the media have also specifically indentified these groups as preferential mates. One report noted that young women in rural areas sought mates among army men, factory workers and cadres rather than peasants.[54] Several reports suggested that there was much evidence that young peasant girls were seeking mates who were government cadres, or factory workers in the cities.[55] In the correspondence columns of the 1960s and 1970s there is every evidence that these groups continued to form the preferred groups. At times government policies have contributed to the importance of each status system relative to the other. For instance during certain periods, such as the Cultural Revolution and its aftermath, there was much more attention and recognition given to groups of high political status or greater 'red' qualities. At other times and currently (1983) it is the technicians or the 'experts' with formal educational qualifications who have been awarded a higher political status.

The location of clearly defined preferential mates according to political and socio-economic criteria would suggest that marriage is still viewed as an avenue of social mobility and that homogamy, or marriage between those of similar political and socio-economic status, is the norm and confirms the status of certain advantaged and disadvantaged groups. One means by which status groups may enhance their distinctiveness is through the positive encouragement of endogamy or in-group marriage. In China one of the most clearly bounded of status groups is to be found at the apex of the political status gradient, that is among those who were members of political organisations. It would not be surprising to find that this group tried to maintain their social distance by placing restrictions upon those marrying out. Certainly rules prohibiting marriage to those who were not fellow-members of the Youth League or Party were said to be widespread in the 1950s and at that time there were fears expressed in the national newspaper that once persons were encouraged to marry within their own organisation that group was on its way to becoming a new class.[56] Although formal rules have been abolished, there is no doubt that in the last two decades the Communist Party and especially the Youth League have provided unique opportunities for regular social interaction among young people of similar political status in the urban and especially the rural areas. In the rural areas it was the young political activists, the Youth League members, Party members, members of the local drama troupes and those rewarded by the political authorities such as 'good commune members' who had occasion to attend meetings, conferences and festivals outside the village and who had the opportunity to meet and become attracted to a partner of their own choice. These opportunities, outside the confines of the village where the norms of segregation and surname exogamy apply, laid the foundation for a certain amount of organisational endogamy.

There was not only some endogamy to be observed among those particularly advantaged, but also the barriers discouraging the disadvantaged from improving their political status through establishing marriage alliances with those of 'good' class origins must have caused some exploiting class endogamy. Whether or not there is widespread endogamy, it is apparent that homogamy and assortative mating or marriage of 'like with like' may well be the norm in Chinese society despite an ideology which recommends free-choice and heterogamy. It is not that there are no heterogamous marriages; there are, but the maximum publicity which they receive and the popular disapproval with which they are greeted suggests that heterogamy is a less common or popular marriage pattern.

HETEROGAMOUS MARRIAGES

Heterogamous marriages usually involve wide disparities between the political and social status of marriage partners, and in China the preferred maximisation of both political and socio-economic status has been more difficult to achieve for those at each end of the spectrum on each of the gradients of status. Individuals choosing a marriage partner frequently had to settle for one or the other attributes and the further apart their locations on each of the continua the more likely it was that the match would be heterogamous and generate tension and conflict. The most common social categories involved in heterogamous marriages were those who had high salaries but less political status such as technical personnel, and peasants who ranked higher in political status but had less social status than almost any other large group in Chinese society. An examination of the tension and conflict generated by heterogamous marriages explicitly reveals that norms and expectations of homogamy still underlie the choice of marriage partners.

In this context two sets of prolonged correspondences in 1957–8 and 1963–4 featured in *Zhongguo funu* and current materials in the 1980s provide very interesting case materials. The first correspondence was initiated by a letter from a typist who had fallen in love with a chauffeur, but was thrown into a state of great conflict and anxiety as a result of the criticisms of her sister and her peers that they were not well-matched. According to the editors of the women's magazine, the publication of this letter elicited more than a thousand replies from readers and over 700 of these were in favour of her marrying the driver.[57] Among the letters selected for publication were those which included a number of similar case histories. These consisted of matches between a college-educated wife and a grade school educated soldier, a technician and a worker, an elementary school teacher and an automobile driver, a high salaried (16th grade) wife and low (21st grade) salaried husband.[58] In all cases the women enjoyed a much higher social position than the husband and in each case she had experienced considerable anguish as the result of criticisms from colleagues and close relatives. The college-educated wife of the soldier husband withstood the negative reactions of her sister and schoolmates to the difference in their educational and occupational status, and with the support of the Party and Youth League she married the soldier.[59] This was in contrast to the bank official who, after listening to the criticism and warnings of her friends and family, broke off her relationship with a book-keeper and married a college student instead.[60]

In 1963–4, *Zhongguo funu* again invited correspondence on the subject of 'What to Look for in Choosing a Spouse', and many readers took the opportunity to describe the types of opposition they had encountered in choosing a marriage partner of a lower social status than themselves. One woman, a doctor, described the attitudes of her relatives towards her fiancé whom she said was loyal to the revolutionary cause, but who had a minor government position and was low paid. Her sister had fiercely opposed her marriage and tried to caution her with the words:

You are young, clever and have professional skills. You needn't worry about finding an ideal husband. What a foolish thing to marry such a man! His income is low and he isn't skilled in any field. What happiness will there be if you marry him?

Her sister urged her to be through with him right away and her sister's husband made a point of introducing her to his friends and colleagues who were engaged in more suitable 'conditions of work and economic situations'.[61]

In another case the boyfriend was of good class origins, progressive in thought, hard working and simple in life-style. He had all the characteristics that a girl could want, but for the fact that his job was ordinary and his wages low. Simultaneously this girl met a technician who earned a high salary although he was not very 'progressive in thought'. Influenced by the new ideology of free choice she rejected the technician on the grounds that 'to rest love on the foundations of money was undesirable'. Her family and neighbours were dismayed by her choice. Some advised her, 'You still do not face reality even when you are not well off.' Still others called her a 'fool' by saying 'You simply ask for it.' She described how reactions like these had begun to shake her resolve. She thought that:

while it is not right just to seek enjoyment in life in choosing a husband, is it not so that the problem of livelihood remains a problem of livelihood? After all, reality is reality and after getting married one will still have to organise family life.

She continued to struggle with her mixed thoughts: on the one hand it was not good to marry for money, on the other hand she wanted to have a secure financial foundation.[62] Some girls withstood the pressures and criticisms of their peers and kin while others gave in and chose again. One woman, a doctor, reported how she married a grade 3 worker, against the advice of her friends and parents;[63] another girl, dissatisfied with the low rank and small salary of a Party member, gave him up once she had the good fortune to be introduced to a cadre who also had a high grade and a high salary.[64] These cases all illustrate the tension generated by heterogamous marriages where there were discrepancies between socio-economic and political status, but the maximum disapprobation was reserved for those heterogamous matches in which one partner was a peasant residing in the countryside.

Although poor and lower middle peasants enjoyed a measure of political status, it could in no way make up for their position of low socio-economic status. In the ranking of occupations, peasants were placed on the lowest rung. Indeed social mobility was viewed as an urban phenomenon and it was often said that life in the country-side had 'no future'; peasants had low salaries and their cultural level was usually lower than those of other occupations.[65] In a correspondence column on marriage in the Hunan newspaper, some girls wrote that, despite official moves to elevate the political and social status of peasants, they had their reasons for not wanting to marry them. 'Farming', they said, 'meant labour, hard living, no future' and peasants had no 'education'. One girl left no room for doubt as to her intentions. 'Farming', she concluded, 'was dark and dirty and without a future.'[66] For a peasant girl then an offer of marriage in the city was cause for congratulations. When one village girl was pressed by a young man to come to the city to be married, her mother was said to be extremely happy, and the women in the neighbourhood were heard to say, 'Hurry up and go with him. Enjoy yourself. Such a good son-in-law can't be found anywhere even if you look with a lantern.'[67]

Residential propinquity has served to circumscribe the number of marriage alliances crossing the urban–rural divide, but the tension and conflict which such matches aroused has been brought into sharp relief by the recurrent government policy to encourage young urban school graduates to migrate from the cities to the countryside and settle permanently. There is evidence to suggest that the problem of marriage has proved a major obstacle to the integration of the *xiaxiang* ('sent down to the countryside') youth into village society and caused much dissatisfaction and disaffection among the youth who had been sent to rural areas. Each decade the media has publi-cised cases of inter-marriage between urban-educated girls and peasant boys and in all cases the initial opposition to their marriage has been substantial. In 1957, a young girl student agonised over whether or not her schoolmates would laugh at her choice of a poor peasant boy who was a Youth League member and popular in the village. She wondered whether it might be better to find a cadre or a worker who 'were more suitable matches for middle-school graduates'. She eventually decided to go ahead and marry him and the wedding was much applauded for breaking down traditional social class barriers and illustrating a reversal of the trend of village girls 'looking down on peasants' and moving to the city on marriage. Another girl student in the same village was already said to have followed her example and fallen for the Secretary of the Youth League Branch.[68]

In the 1960s there were a number of cases where parents strongly opposed their daughters' plans to marry and settle in the countryside. One set of parents said to their daughter time and again that there were no 'prospects' for her if she got married and went to live in the countryside. 'Since you have over ten years of schooling,' they said, 'how can you marry a teacher of an agricultural middle school resident in the countryside.' To show the measure of their disapproval, they insisted that if she was to proceed with these arrangements she must return to them a sum of Y3000 to defray the expenses of her upbringing. At the same time they embarked on a search for a suitable husband for her in the city.[69] Another girl who made a similar choice was much pressured by parents and relatives to find a good prospect in a high position, make her mother satisfied and do credit to her relatives.[70] In 1974 a match between a girl teacher of a commune middle school and a peasant boy was ridiculed by those who thought that a university student should marry another university student and not a peasant in the countryside.[71] This was also the experience of another teacher who found that the comment 'it is ridiculous for a Peking-born college graduate to marry a peasant' was a common reaction to her plans for marriage. Her father, who was among those expressing this disapproval, asked of her: 'What future will you have if you marry a peasant and live in the countryside all your life?' A fellow teacher called it a 'scandal'. The girl concerned thought that these comments showed that people still thought college graduates should only marry workers and cadres. She surmised that it was because peasants were still associated with the idea of 'dirty' manual labour.[72]

What is common to all the examples cited above is not only the conflict which such a heterogamous match arouses in the families involved, but also that the peasant families and peasant boys themselves had not expected to be so fortunate in the choice of bride or daughter-in-law. They never thought that an urban girl would want to live in the countryside and share the rigours of peasant life.[73] It is also noticeable that the girls chose peasant boys who were members of the Youth League and Communist Party and who were renowned for their physical labour and popularity, and in rural terms they had as much 'future' as could be expected. They were thus carefully chosen. As one *xiaxiang* girl said on the occasion of her friend's wedding to a peasant boy, 'I'm positive about looking for a peasant boy, but it might take longer to find a more suitable one.'[74] Interestingly there are few if any cases reported of peasant girls marrying *xiaxiang* boys. This is probably because in comparison to peasant boys, *xiaxiang* boys were much disadvantaged and their difficulties in arranging marriages were the source of much disquiet.[75]

In the past five years there has been increased publicity given to similar examples. In one well publicised case the girl's parents were so incensed by their daughter's choice of a peasant boy that they resorted to violence and it took some effort to convince the local cadres and courts that their support of the parents was violating the law.[76] There have been several recent articles in the media congratulating young educated girls who have married peasant boys and settled in the countryside. Perhaps as a result of ending the enforced migration of young people to the countryside, or the *xiaxiang* policy, it is more common for stories, plays and the media to draw attention to heterogamous marriages within either the rural or urban social field. It has to be said that when this paper was first drafted it was still difficult to assess the influence of the Cultural Revolution on marriage choice. During that period there were criticisms of the high political status automatically assumed by political cadres and members of the Communist Party and the Youth League, the presumed association of class origins and levels of political consciousness and the new differentials which had emerged since 1949 in wealth and educational opportunities, all of which might be expected to have influenced marriage patterns. Even before the Cultural Revolution it was suggested that inter-class marriages would increase in the future;[77] however, all the evidence, and there have been a number of commentaries on the subject published in the media in 1979, 1980 and 1981, suggests that the differences between urban and rural areas and between professional and manual workers continue to be directly or indirectly reflected in marriage choice. For instance media reports of heterogamous marriages, especially those between girls from intellectual or cadre families and male service or factory workers who have little formal education but are 'progressive' politically, reveal the social scorn which such matches continue to attract. Government documents draw attention to the general association of marriage negotiations with socio-economic and political mobility and the continuing discrimination against young people in service occupations with low wages and status. Plays and short stories highlight the theme of free-choice marriage between partners of differing social and economic status.

However, the most interesting evidence to emerge in support of the continuing influence of status on marriage choice comes from the application forms in the new Marriage Bureaux. Apparently the problem of finding a suitable marriage partner is such that it has caused the present government to give its consent to the establishment of Marriage Bureaux in all the major cities. During the last two to three years these have been set up by the Municipal authorities in conjunction with the Women's Federation and Youth League to provide an introduction service to potential marriage partners.[78] Clients fill in a form listing their name, age, occupation, skills, wage, educational level, interests, height and weight plus description of their ideal marriage partner. According to surveys of the clients, applications mainly come from persons who are nearing the age of thirty years, work in occupations and enterprises largely made up of a single-sex labour force and who have low socio-economic or political status (such as co-operative factory workers, miners, sailors), and those with a delinquent or court record. According to cadres of the Bureaux, the expectation of young persons and the definition of their ideal partner frequently outmatches their own conditions. At first the applications were mostly from men with low status, but women now frequently make up half the applicants. A survey of the forms of 100 unmarried women of thirty years of age showed that 45 per cent were university students and 13 per cent senior middle school graduates. They usually requested a partner from an intellectual family who had a similar educational level and held the position of a technician, middle school teacher, doctor or cadre.[79] The information required of applicants and the examples cited in the literature suggest that homogamy probably forms the major principle in matching clients.

Another source of evidence suggesting that homogamy continues or is even increasingly common at the present time comes from the details of divorce cases, the number of which seem to have increased in recent years. One reason given for the divorces, and this is not a new one, is that one partner who has recently been promoted through higher education or a change in occupation or migration to the city may seek a more appropriate spouse.[80] The second, and new, cause of the recent increase in divorces among young persons is that during the Cultural Revolution peasants and workers with high political status were officially defined as preferential marriage mates and many intellectual and other young people with high economic status deemed it prudent to select such mates. Now that the balance of the status systems has swung in favour of socio-economic status, they regret these matches and have pursued a divorce.[81]

MARRIAGE AND STATUS GROUPS

The data presented in this paper strongly support the proposition that both political and social status continue to influence the choice of marriage partner, and that this is so whether the older or younger generation select the marriage partner. In both urban and rural areas the criteria governing marriage choice reveal that there are clearly defined status groups in Chinese society and a hierarchy can be diagrammatically represented (see Figure 3). The tension aroused by heterogamous marriages between partners from different status groups which has not abated over the past three decades gives some impression of the social distance between status groups.

Despite a long campaign to institutionalise free-choice marriage as a means to reduce stratification in contemporary China, all the evidence suggests that marriage choice continues to be structured by socio-economic and political status criteria which, though exhibiting some differences from the past, reflect the present hierarchical arrangement of status groups in Chinese society. The reason for this discrepancy between policy and social practice may well be due to the way in which marriage reform has been con-

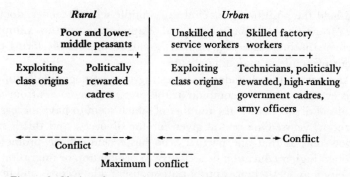

Figure 3 Choice of mate: the gradient of political and social status

ceptualised in China and its relation to other government policies. The Chinese government has defined marriage reform almost exclusively in terms of effecting ideological changes as a result of sustained educational campaigns to familiarise the population with the desirability of free choice without regard for social status, occupation or property, and its contribution to reducing undesirable systems of stratification. The premises underlying the policies assume that as long as the people have a 'raised consciousness' and are aware of the meanings behind traditional symbols and rituals they will of their own accord reject outmoded customs. At the very least, the government has assumed that ideological and economic reforms have been working in a uniform direction of change, progressively institutionalising free-choice marriage. However, at the same time as the government has utilised the ideology of free choice to initiate change in one direction, economic and political policies have with a few exceptions been mainly concerned with defining and confirming the relative positions of status groups in Chinese society.

The degree to which marriage choice has continued to be structured by political and socio-economic status is thus also a direct reflection of the degree to which government policies have been able to equalise educational opportunity, incomes, the redistribution of land and capital, access to the means of production, reduce the corporate interests of the household and redefine the concept of 'class'. Interestingly there is a direct correlation between the periods of more intensive campaigns to reform marriage patterns of the early 1950s, early 1960s and late 1970s and periods when policies towards the private sector of the economy, education and income distribution all contribute to and confirm socio-economic and political status differentials in Chinese society. It is probably this continuing conflict between two sets of policies which has been responsible for the structuring of marriage choice not according to the ideology of free choice, but according to the rating of crystallised status groups in contemporary Chinese society. Marriage policies alone cannot effect a reduction in social stratification and any future social changes will depend on government policies taking cognisance of the fact that patterns of marriage do not only have consequences for social stratification, but that they are also a consequence of stratification systems maintained by current socio-economic and political policies.

9

SEXUAL INEQUALITY UNDER SOCIALISM: THE CHINESE CASE IN PERSPECTIVE

Martin King Whyte

Sexual inequality seems a ubiquitous phenomenon, and its roots are not well understood. Some of the roots are clearly biological and involve factors such as women's role in bearing children and the greater body strength of men. Other sources are disputed and yet poorly understood, in spite of abundant research. In the last century or so, as the worldwide commitment to equality has grown, increasing efforts have been made to reduce the extent of sexual inequality. In modernizing and developed societies hopes for reducing even the influence of biological differences have increased. As fertility became controllable and as mechanization, automation, and the ballooning of the service sector of the economy made physical strength less important in many jobs, advocates of sexual equality began to feel that the most important barriers to their goal were about to be overcome. In the twentieth century these trends were increasingly reinforced by the actions of political elites and state power which, through court decisions, legislation, and mass movements, entered the battle for equality. But if one takes stock of the results of this major change effort so far, the picture everywhere seems somewhat disappointing. Furthermore, in those socialist states in Eastern Europe where the state commitment to sexual equality has seemed most forceful, the record in most areas is not much better than in the capitalist West.[1] China, to some, has suggested that a certain kind of socialism could provide more thorough-going progress toward sexual equality. In the pages that follow we want briefly to review evidence on the sorts of systematic sexual inequalities that still exist in both the capitalist West and in socialist Eastern Europe. Then we will present some new data for urban China which we will use to analyse whether, in the land where women

198

are said to 'hold up half the sky', their lot departs in any major way from this generally disappointing picture.

For the most part this paper will remain at the descriptive and broad comparative level. Our primary aim is to set out data on sexual equality/inequality in several important realms so that cross-national similarities and differences can be assessed and pondered. Some thoughts will be offered on the reasons for the patterns found but these are still preliminary, and the enigma of how and why women's lot differs from that of men is, as already noted, still far from being understood.

We must also deal with the issue of how fair it is to compare the Chinese case with data from much more highly developed countries, capitalist and socialist. Our reasons for doing so in part derive from the fact that some observers have made great claims for the liberation of women in China, even when compared with much more advanced countries. But, to make the comparison more 'equal', we will use here primarily data from urban China, in comparison with national samples from other countries (or occasionally, with urban samples from other countries). In this way, we leave out of the comparison the large bulk of the Chinese population that is rural. The lot of women in rural China is admittedly distinctive and not very comparable with the other countries we will be looking at, and we have already examined the rural scene in previous work.[2]

We would also argue that it is not clear at the outset that comparisons of the position of women in countries at different stages of development are inherently unfair. If economic development was the major prerequisite for sexual equality we would not have to puzzle out why in advanced countries we do not have more of it now, and in fact there is a spirited debate in the literature on whether or in what sense economic development improves the lot of women or leads to more sexual inequality.[3] At the outset it seems to us that some of the things we will be looking at, such as the percentage of female students, are likely to be influenced by the level of development, while others, such as the degree of occupational segregation by sex, do not seem to be so influenced, in any clear sense.[4] Thus we feel warranted in going ahead and making our comparisons while keeping in mind that China's lower level of development may be a factor influencing some of the patterns we find.

Table 1. *Indicators of sexual inequality in the capitalist West (figures are female % of total circa 1970, except as indicated)*

	Austria	Belgium	Canada	Denmark	Finland	France	W Germany	Greece	Italy	Netherlands	Norway	Portugal	Spain	Sweden	Switzerland	United Kingdom	United States
Illiteracy (female% − male%)	0%	0%	0%*					17%	6%*			16%*	8%	0%	0%	0%	−1%*
Primary school	49%	48%	48%	49%	47%	49%	49%	48%	48%	49%	51%	49%	50%	49%	49%	49%	49%
Secondary school	42%	47%	49%	51%	51%	51%	46%	42%	44%	43%	48%	45%	42%	52%	41%	49%	49%
Tertiary school	29%	29%	39%	36%	48%	32%	27%	32%	38%	28%	30%	44%	27%	37%	23%	32%	41%
Labour force	39%	30%	33%	37%	45%	35%	36%	28%	27%	26%	28%	25%	20%	35%	34%	37%	37%
Occupational segregation (index of dissimilarity, 7 categories)	34	40	44	45	39	39	35	24	23	45	49	23		40	37	42	40
Occupational segregation (86 categories)*			67				60		44		73			73		64	64
Relative earnings		73%				69%	60%			60%					63%	50%	59%
National legislature representation											22%			12%		4%	3%

| Female hours on domestic chores – male hours | + 3.4 | + 3.5 | + 4.8 | + 3.2 |
| Female hours of leisure – male hours | – 1.0 | – 1.1 | – 1.1 | – .7 |

* = Data for 1960–1   Blank = data not available

Sources

Illiteracy: Sharon Wolchik, 'Politics, Ideology, and Equality: The Status of Women in Eastern Europe', unpublished PhD dissertation, University of Michigan, 1978, p. 24. UNESCO, *Statistical Yearbook 1974* (Paris: UNESCO, 1975), pp. 40–80.

School enrolments: UNESCO, *Statistical Yearbook 1971*, pp. 130–50, 159–97, 325–38. Abbott L. Ferriss, *Indicators of Trends in the Status of American Women* (New York: Russell Sage Foundation, 1971), pp. 304–9 (figures for 1968 for US).

Labour force participation: International Labour Office, *Yearbook of Labour Statistics* (Geneva: ILO, 1972), pp. 22ff. Also Wolchik, *op. cit.*, p. 60. Occupational segregation, seven-category occupational breakdown: K. Gaskin, 'Occupational Differentiation by Sex', unpublished PhD dissertation, University of Michigan, 1979. International Labour Office, *Yearbook of Labour Statistics 1972* (Geneva: ILO, 1972), pp. 150ff., and comparable figures from subsequent yearbooks.

Occupational segregation, eighty-six-category breakdown: Gaskin, 'Occupational Differentiation by Sex; An International Comparison'.

Relative earnings (caution: the measure and extent of labour force included varies somewhat from country to country, making comparisons inexact): Figures for Belgium (average hourly earnings of adult workers in industry, October 1975), France (average annual earnings of full-time labour in private and semi-private industry, 1973), from Michael Swafford, 'Sex Differences in Soviet Earnings', *American Sociological Review*, 43 (1978), p. 670. Figures for West Germany, the Netherlands, Switzerland, and the United Kingdom are for c. 1965 from John Echols, 'Politics, Policy and Equality under Communism and Democracy', unpublished PhD dissertation, University of Michigan, 1976, p. 195. Figure for the US is for median annual earnings of year-round full-time civilian workers in 1968, from Ferriss, *op. cit*, p. 141.

National legislature representation: Figures cited in Wolchik, *op. cit.*, p. 131.

Time budget figures: John Robinson, Philip Converse, and Alexander Szalai, 'Everyday Life in Twelve Countries', in A. Szalai, ed., *The Use of Time* (The Hague: Mouton, 1973), pp. 126, 133 (figures for hours per day averaged over workdays and weekends, for employed women and employed men only).

201

SEXUAL INEQUALITY IN ADVANCED CAPITALIST
SOCIETIES

In some areas women have made major gains in the past century in the industrialized West. Women's suffrage has triumphed, many forms of legal discrimination against women have been struck down, and female political leaders have appeared in towns, states, and even nations. But if we look at a variety of indicators that are commonly referred to in studies of this type, women still have a long way to go to achieve full equality. In Table 1 we bring together several indicators of women's relative position in various countries in Europe and North America. From this table we can see, first, that there is not much difference in the most advanced capitalist countries in the literacy rates for men and women or in their rates of attendance in primary and secondary schools. But at the university level women are still underrepresented to some degree, with figures ranging from a low of 23 per cent for Switzerland to a high of 48 per cent in Finland.

Women in the West have entered the job market in increasing numbers in recent years, but they are still underrepresented there relative to men, with the range from 19.6 per cent in Spain to a high of 45.1 per cent in Finland. But even the women who are employed tend to earn less than men. Here we have less information available, but the typical range for earnings by full-time women workers seems to be of the order of 45–75 per cent of what men earn. Furthermore, this differential has not shown much sign of being eliminated in recent years, in spite of the increasing job commitment and labour force participation of women.[5] A number of factors lie behind this wage differential. A major factor is simply that in all of these countries the occupational structure is highly segregated by sex. Some occupations are sex-typed as female, and are predominantly filled by women, while others are thought of as male jobs, and are mostly occupied by men. And more often than not the 'female' jobs are ones that have relatively low pay, while many of the highest-paid jobs tend to be dominated by men. Table 1 allows some rough comparisons between countries by showing the index of dissimilarity computed for the sexual distribution across occupations, using grosser and finer occupational breakdowns. This index can be interpreted as indicating the percentage of women (or of men) who would have to change occupations in order for their representation in each occupational category to match their overall representation in the labour force.

At this point we should pause to point out that all three of these economic indicators – level of labour force participation, relative wage level, and occupational segregation, are at least potentially independent of one another. In other words, if in a country women constitute only a small portion of the labour force, but the women who work are spread fairly evenly across all occupations, then for that country the occupational index of dissimilarity will be low, while in another country with high women's labour force participation but very uneven occupational distribution of women the index will be a high one. Similarly, it is conceivable for women to be represented poorly in the labour force but earn wages comparable to men, or for women to be highly segregated in the occupations they hold, but to dominate highly paid occupations as well as lowly paid ones, so that their earnings will be on a par with men.

We can see from Table 1 that in the real world women are on the short end of each of these indicators. Interpreting the index of dissimilarity figures is not simple, since, depending on how many occupational categories one uses in the computation, the index will be lower or higher (generally with a higher index for a finer occupational breakdown). Nonetheless, the picture is clear here as well. In all of the countries for which we have information, it is clear that very substantial occupational segregation by sex exists, indicating that men and women tend to hold different kinds of jobs.[6]

Another factor in women's lower earnings is not visible in the figures in Table 1. This is the fact that, even within occupations, the leading and most highly paid posts tend to be held by males. There is substantial debate in the literature on just what are the mechanisms by which women end up in different sorts of jobs than men, and ones that are generally less well paid. However, we will not go into these debates here, but simply note that the pattern exists in only somewhat varying degrees in all of the countries in the capitalist West.[7]

In politics the gaps are if anything even more marked. Studies a generation ago indicated that women made up only 15–30 per cent of the members of democratic parties in various Western countries, but Party membership is obviously nowhere near as important in the West as in the East.[8] Women are also greatly underrepresented in positions of national and even local leadership. We do not have as much systematic data as we would like, but the figures cited on women in national legislative bodies make the general picture clear. In recent years women have clearly been in the minority in all of these countries, with figures ranging from 2.5 per cent in the United States to 22 per cent in Norway. More recent (1977) figures for the United States reveal the following picture: women at that point constituted 3.4 per cent of the numbers of Congress, 10.7 per cent of the state executive officers (elected or cabinet-level appointed), 9.2 per cent of the membership of state legislative bodies, 1.8 per cent of the state judiciary posts, 3.1 per cent of county commissioners, and 7.8 per cent of the membership of local mayoral and township council bodies.[9] Clearly in the political realm women do not fare as well relative to men as they do in the economy.

In the United States and in Western societies generally there is increasing change in sex-role attitudes toward accepting egalitarian standards in the abstract. But when we look within homes to see how families manage their lives, things do not look so equal. In particular, in all of the countries for which we have data, women end up doing the bulk of the domestic chores, even if they work full-time outside the home. In fact, there is some debate among those who do research on American society over whether when women work outside the home, rather than being housewives, this makes any difference at all to the amount of work their husbands do around the house.[10] But in any case women end up spending more time on chores than men do, and as a result they generally have less time for leisure than men, and less opportunity to engage in other activities outside the home that would conflict with their domestic burdens. In Table 1 some rough indicators are given from time budget studies that attest to this double burden – that employed women have in essence two jobs, one at work, and one in the home. Time budget studies involve asking individuals to record the amounts of time spent on various activities for the full twenty-four hours each day, and often over a span of several days or a week. In the table we display two kinds of figures where they are available: the difference between the time employed women spend on house-hold chores and men do and the difference in amount of leisure time recorded (per twenty-four-hour period). In general these figures make the 'double burden' situation of women fairly clear. A number of authorities feel that these domestic burdens are at least one of the reasons that women are not able to compete better in the occupational and political arena, and they may not be unrelated to the fact that studies in the US generally show that women have higher rates of mental illness, neuroses, and psychosomatic complaints than men.[11]

In spite of the Women's Liberation Movement and dramatic changes in public opinion about sex-roles, and even evidence of changes in the way parents are rearing their sons and daughters (all tending to foster more equality or an androgynous orientation), there is little indication that anything other than the slightest, glacial changes are occurring in these overall indicators of sexual inequality in the West, except in regard to the proportion of women working. It is this persistence in the face of so much apparent effort and change that leads to the sense of disappointment and frustration referred to at the outset of the paper. But we shall see below that the picture in the socialist countries of Eastern Europe is not far different.

SEXUAL INEQUALITY IN EAST EUROPEAN SOCIALIST COUNTRIES

There is one strikingly different feature of women's roles in Eastern Europe, and that is that much higher proportions of women work than is the case in the capitalist West. In Marxist theory it is assumed that the elimination of private property in the means of production and general female labour force participation are the necessary conditions for promoting sexual equality. However, when we look at the evidence in other spheres, it becomes rapidly apparent that these conditions are at least not sufficient to produce substantial sexual equality. The overall picture for the socialist countries of Eastern Europe is one that does not differ dramatically from the one we have already sketched for advanced capitalist nations. We will briefly touch on some of the indicators here, but the reader should be aware that problems of data availability and comparability make any firm conclusions difficult. There are a host of questions and problems about most of our indicators (e.g., does one count part-time students, what items are included in the earnings calculations) that we will not give their proper due here, but which would have to be dealt with thoroughly before any firm conclusions could be reached about the relative amounts of sexual inequality in East and

Table 2. Indicators of sexual inequality in socialist eastern Europe (figures are female % of total circa 1970, except as indicated)

	Albania	Bulgaria	Czechoslovakia	E Germany	Hungary	Poland	Rumania	Yugoslavia	USSR
Illiteracy (female% – male)		10%			1%	2%		21%	0%
Primary school	47%	48%	49%	50%	48%	48%	49%	47%	49%
Secondary school	38%	48%	58%	46%	43%	57%	42%	45%	55%
Tertiary school	32%	51%	38%	36%	43%	42%	43%	39%	49%
Labour force	39%	41%	47%	47%	41%	46%	30%	31%	51%
Occupational segregation (index of dissimilarity, 7 categories)		26	33		28		31	24	36
Relative earnings			66%		66%	63%		84%	65%
Party membership	22%	25%	27%	23%	24%	23%	23%	20%	23%
Party Central Committee	15%	11%	9%	12%	9%	9%	6%	8%	3%
National legislature	17%	18%	26%	32%	24%	14%	14%	8%	31%

206

Female hours on domestic chores – male hours	+ 2.6	+ 2.8	+ 3.8	+ 4.2	+ 3.4	+ 3.9	+ 2.6
Female hours of leisure – male hours	– .6	– 1.6	– 1.3	– 1.3	– 1.3	– 1.2	– 1.9

Blank = data not available

Sources

Illiteracy: Wolchik, *op. cit.*, p. 22; UNESCO, *Statistical Yearbook 1974*, p. 77; Tsentral'noe Staticheskoe Uprevlenie, *Narodnoe Khoziaistro SSR v 1970g* (The National Economy of the USSR in 1970) (Moscow: Statistical Publishing House, 1971), p. 23 (only ages 9–49).

School enrolments: UNESCO, *Statistical Yearbook 1971.*

Labour force participation: Wolchik, *op. cit.*, p. 57.

Occupational segregation: International Labour Office, *Yearbook of Labour Statistics 1972* (Geneva: ILO, 1972), pp. 150ff., and comparable figures from subsequent yearbooks. Tsentral'noe Staticheskoe Uprevlenie, *Itogi Vsesoyuznoi Perepisi Naselenia 1970 goda* (Results of the All-Union Census Population of 1970) (Moscow: Statistika Publishing House, 1973), vol. 6, Tables 2 and 18.

Relative earnings: Echols, *op. cit.*, p. 195; Wolchik, *op. cit.*, p. 71; Swafford, *op. cit.*, p. 661.

Party membership: Wolchik, *op. cit.*, p. 116.

Central Committee membership: Wolchik, *op. cit.*, p. 153.

National legislature membership: Wolchik, *op. cit.*, p. 133.

Time budget figures: Robinson, *et al.*, *op. cit.*, pp. 126, 133 (figures for hours per day averaged over workdays and weekends, for employed women and employed men only).

West. Since our main interest is in setting a framework for introducing our Chinese data, we will content ourselves here with a simple, rough comparative look.

In Eastern Europe the indicators at the low end of the educational distribution (see Table 2) do not look much different from those in the West, with noticeably higher female illiteracy rates only in the less developed countries and near parity in primary enrolments. At the secondary level there is more diversity in Eastern Europe, with figures ranging from a low of 38 per cent in Albania to a high of 58 per cent in Czechoslovakia (and figures nearly as high in Poland and the Soviet Union). These figures are outside of the narrower, near parity range for the secondary school enrolment figures in the West. At the tertiary level the figures for Eastern Europe look somewhat better than those from the West, with the range from 32 to 51 per cent female attendance, compared with a range from 23 to 48 per cent in the West. In general, then, the way women fare educationally in East and West does not look all that different, although perhaps given the generally lower levels of economic development in the East the comparison (particularly at the university level) should be judged in favour of the socialist countries.

From the fourth row in Table 2 we can see the higher level of labour force participation in the East already referred to. Only Rumania and Yugoslavia show women representing much less than 40 per cent of the labour force, while in the West only Finland shows more than 40 per cent of the labour force composed of women. Looked at in another way, several East European countries have from 75 per cent to around 90 per cent of their adult women in the labour force, while in the West the highest levels are generally in the 50–60 per cent range.[12] If we examine occupational segregation we are hampered by differing definitions of occupational categories and the lack of any figures for as detailed an occupational distribution as the eighty-six categories for which we have computations for some Western countries. Looking at the indexes of dissimilarity for the crudest, seven-category occupational breakdown, it looks as if occupational segregation in the East is slightly less marked than in the West, but not dramatically so. But in the East as well as the West, the dominant picture is one of extensive occupational segregation, with men dominating managerial positions, higher professional ranks, and heavy industry, construction, and mining, while women dominate lower professional, clerical, sales, and service occupations, as well as much of light industry. A computation using thirty-nine occupational categories for the Soviet Union in 1970 shows an index of dissimilarly of forty-six, or in other words 46 per cent of the women (or men) in the Soviet labour force would have to change jobs in order for the sexual division of the labour force to be comparable across all occupations.[13] Furthermore, Michael Sacks made a detailed comparison of this same range of occupations in the 1939, 1959, and 1970 Soviet censuses, and concluded that there had been little if any reduction in occupational sex segregation over this time period, in spite of significant increases in women's labour force participation and growing parity in educational attainments.[14] Sacks also presents data to show that, within occupational categories, the more responsible and highly paid jobs tend more often to be occupied by males.[15] We do not have comparable detail for all Eastern European countries, but what figures there are indicate that the same situation applies in all of these socialist countries.[16]

When it comes to female wages in comparison with male wages, the socialist countries do not look all that different from the capitalist West, with the puzzling exception of the high figure for Yugoslavia. And in all of the socialist countries except Yugoslavia, there is a strong negative correlation between the percentage of women in a sector of the economy and the average earnings of people employed in that sector.[17] For the Soviet case additional details are again available. A local study of families in the city of Odessa concluded that in 73 per cent of the cases the husband's salary was higher than his wife's, that in 20 per cent of the families their wages were about equal, while in only 7 per cent of the cases did the wife earn more.[18] Another local study in Yerevan, in Soviet Armenia, was used to provide the figure of 65 per cent included in the table as the ratio of female earnings to male earnings. Secondary analysis of the Yerevan data by Michael Swafford shows that even when one controls for age, educational attainment, branch of industry, and occupational level women still end up earning only 72 per cent as much as men. In other words, the lower earnings of women do not appear to be primarily a result of their working in different kinds of jobs than men, or having less education, but appear to be a 'pure' gender effect, at least in this one Soviet city.[19] To sum up, the higher labour force participation rates of these socialist countries do not get translated very effectively into either comparable earnings with men or minimal occupational segregation.

When we enter the realm of politics comparisons are more difficult, given the very different natures of political systems, East and West. It is clear, for instance, that Party membership is much more important in the East, while membership in national legislative bodies carries far more power in the West. Several conclusions can be drawn from this comparison. One is that everywhere, regardless of political system, women are severely underrepresented in political leadership. Another is that, the higher one goes in the political system, the fewer women one is likely to find.[20] A third conclusion comes from comparing the range of representation in Western national legislatures and Party central committees in the East, assuming that these bodies are to some extent comparable, in terms of power. In general the range of representation of women does not look much different between East and West, so we tentatively conclude that women do not have much more of a political voice in the socialist countries, in spite of their more important economic role.

In our household time budget figures the pattern in the East is also quite similar to that in the West. In both Table 1 and Table 2 the figures refer only to employed men and women, which helps us exclude the influence of the different levels of women's labour force participation in East and West. The patterns in Table 2 again show a clear 'double burden', with women doing much more domestic work than men, and largely as a consequence ending up having less leisure time each day than men. Again we have additional information on the Soviet case. Michael Sacks has analysed time budgets for that country from the 1920s and the 1960s. He concludes that, over this stretch of time, which spanned the period during which women moved from low to high levels of labour force participation, men did not, on the average, increase the amount of time they spent on domestic chores.[21]

Several features of life in the Socialist Bloc make the double burden borne by women especially tedious. First, as may be clear, no serious effort has been made to get men to help out around the house, comparable to the major effort devoted to getting women out into the work force. Second, the pattern of economic priorities in these countries has emphasized heavy industry and deemphasized the development of services and consumer goods. As a result, the development of appliances and services that might relieve some of the burden of household work has been much slower in the East than in the West (except in the realm of providing pre-school child-care institutions). As a result, doing the laundry, shopping, and coping with other chores are generally more difficult and tedious in the socialist countries than in the West.

In the foregoing pages our discussion has been limited to aspects of male and female roles that are readily measurable, and subtle aspects of interpersonal relations and power and deference between men and women have been ignored. We cannot claim that our indicators present an overall picture of all aspects of male-female roles in these two types of societies. But we do feel that our indicators and discussion are sufficient to draw several overall conclusions, which have been hinted at already in our introduction. Some differences are clearly visible, and the major one is that women are much more fully represented in the labour force in most East European countries. There are marginal differences, perhaps, in university enrolments and occupational segregation, with women faring somewhat better in socialist countries. But the overall picture is still one of substantial similarity in how women fare in the two types of systems. In both East and West women are slightly under-represented in higher education and in the labour force, the jobs they hold tend to be different ones than those men hold (and ones that are less well paid), they are more severely underrepresented in politics and leadership positions, and they continue to do the lion's share of domestic work even when they hold full-time jobs. And where information is available over time, there is not much evidence of major change taking place in any of these features of male and female roles, except in regard to female labour force participation. Socialism and women's labour force participation do not seem to have fulfilled their Marxian promise more fully to liberate women, who continue to suffer multiple disadvantages in both East and West. We now need to turn to the major task of this paper, considering whether the lot of women is different in any major way in urban China.

THE POSITION OF WOMEN IN URBAN CHINA

When we turn to the Chinese case we confront even more difficulty in making comparisons. Systematic data published in China are available on very few of the indicators we have used in the earlier parts of this paper. So for the bulk of our analysis we will have to turn to data we have collected from informants from cities in various parts of China.[22] Most of the data we will be analysing come from what we call a 'Neighbour census' that was collected via intensive interviews in Hong Kong in 1977–8. As part of broad-scale interviews with 133 former residents of urban places in China, informants were asked to fill out forms describing the household compositions and member characteristics of five or so of their immediate neighbours whose family situations they knew in detail. (That informants were generally able to provide such details is an interesting commentary on the degree of solidarity and lack of privacy in urban neighbourhoods.) Detailed probes resulted in information about ages, marital statuses, jobs, income levels, educational backgrounds, seniority, and other characteristics. In some cases we were also able to obtain detailed information on the role played by various family members in household chores. The result of these portions of our interviews was a neighbour census of 581 urban households, consisting of 2865 individuals. We use this technique to obtain a sample to analyse that is less biased and selective than the families of our informants or their kin or friends would be. However, it needs to be stressed that, strictly speaking, this is not a sample that is in some full sense representative of China's urban population. The sample includes people from cities large and small from all over China, but with a heavy overrepresentation of localities in Guangdong and Guangxi provinces. And while on some indicators (e.g., the proportion of people working in state versus collective enterprises) our sample looks fairly similar to distributions published for all of urban China, we do not have enough detailed statistics on the urban population published in China to establish how representative or unrepresentative our sample is. In the absence of better data, it seems best to proceed cautiously to use this information for investigating the position of women in urban China.[23] Because of the lack of comparability of our data and our particular interest in the Chinese case, we will proceed here to investigate the same areas we looked at in other sections of the paper, but in more detail, rather than collapsed into a single, summary table of indicators.

In regard to education we do have national statistics published for 1978, and these indicate that females made up 45 per cent of the primary school enrolment, 41 per cent of the secondary school enrolment, and only 24 per cent of the tertiary enrolment.[24] These figures are for all of China, not just the cities, and they show China coming off somewhat worse than any of the countries in Tables 1 and 2, as we might expect given her much lower level of economic development. (The figures are not far different from those for the poorest countries in those tables, such as Greece, Spain, and Albania.) Of course these Chinese figures reflect considerable progress from the picture in traditional China, but not consistent progress, and even retrogression in recent years. (As early as 1952 women made up 23 per cent of the tertiary student enrolment, a figure which rose to 27 per cent in 1965 and 33 per cent in 1976.)[25]

If we look at data from our weighted urban sample the situation looks somewhat better, as does the trend over time. If we count as illiterate only those who had no education at all (a conservative procedure), then in our sample the female illiteracy rate for all those over age 20 is 22 per cent and the male rate is 2 per cent, producing a substantial differential. However, there are very few individuals with no education below the age of 40 in our sample, and in the 20–39 age range the illiteracy rates are 4 per cent and 0 per cent for females and males, respectively. In other words within our urban sample illiteracy is on its way to being wiped out in the younger cohorts, with the sex disparity in the illiteracy rate departing with it.

In Figure 1 we present figures on the mean levels of educational attainment by males and females in our weighted sample, differentiated by the period in which schooling was begun. Here again the trend over time is quite marked.[26] From the figure we can see that, for those who began their schooling before 1918 (or received none at all, but would have begun then), women received little more than one year of schooling on the average, while men received almost seven years. So the gap in mean educational attainment for this cohort is almost six years. Over time the male average educational attainment generally rises, to eventually surpass nine years, but then falls back as a result of the Cultural Revolution 'gearing down'

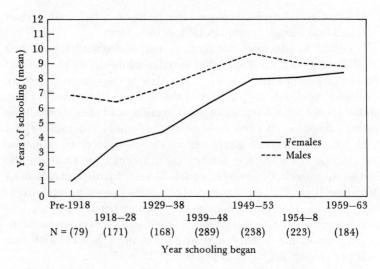

Figure 1 Education by year schooling was begun and sex

N = combined male and female sample sizes.
Year schooling was begun = year reached age seven.

Source: weighted urban neighbour sample.

of schooling to a mean level for our final cohort that is less than two years more than our first cohort, a rather surprising result. Over this period the gains for women are more constant, so that in our final cohort the average female is receiving only 0.44 fewer years of schooling than the average male. The difference is still significant, and favours males, but it has been almost eliminated. Finally we can look at the highest end of the educational distribution. Very few of the younger people in our sample were attending university, again in part due to the 'gearing down' of the Cultural Revolution, but we can examine the sex ratio of all adults in our sample who had acquired some post-secondary school education. Of 201 such individuals in our sample, 30 per cent are female, a figure that compares more favourably with the tertiary enrolment figures for other countries than does the national tertiary enrolment figure cited earlier, even if it is still short of equality. In general our various measures of educational attainment from our sample indicate that the educational disparity between men and women in

Table 3. *Proportion of women and men employed*

Age	Female (%)	Male (%)	N
10–19	21	19	362
20–9	93	93	461
30–9	94	97	355
40–9	89	98	223
50–9	73	99	175
60–94	20	38	151

Source: Weighted urban neighbour sample.

urban China has been dramatically reduced, but not totally eliminated. This represents impressive gains, but still does not make the Chinese case stand out in comparison with the experience of the countries we considered earlier.

When we examine women's labour force participation, we can see from the figures in Table 3 that in our weighted urban sample Chinese women are very fully involved up until about age 50, after which their rate begins to decline more rapidly than does the rate for males. (In common with other socialist countries, regulations in China provide for retirement pensions at earlier ages (45–55) for women than for men (50–60), and retirement is not obligatory, particularly for professional, managerial, and highly skilled personnel.) Overall, about 93 per cent of the women in the 20–49 age range in our weighted sample are employed, compared with 96 per cent of the men. So in the prime working years there is not much difference by sex in labour force participation. It is only after the age of 50, when women begin retiring earlier, and when we find more women who were never fully employed, that a sizeable gap between the rates is visible.

But do women work in substantially different kinds of jobs than do men? In other words, is there the same sort of occupational segregation by sex as we have seen in national figures for countries in the West and the European Socialist Bloc? A firm answer is difficult, because we do not have comparable occupational breakdowns for our Chinese sample to those used in our earlier tables.

215

Table 4. *Average wage levels and female representation in occupational groups*

Occupational grouping	Average wage (yuan)	Female (%)	Occupational grouping	Average wage (yuan)	Female (%)
University profs., school principals	103	39	Construction workers	53	18
Engineers, technicians	90	29	Accountants	53	47
Doctors, pharmacists	81	31	Expediter/procurer	53	0
Gov't administrators	75	22	Teacher, unclassified	51	57
Other cadres, military offic.	74	30	Sales supervisor	50	53
Managers, shop heads, etc.	67	23	Other clerical	48	66
Other professionals	63	33	Nurses	45	97
Foremen	63	0	Primary school teachers	44	80
Secondary school teachers	62	67	Cashiers, sales clerks	42	68
Drivers, transport workers	60	13	Cooks, waiters, barbers	42	48
Skilled production workers	60	7	Ordinary workers	41	54
Indep. sales workers	57	33	Street cleaners	38	86
Artists and authors	56	71	Pre-school teachers	37	100
Policemen & soldiers	56	7	Nursemaids, servants	29	93
Trans. conductors, postal work	55	55	Temporary workers	27	75
Rank-and-file gov't officials	54	53	Apprentices	22	55

Source: 1977–8 Chinese urban neighbour sample.

But several patterns are clear. First, there is a general tendency to see women concentrated in the same sorts of jobs – light industry, services, clerical, etc. – and underrepresented in others – heavy industry, managerial positions, etc. – as in other countries. And just as in other countries, the jobs that women hold are likely to be ones that are paid less than the jobs men hold. This can be seen at a glance from the figures in Table 4. There we list a detailed grouping of thirty-two occupational categories represented in our sample, along with their average pay levels and the percentage of that category that is female in our sample. A glance shows that there is a strong negative relationship between the income level of an occupational category and the percentage of females who are likely to be found there. (The correlation coefficient for these two variables is $r = -.54$.) Inspection of the categories also supports our claim that the pattern of occupational segregation is similar to that found in other societies.

In China there is another factor to be considered, which involves the distinction between state and collective enterprises. In discussions of occupational segregation by sex in the West it is often argued that there is a 'dual labour market' at work, and that women and other minorities often get channelled into inferior jobs, ones that have fewer benefits as well as lower pay, while white males tend to monopolize the high pay and high security jobs in the primary sector of the labour market.[27] In China there is, in effect, a formally institutionalized dual economy, even though there is no free labour market as such. Urban economic enterprises are classified as either state or collective enterprises. The former, which employed about 78 per cent of the urban labour force in the late 1970s, tend to have higher pay, more fringe benefits, and more job security. The collective sector, which includes things like neighbourhood factories and service shops, is characterized by lower pay, fewer benefits, and more uncertain career prospects (less chance for mobility and more chance of losing one's job). And in our sample 45 per cent of those employed in state enterprises are female, while 59 per cent of those employed in neighbourhood collective enterprises are female. Clearly this distinction is not the only factor in women's segregated job situation and lower income, but it is an important factor.

We can delve somewhat further into the question of the income differences between men and women. In Figure 2 we graph the

217

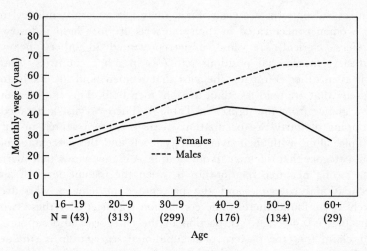

Figure 2 Monthly income by age and sex

N = combined male and female sample sizes.

Source: weighted urban neighbour sample, employed persons only.

mean wages of men and women broken down by age. From the figure it appears that men and women start off with fairly similar wages, but then at later ages men are able to progress into higher wage brackets while women do not continue to make equal progress. However, the figure cannot tell us for sure if this interpretation is correct, since women in older cohorts may simply have less of the important determinants of wage levels (education, seniority, skill, etc.) than do younger women, who might turn out to have different futures. Some additional light on the question is provided by performing a regression analysis of our reported earnings data. Table 5 shows the results of this analysis, for the whole sample, and for men and women separately. Regression analysis is a statistical technique that allows us simultaneously to control for the influence of several other variables so that we can separate out and examine the 'pure' influence of one variable on another.

Several things are apparent from examining Table 5. First, the mean income of women in our sample is about 74 per cent that of men (77 per cent in our weighted sample) which compares relatively favourably with the figures cited in Tables 1 and 2 for other countries.

218

Table 5. *Linear regression analysis of individual income levels*

For the entire sample: Panel A
N = 666 Mean income level = 50.13 yuan Regression constant = − 14.42
$R^2 = .47$

	Sex	Education	Seniority	Occupation*
Metric regression coefficient	4.38	1.00	1.57	.69
Standardized regression coefficient	.074	.129	.441	.341

For females only: Panel B
N = 302 Mean income level = 42.16 yuan Regression constant = −7.59
$R^2 = .50$

	Education	Seniority	Occupation*
Metric regression coefficient	1.05	1.19	.62
Standardized regression coefficient	.203	.431	.382

For males only: Panel C
N = 364 Mean income level = 56.75 yuan Regression constant = − 15.1
$R^2 = .43$

	Education	Seniority	Occupation*
Metric regression coefficient	1.03	1.81	.72
Standardized regression coefficient	.110	.467	.321

Note: Metric coefficients indicate the monthly return in yuan for each additional year in school, year of education, unit in occupational rank, or difference in gender. Standardized coefficients indicate the relative importance of all of these variables in determining income. All coefficients are significant at p < .01.
*Occupation is represented by the average income level of 32 occupational groupings.
Source: 1977–8 Chinese urban sample.

219

Second, the metric regression coefficients show that men benefit slightly more from each step up the occupational ladder, and considerably more for each added year of seniority, than do women (see the top rows in Panels B and C of Table 5). This is important because, as the standardized regression coefficients in those same panels show, occupational placement and seniority have stronger independent effects upon income than does education. But the top panel in the table reveals another important fact: when one controls for the other variables the independent influence of gender is considerably reduced, although not totally eliminated. The metric regression coefficient for sex in Panel A shows a considerable reduction from the 14.6 yuan gap in mean incomes before other variables are taken into account. What this means is that much, but not all, of the difference between male and female incomes in our sample can be attributed to the fact that women get placed in less remunerative occupations and benefit less than men from seniority, rather than being a residual gender effect, a conclusion which differs from the one noted earlier emerging from Swafford's analysis of Soviet wage data.[28]

Our analysis has shown that women in our urban sample are occupationally segregated to an important extent, and that they have lower earnings than men. But how do these Chinese patterns look in comparative perspective? We have just noted that the earnings gap is somewhat more modest than in most of the other countries we have looked at. Several other kinds of data speak to this issue as well. In our sample, if we look at employed couples' earnings alone, we find that in 73 per cent of such couples the husband earns more, in 12 per cent of the cases the earnings are about equal, and in 16 per cent of the cases the wife earns more (N = 354 couples). These figures are not too different from the figures cited earlier for Odessa in the USSR (73 per cent, 20 per cent, 7 per cent), except for a slightly higher proportion of cases in our sample in which the wife earns more. Another figure from our sample is that married women on the average earn about 37 per cent of the household income. (Married men on the average earn 57 per cent, the rest being earned by other family members.) In one socialist society for which we have figures, Czechoslovakia, wives earn somewhat less, only 18–20 per cent of household income on the average. In the United States in 1974 the average married woman with husband present earned 26 per cent of her family's income if she worked, and this figure looks as high as it does only because in the US there are unlikely to be other earners in the family besides the husband and wife.[29] In terms of income, then, women in our Chinese urban sample do somewhat better than in comparable countries.

If we consider the question of occupational segregation, the issue is complicated by the difficulty of arriving at comparable occupational breakdowns to make comparisons. If we compute an index of dissimilarity for the distribution of males and females in our most detailed, fifty-category occupation code, we get a figure of 34, which means that about a third of the women (or the men) would have to change jobs to make the sex ratio of each occupation comparable to that for the sample as a whole. If we use a collapsed, ten-category occupational breakdown (high professional, administrative cadres, managerial cadres, low professional, clerical and sales, skilled manual, service workers, ordinary and semi-skilled manual, unskilled and marginal workers, and other) we compute an index of dissimilarity of 31, only slightly less. However, if we try to rearrange our occupations into an even more collapsed, seven-category code more or less comparable to that used in Tables 1 and 2 (with the following categories: professional, technical and related; administrative and managerial; clerical and related; sales; agriculture, forestry, animal raising; production, transport, and mine workers; and service workers), we compute a much lower index of dissimilarity of 15. If we glance back at earlier tables, we will see that even for the most detailed breakdown of our Chinese data, these are fairly low values by international standards. In sum, the pattern of occupational segregation by sex in our sample is not very distinctive, but it appears to be somewhat less sharp than in other societies. However, before jumping to conclusions about what in the nature of Chinese socialism might have produced this moderation in segregation, we must take note of the fact that a computation of an index of dissimilarity for the seven-category occupational distribution by sex in capitalist Hong Kong yields a value of 9, even lower than for our urban sample within China. Since the way such indexes of dissimilarity are affected by economic, cultural, and other factors are as yet poorly understood, it is difficult at this point to draw firm conclusions, and we will defer further comments until our conclusion. We simply want to stress here that both the degree of handicap in wages and occupational segregation of women in our Chinese urban sample look somewhat more moderate than most of our comparison figures for both Western capitalist and East European socialist societies.

In the realm of politics we have some limited national figures to cite. We have not been able to find a current figure on the percentage of all Party members who are women. However, 19 per cent of the 1510 delegates to the 11th Party Congress in 1977 were women; women constituted 11.4 per cent of the membership of the Central Committee selected at that Congress (and 7 per cent of the full, as opposed to alternate members of the CC), and only one out of twenty-eight politburo members (3.8 per cent), who was only an alternate member. These figures do not constitute any clear increase from previous Congresses.[30] If we switch over to the state organs, we find that one out of fourteen (7.1 per cent) vice-premiers chosen at the 5th National People's Congress in 1978 was a female, as was one out of thirty-seven ministers chosen (2.7 per cent). (Actually, the one female in all of these computations is Chen Muhua, who is doing multiple duty in our figures.) Women do somewhat better in the somewhat more honorary, less powerful state positions. They constitute 14.3 per cent of the chairperson and vice-chairperson and 20 per cent of the members of the standing committee of the NPC who were named at that time. Women also make up 26 per cent of the more than 18 million state cadres in China, but only 3–6 per cent of the high-ranking state cadres (those above rank 13 in the official system of 26 state cadre ranks).[31]

In our own weighted urban sample we find the following picture. Women make up 62 per cent of the members of the Communist Youth League in our sample, but only 12 per cent of the members in the more selective Chinese Communist Party. In Figure 3 we display the pattern of membership by sex in both of these organizations, broken down by age cohorts. There we can see that at their peaks in the 40–9 age cohort, close to a quarter of the men in our sample belong to the Party, but less than 10 per cent of the women. Both the national and our own figures testify to both the under-representation of women in politically important positions, and the increasing male dominance at the higher levels. If we look at the other end of the leadership scale, the picture is different. Our informants were asked the gender of the people serving as heads of the

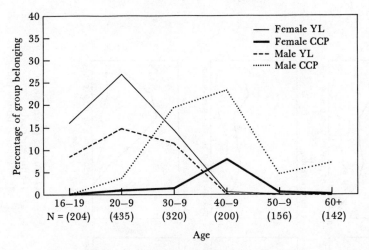

Figure 3 Youth League and Communist Party membership by age and sex
N = combined male and female sample sizes.
Source: weighted urban neighbour sample.

residents' committees and residents' small groups where they lived –
the lowest and most menial positions of authority in Chinese cities.
Fully 70 per cent of the residents' committee chairpersons and 88
per cent of the heads of the residents' small groups mentioned
were women.[32] In general these data on leadership do not make the
Chinese case look particularly different from the socialist countries
of Eastern Europe.

The final area for detailed analysis here concerns the division of
labour within the home. We want to know whether Chinese women
suffer from the same sort of double burden that working women in
other countries do, by being the primary performers of domestic
chores. Since we are dealing with reports on people's neighbours,
we were not able to obtain the sort of detailed, hour-by-hour time
budget calculations reported for other countries in Tables 1 and 2.[33]
But we did use special forms to collect a somewhat different kind of
report on the household division of labour. On these forms we asked
informants to report what sort of role each member of neighbouring
households played in the following chores: shopping for vegetables,
cooking, washing the dishes, sweeping, washing clothes, emptying

223

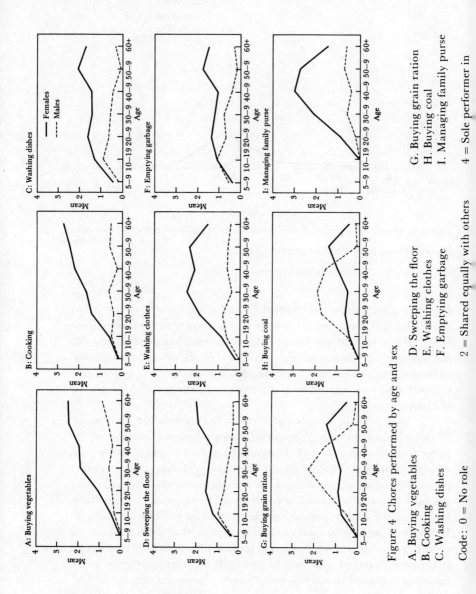

Figure 4 Chores performed by age and sex

A. Buying vegetables   D. Sweeping the floor   G. Buying grain ration
B. Cooking   E. Washing clothes   H. Buying coal
C. Washing dishes   F. Emptying garbage   I. Managing family purse

Code: 0 = No role   2 = Shared equally with others   4 = Sole performer in

224

the garbage, buying the family's grain ration, buying the family's coal ration, and managing the family money. The available alternatives were: no role, a minor role, an equal role, the major role, and the sole role in performing the given task. These data serve as a device for comparing the domestic burdens of men and women, and they will also permit us to make some rough comparisons with data from other countries.

In Figure 4 we show the mean scores of men and women on the performance of each chore, again differentiated by age cohorts. From the figure we can see several patterns. The first five chores we can consider prototypically 'feminine', and for each of these, females at all ages are more likely to perform them than men. There is not much difference in performance of these chores by young sons and daughters in the family, but thereafter the gap increases, although for washing dishes and clothes the gap closes somewhat at the end, as older women cede these chores to younger women. At all ages males are on the average not likely to play more than a minor role in any of these chores. The pattern is similar for emptying garbage, except that here teenage boys are somewhat more likely than daughters to help out. For buying grain and coal the pattern is somewhat different, as these involve carrying heavy loads back home, and often up long flights of stairs. For these chores we see that men in the prime years are more likely to be the ones to perform them, although in the oldest two cohorts women again end up with more of the burden. Finally, managing the family money is the most overwhelmingly female task of the whole set. We note that this task is different in nature from the others, involving responsibility and power as much as a burden. Still, on balance, the evidence in the figure indicates a very familiar situation of women who work outside the home also bearing the major responsibility for tasks within the home.

We made some effort to try to determine under what circumstances men are more likely to help with chores around the home in the families in our sample. To do this we constructed a mean scale of the five 'feminine' chore items and examined how this varied in relation to the background characteristics of males and females. In Table 6 we summarize the results of that analysis. The correlation statistic is used to measure the strength of the associations. (The partial correlations in columns 2 and 4 of the table allow us to control for age and

Table 6. *Factors affecting participation in 'feminine' household chores (correlation coefficients)*

Variables	Wife	Wife[a]	Husband	Husband[a]
Job characteristics				
Income	−.27*	−.35*	−.14*	−.13
% of family income contributed	−.07	−.12	−.12	−.16*
Whether employed	−.12*	−.18*	−.01	−.21*
Seniority	−.29*	−.39*	.01	.14*
Type of industry	.17*	.15*	.10	.07
Type of occupation	.14*	.19*	.07	.13*
Ownership of unit (coll. vs state)	−.25*	−.22*	−.06	−.06
Personal characteristics				
Age	.01	XX	.13*	XX
Education	−.03	−.03	.08	.05
YCL or CCP membership	.05	.04	.00	−.04
Class background	−.02	−.02	.00	.02
Family situation				
Family structure (nuc. vs extend.)	−.15	−.06	−.16*	−.01
Unemployed females at home	−.21*	XX	−.27*	XX
Eat lunch in canteen	.18*	.21*	.13*	.12
Work long hours	−.11	−.13*	.15*	.13*
Frequency of evening meetings	.03	−.01	.05	−.01

Family living standard				
Relative living standard (inf. jud.)	.11	.10	.14*	.12
Consumption index (bike, radio, watch, sewing machine)	.33*	.37*	−.02	.00
Facilities in home (running water, bathroom, kitchen, toilet)	−.01	−.02	.13	.16*
Own house lived in	.11	.14*	.05	.12
Characteristics of urban place				
Level of city	−.13*	−.31*	.08	.15*
City in Guangdong or Guangxi	.07	.10	−.18*	−.17*
Level of relations and supplies	.05	.01	−.22*	.25*
Frequency of household inspections	.15*	.21*	.15*	.24*
Median N	(120)	(108)	(103)	(111)

Note: **XX** = controlled relationship, cannot be computed.
*Relationship significant at p. 10.
[a] Partial correlation coefficients, with age and presence of unemployed females in the home controlled for.
Source: Currently married men and women in urban neighbour sample.

227

whether there were unemployed females at home to see if the associations still hold under these controls.)

Several things can be concluded from Table 6. First, general class
variables do not make much difference in chore participation for
either sex – the correlations with education, Party membership, and
class background are all very low. Second, wives who are employed,
earn high incomes (absolute more than relative to their total family
income), have high seniority, and work in state enterprises do
significantly fewer chores than other wives. For husbands the effects
of these variables are less clear, with high income employed males
also tending to do fewer chores, but those with high seniority perhaps
doing more chores than other husbands. There is no linear relation
between a wife's age and her share in the chores, but older husbands
tend to help out less than younger ones. Family structure is also
important, and it is particularly notable that husbands and wives
both do fewer chores when there are other unemployed females in the
household who can manage these tasks. Curiously, having a work
schedule that keeps one away from home does not lead to performing
fewer chores at home; in fact husbands and wives who eat lunch in a
unit canteen, and husbands who have late hours of returning from
work, do more chores than the average. The other relationships in the
table suggest that wives do more chores where they have lots of consumer durables, perhaps when they own their own home, when they live
in a smaller town, and when there are frequent household cleanliness
inspections. For husbands the patterns here are weaker and somewhat
different, with men doing more chores where there are frequent cleanliness inspections, where rations are insufficient, in cities outside of
Guangdong and Guangxi, and perhaps in larger cities and in homes
with more facilities. We do not have a general explanation that makes
all of these associations interpretable, and the figures for husbands are
particularly hard to explain. However, for women at least we would
argue that the figures in the table do show one broad pattern.
Women have divided obligations in the home and on the job. Factors
which increase the level of obligation and emotional investment in
the job, such as work in a state enterprise, high seniority, and high
pay, will cut into the time a woman spends doing domestic chores.
On the other hand, factors that increase the domestic obligations and
emotional investment, such as not having other women at home to
help, having high consumption standards, and having frequent

household cleanliness inspections, tip the balance in favour of putting more effort into domestic chores. So there is a general pattern of family chore divisions which gets modified to suit the situational pressures that families, and in particular wives, face. Again, factors of class and personal resources do not seem to explain the associations in the table.[34]

We have argued that in urban China we find a common, perhaps universal, pattern of employed women doing more of the household chores than men. We still need to try to place these results in comparative perspective. Since we do not have time budget data for our sample, we need to try to take studies using other methods from different societies and try to make them comparable to our Chinese data. The comparison will be quite a rough one, since we will be converting scores derived from studies using slightly different methods and questions. For our data we will use the ratio of the mean score of husbands on a given chore to the mean score for wives. Thus a score of 0 means the husbands do nothing, a score of 1.0 indicates that husbands do as much as wives, and scores over that indicate husbands do more. For comparison purposes we use studies done in other countries using the methodology devised by Blood and Wolfe. This involves asking a sample whether a given task is always done by the husband, usually done by the husband, done by both spouses equally, usually done by the wife, or always done by the wife. To compute the male contribution for such figures, we assign values of 4, 3, 2, 1, 0 to these alternatives and then compute the average. For females we perform the same computation using 0, 1, 2, 3, 4 for these same alternatives. Then we take the ratio of the male to the female score and use it as our measure.[35] Where possible we will examine only the responses given by employed wives to such questions.

In Figure 5 we draw bar graphs to compare our results with studies conducted in the United States, Finland, Sweden, Austria, Belgium, East Germany, Rumania, and the Soviet Union, using our five 'feminine' chores and the issue of money management. From the figure we can see that, for the five feminine chores, there is nothing remarkable about our Chinese results in relation to the other studies. In other words, if this rough comparison is correct, there is no special tendency for Chinese men to help out around the home more than husbands in other countries, and women in China seem to suffer under a double burden that is as bad as is common elsewhere.

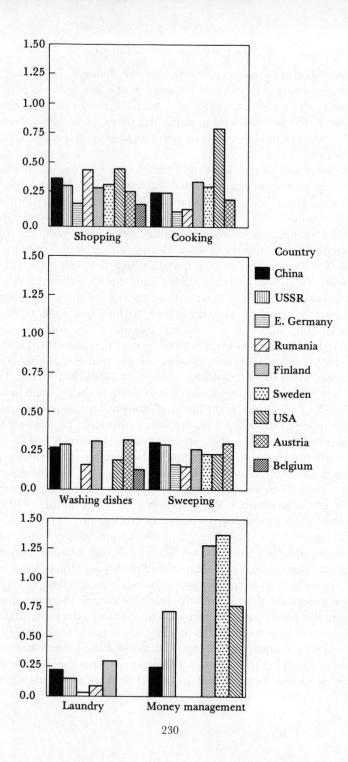

Figure 5 Ratio of mean husband/wife task performance scores

Cooking = breakfast for USSR, Finland, Sweden, and the USA.

Sources

China: 1977–8 urban neighbour chores sample.

USSR: A sample of 430 married women in 1966 in the cities of Moscow, Leningrad, and Penza. The self-report chore questions were: payment of bills, buying groceries, preparing breakfast, preparing dinner, washing dishes, everyday cleaning, and laundry. See G. Slesarev and Z. Yankova, 'Zhenshchina na promyshlennon predpriatti i v sem'e', (The Women in the Industrial Enterprise and in the Family), in G. Osipov and J. Sczepanski, *Sotsial'noe Problemy Truda i Proizvodstva* (Moscow: Mysl', 1969), p. 430 (all employed women).

Rumania: A subsample of responses of working wives from a larger sample in Bucharest in 1976. The chore questions were: daily shopping, meal preparation, dishwashing, clotheswashing, and daily cleaning. Reported in William Moskoff, 'Sex Discrimination, Commuting, and the Role of Women in Rumanian Development', *Slavic Review*, 37 (1978), p. 450.

Finland and Sweden: Samples of 271 married women in Helsinki and 442 married women between ages 20 and 45 in Uppsala, both from studies conducted in 1966. (Working wives make up only 65 and 52 per cent, respectively, of the samples.) Reported in Elina Haavio-Mannila, 'Convergences between East and West: Tradition and Modernity in Sex Roles in Sweden, Finland, and the Soviet Union', *Acta Sociologica*, 14 (1971), p. 121. The chore questions were: buying the food, preparing breakfast, preparing dinner, washing the dishes, daily cleaning, washing clothes (in Helsinki washing the husband's shirts and socks), and paying the regular bills.

United States: Sample from 1971 Detroit Area Study interviews with over 2000 residents of that city. Responses of wives were used here. The chore reports concerned preparing the husband's breakfast, grocery shopping, straightening up the living room before company comes, doing the evening dishes, and keeping track of the money and bills. See Beverly Duncan and O. D. Duncan, *Sex Typing and Social Roles* (New York: Academic Press, 1978), p. 198 (working women only).

East Germany: An extensive survey (sample characteristics unclear) published in the paper *Der Morgen* on 22 Sept. 1968. Cited in B. Jancar, 'Women under Communism', in J. Jaquette, ed., *Women in Politics* (New York: John Wiley, 1974), p. 225.

Austria: A sample of 1370 Austrian working women in several cities and towns, all in the 20–30 age range. Chore reports concerned shopping for daily needs, cooking, washing dishes, and vacuum cleaning. See M. Szinovacz, 'Role Allocation, Family Structure, and Female Employment', *Journal of Marriage and the Family*, 39 (1977), pp. 781–91.

Belgium: A sample of 500 representative families in Louvain, Belgium, interviewed in 1961–2. See W. Silverman and R. Hill, 'Task Allocation in Marriage in the United States and Belgium', *Journal of Marriage and the Family*, 29 (1967), pp. 353–9.

However, the final item on money management looks quite different. There it appears that Chinese men play much less of a role in managing the family money than do men in other societies. (However, since in the other studies the question offered concerned 'paying the bills' rather than 'managing the money' part of this difference may be due to variation in questions used.) Unfortunately we do not have clear enough data for the pre-1949 period to be certain about whether this pattern of female money management represents a real change over time or not, but it certainly differs from the stereotype of men dominating affairs in 'traditional' Chinese families. To conclude, women may have an unusual predominance in managing family finances in urban China, but when it comes to household chores as usually defined, their situation does not seem to be at all unusual compared with the situation in other societies.

These numerical data do not portray very effectively what it means for Chinese women to have to cope with both a job and family chores. It is debated whether, in the West, household appliances and conveniences actually reduce the time spent on housework, but they certainly relieve some of the physical drudgery.[36] In China there is no such relief; the policy of scrimping on state expenditures, on social overhead, and on services makes the situation more difficult. Work schedules in China involve six days a week, and the one day off for rest is often occupied as much with doing the cleaning and laundry as it is with leisure and rest. And to daily work schedules must often be added time spent commuting to and from work and obligatory after-work meetings and other activities. Shopping for food is also a major chore. Much food is of course rationed, and for these items complicated management and planning of the use of coupons, booklets, and so forth are required. Even unrationed items are often in short supply, and shopping involves making the rounds of different kinds of shops specializing in particular foods, and sometimes lining up early in the morning to insure that one can make a purchase. Refrigerators are practically nonexistent, so that shopping is generally a daily chore. Cooking is also no easy matter. Gas is only beginning to be available in some newer housing in the largest of Chinese cities, but for most urban families cooking requires lighting and tending a fire made from 'beehive coal' as well as undertaking the labourious slicing and dicing that are basic to Chinese cuisine. Some work unit

232

and neighbourhood canteens ease the burden by preparing relatively low cost meals (and the government has shown signs of trying to encourage cold meals and fast foods), but most families eat at home at least for two meals a day, and often all three. Doing the dishes, bathing, and doing the laundry generally involve heating water, and may sometimes involve fetching pots of hot water from special stands on the street. Washing the laundry and bedding seems to be the most laborious task of all. Washing machines are again almost nonexistent, so that things have to be scrubbed and washed completely by hand. Public or neighbourhood laundries are very rarely available as a substitute for family labour in this chore. There are other complications as well, but by now the picture should be clear. Women are the dominant performers of household chores in urban China, as they are elsewhere, and these chores are very burdensome indeed. We assume that these burdens are one factor, in China as elsewhere, why women do not play a more active role in politics, advance more rapidly up career ladders, and have more time for leisure and self-improvement.[37]

There are other aspects of female roles that we want to touch on briefly here, even though in these cases we have no cross-national comparisons to make. Instead, there are several features of women's roles in urban family life that present an interesting contrast with earlier work on rural family patterns in China.[38] First, there seems to be some residual preference for bearing sons, but it does not appear to be as strong as in the countryside. Increasingly couples seem to be willing to stop at two children (and the government is trying to pressure them to stop at one), even if they have not yet borne a son. There are only relatively isolated cases in our interviews of women continuing to bear child after child until a son arrives, a situation that was still common in rural Guangdong in 1973–4. (However, in some cases in urban areas this persistence can take extreme forms, even to the extent of a woman binding her body to disguise a pregnancy and escape the birth control enforcers.) However, family limitation still seems to be seen mainly as a woman's responsibility, as it does in the countryside. We feel that son preference in urban areas has weakened as factors such as retirement pensions, lack of family control over jobs and housing, and so forth make the reinforcement of patrilineal ties less essential.

Several other features of urban family life suggest a weakening of

233

Table 7. *Initial post-marital residence patterns*

	All marriage cases (%)	Post-1966 marriages (%)
With groom's family	36	38
With bride's family	4	3
In groom's unit housing	12	15
In bride's unit housing	2	3
Unit housing – both in same unit	8	12
Non-unit housing, separate neighbourhood	34	23
No joint residence for couple	5	7

Source: 721 marriage cases from interviews.

the traditional emphasis on patrilineal ties. One concerns the pattern of residence after marriage. Some informants claimed that a new trend toward married couples moving in with the bride's family had emerged in recent years, and that this matrilocal arrangement produced more family harmony than the traditional patrilocal arrangement. However, when we examined our data on marriage cases systematically, no such trend toward residence with the bride's family was apparent (see Table 7). What is apparent, though, is that a neolocal pattern, with the married couple living separately from either set of parents, has been more common than the traditional patrilocal arrangement throughout the post-1949 period. Some preference for the patrilocal form persists, but couples show considerable flexibility in seeking out housing, and in a majority of cases the watchful eye of the mother-in-law will not be there to reinforce obligations between generations.

Clearer evidence of the weakening of the patrilineal emphasis in family life can be seen in the way urban families reacted to the campaign to send educated youths to settle in the countryside. In this campaign, which sent more than 17 million educated urban youths to the countryside in the decade after 1968 and still continues in reduced form, there have generally been provisions to exempt one child in the family from going, and in some cases arrangements to allow one child to take the place of a retiring parent in their job or work unit. In this situation urban families have to weigh their desire to foster patrilineal continuity against another concern – the dangers to the virtue of their daughters of living unsupervised in a distant village. In this situation the concern for the daughter's virginity may win out, and in fact in our weighted sample 61 per cent of those who were or had been in the countryside were sons. This is not a large difference, but it does illustrate the way other concerns can override the desire to foster patrilineal continuity.

Comparisons with the contemporary rural scene highlight several other aspects of weakening patrilineal ties. For one thing, generally in urban China daughters as well as sons now share the obligation to help support ageing parents, and daughters as well as sons can inherit what little family property there is (mainly consumer durables in large cities, but often housing as well in smaller ones). Another indication comes from our analysis of divorce cases. In our rural study we found that, while women initiate the majority of divorces now, in any settlement they tend to lose out. They do not generally get to take any share of family property, they do not usually get custody of the children, and they may even have to repay the bride price that was paid out at the time of their marriage. In our divorce cases from urban China the picture is different. Women do initiate the divorce cases more often (in 77 per cent of our cases). But they got custody of the children in 58 per cent of the cases, while the husband got custody in only 25 per cent (in the remainder, custody was split). This may seem like more preference for the husband than is common in the West, but it does differ sharply from the predominance of male custody in rural Guangdong, and fits the balanced-with-slight-female-preference emphasis of the provisions of the 1950 Marriage Law. In urban divorces women more often than not were also favoured in the division of family property (in 58 per cent of the cases), which is again not the situation in rural China. In general, then, we conclude that urban women are less fully subordinated to patrilineally oriented family units than is still generally the case in the Chinese countryside.[39]

There are many important aspects of women's roles that have not been discussed in this paper. What about the way boys and girls are treated in school, or the attitudes of work authorities to male and female employees, or the power of male family heads (and males, when present, are still recognized as such)? There are many subtle aspects of women's roles relative to men that we cannot say much about based upon our interviews, particularly in terms of cross-national comparison. We cannot make any claims here that we have covered all the important aspects of sexual equality and inequality in urban China, or even necessarily the most important ones. But the evidence we have presented does enable us to make some generalizations about how distinctive the lot of women in urban China is, in comparison with the situation in other societies.

CONCLUSION

We have traversed a complex terrain of indicators, and it is not easy to draw comprehensive conclusions. The weight of all of our evidence leads us to a conclusion that is not very exciting: there does not seem to be much difference in the degree of sexual inequality East and West, or between China and the other countries surveyed. Women in socialist and capitalist countries, and in richer and poorer countries of both types, fall short of equality with men in many important spheres of life.

Still, not everything is uniform. Although the rate of female labour force participation is on the rise in the West, socialist countries (including China) are distinctive in having on the average significantly higher labour force participation by women. Perhaps in connection with this full mobilization of women into the work force, socialist countries seem to have higher representation of women in higher education, and perhaps slightly less occupational segregation, than is the case in the capitalist West. But in other realms, such as relative wages, political participation, and household chores, there does not seem to be much difference between the two kinds of societies. Full labour force participation by women does not directly translate into equality in other realms. In fact, given the greater burden of household chores in socialist societies in comparison with developed capitalist ones, and the relatively obligatory nature of work for women, one can question whether the full mobilization of women into the work force can be thought of as 'liberation' after all.

While we have not examined matters in this way, clearly the degree of economic development affects the representation of women in schools at various levels, with poorer countries included in our survey generally having more male predominance. The degree of economic development also has some impact on the rate of female labour force participation, although here the trend is not one of a simple linear increase, and the political system and prevailing culture also make an important difference. But, it is not clear, at least for the limited range of countries considered here, that the degree of economic development has much impact on things like women's political representation, occupational segregation, relative earnings, and the household division of labour. Just what factors do or might influence these aspects of women's roles is a topic that requires much more research.

If we look at our Chinese case, we can say that in general the lot of women in urban China does not differ too much from the other societies on most indicators. We have been able to discover only a few areas where the Chinese case may differ somewhat, and even in these the problems of comparability make any firm conclusions difficult. But our evidence makes it look as if women in urban China are somewhat less discriminated against in terms of wages and somewhat less occupationally segregated than in our comparison societies, and that women in our sample may have an unusually high degree of control over family funds.

Assuming these are genuine differences, it would be nice to be able to account for them. But we cannot claim to have satisfactory explanations at hand, particularly in regard to family money management, and we invite readers to ponder the matter. In regard to wage and occupation differences, one thing is clear. We have already seen in Figure 2 that the wage difference between men and women is small in our younger cohorts, but is much larger among older employed persons. In a separate analysis not reported earlier, we found that occupational segregation by sex is also much lower in the youngest age cohorts.[40] Unfortunately, without data over time, we cannot be sure how to account for this pattern. But we think it is likely that this age difference is partly attributable to the urban employment crisis in recent years and the effects of the Cultural Revolution on job opportunities of the young. Essentially the educational ladder to well paid, non-manual jobs was pulled out from under our youngest cohort, and only a limited range of jobs, mostly in industry and the service and sales trades, was available to those lucky enough to gain an urban job. In other words, the variation in job opportunities that had existed was sharply truncated,

237

and young males and females scrambled to get whatever urban jobs were available, if they could qualify. In this crisis situation we have already noted that some parents were especially concerned to get their daughters plugged into urban jobs. In these jobs both males and females were usually stuck at a fairly uniform beginning wage level (30–35 yuan) up until the wage adjustments which began late in 1977 (which are not represented in our wage data). We are suggesting, then, that these factors to some degree short-circuited the 'natural' tendency for male and female job destinations (and wages) to differentiate. One implication is that, with the current return to policies of earlier years, the improvement in urban job prospects, and an increasing consideration of individual job preferences, we can expect to see this modest distinctiveness of the Chinese case reduced or disappear.

Perhaps our comparisons in this paper have been unfair to China. We have for the most part ignored the progress women have made in contemporary China, in comparison with earlier decades and centuries, and we have not compared China with other poor developing nations. We do not want to imply that women have not achieved substantial progress in China, and we acknowledge that in many areas of social life even the lot of women in rural China would compare favourably with many developing countries elsewhere. Instead our argument is that both socialist and capitalist development produce certain kinds of improvements in the lot of women, but that these seem to proceed only up to a point that is still far short of full equality. The evidence from our interviews suggests that China has not found policies or institutions that could break through this barrier toward more total equality of the sexes. Whether there are conditions making more substantial sexual equality possible, and what these might be, are puzzles that the case of socialist China does not help us to solve.

NOTES

I. WATSON: INTRODUCTION: CLASS AND CLASS FORMATION IN CHINESE SOCIETY

1 See for example Ch'ü T'ung-tsu, 'Chinese Class Structure and Its Ideology', in John K. Fairbank, ed., *Chinese Thought and Institutions* (Chicago: University of Chicago Press, 1957), p. 245. Ch'ü refers to the scholar-officials as 'the backbone of the ruling class'.
2 Denis Twitchett, 'A Critique of Some Recent Studies of Modern Chinese Socio-Economic History', *Transactions of the International Conference of Orientalists in Japan*, 10 (1965), pp. 28-41. See also Hilary J. Beattie, *Land and Lineage in China: A Study of Tung-ch'eng County, Anhwei, in the Ming and Ch'ing Dynasties* (Cambridge: Cambridge University Press, 1979), pp. 1–21, 127–32.
3 There have been some recent exceptions to this trend, see Hill Gates, 'Ethnicity and Social Class', in Emily Martin Ahern and Hill Gates, eds., *The Anthropology of Taiwanese Society* (Stanford: Stanford University Press, 1981) and Rubie S. Watson, 'Class Differences and Affinal Relations in South China', *Man*, 16 (1981), pp. 593–615.
4 See for example Jing Su and Luo Lun, *Landlord and Labor in Late Imperial China: Case Studies from Shandong*, translated and edited by Endymion Wilkinson (Cambridge, Mass.: Harvard University Press, (1959) 1978). A survey of relevant studies can be found in Philip C. C. Huang, 'Analysing the Twentieth-Century Chinese Countryside', *Modern China*, 1 (April 1975), pp. 132–60.
5 Martin K. Whyte, 'Destratification and Restratification in China', in G. Berreman and K. Zaretski, eds., *Social Inequality: Comparative and Developmental Approaches* (New York: Academic Press, 1981).
6 On the terminology relevant to class labels see Richard C. Kraus, 'Class Conflict and the Vocabulary of Social Analysis in China', *China Quarterly*, 69 (March 1977), pp. 54–74 and his recent book *Class Conflict in Chinese Socialism* (New York: Columbia University Press, 1982).
7 Gordon White, *The Politics of Class and Class Origin: The Case of the*

Cultural Revolution (Canberra: Australian National University Press, Contemporary China Centre, 1976), p. 2.
8 *Ibid.*, pp. 2–3.
9 Martin K. Whyte, 'Inequality and Stratification in China', *China Quarterly*, 64 (December 1975), pp. 684–711.
10 Gordon White, *op. cit.*, p. 3.
11 *Ibid.*, p. 3.
12 See Denis Twitchett, *op. cit.* for a similar argument. Kuhn's view can also be supported by anthropological field data. Villagers in Hong Kong's New Territories (originally part of Guangdong's Xinan xian) do not have an indigenous vocabulary to deal with class differences. This does not mean that they are unaware of differences based on inherited wealth, it is just that they have neither vocabulary nor the inclination to deal openly with socio-economic divisions (cf. Watson, *op. cit.*). There is no reason to assume that people who live across the Anglo-Chinese border were any different prior to the revolution. The notion of social class, as such, is not part of the indigenous culture (at least among Cantonese peasants). The conceptual apparatus of a class system, including the vocabulary, has to be introduced by outsiders. It is little wonder, therefore, that ordinary Chinese are not entirely consistent when they use terms such as *jieji, chengfen,* and *chushen.*
13 For another interesting approach to this subject see Arif Dirlik, *Revolution and History: Origins of Marxist Historiography in China, 1919–1937* (Berkeley: University of California Press, 1978).
14 See e.g., Stuart Schram, 'Mao Zedong and the Role of Various Classes in the Chinese Revolution, 1923–1927', in Muramatsu Memorial Committee, ed., *The Polity and Economy of China: The Late Professor Yuji Muramatsu Commemoration Volume* (Tokyo: Toyo Keizai Shinposha, 1975), p. 299.
15 Martin K. Whyte, 'Inequality and Stratification', pp. 699, 703.
16 *Ibid.*, p. 703.
17 *Renmin ribao*, 18 September 1956, cited in Kraus, 'Class Conflict and Vocabulary' (see n. 6), p. 58.
18 Martin Whyte, 'Inequality and Stratification', p. 703.
19 Kraus, 'Class Conflict and Vocabulary', p. 70.
20 Martin Whyte, 'Inequality and Stratification', p. 705.
21 That is, the process by which new classes emerge from old. This, more than the analysis of existing classes, is a problem that preoccupies many anthropologists.
22 See also Lynn White, *Careers in Shanghai* (Berkeley: University of California Press, 1978).
23 Milovan Djilas, *The New Class: An Analysis of the Communist System* (New York: Praeger, 1957). Stuart Schram notes in Chapter 3 that Mao did not actually use the term 'new class'.

24 Suzanne Pepper, 'Chinese Education After Mao: Two Steps Forward, Two Steps Back and Begin Again?', *China Quarterly*, 81 (March 1980), pp. 1–65.

25 See also Elisabeth Croll, *The Politics of Marriage in Contemporary China* (Cambridge: Cambridge University Press, 1981).

26 Communist authorities consciously created these new pariah groups; they did not emerge 'naturally'. A similar pattern of conscious creation was responsible for the appearance of pariah groups during the imperial era. As Kuhn notes in Chapter 2, the 'mean peoples' were 'man-made' through judicial processes.

27 See G. William Skinner and Edwin A. Winckler, 'Compliance Succession in Rural Communist China: A Cyclical Theory', in Amitai Etzioni, ed., *Complex Organizations, A Sociological Reader*, 2nd edn (New York: Holt, Rinehart and Winston, 1969).

28 Martin K. Whyte, *Small Groups and Political Rituals in China* (Berkeley: University of California Press, 1974), pp. 165–6.

29 On the critical role of rural-to-urban migration in late-imperial China see G. William Skinner, 'Mobility Strategies in Late Imperial China: A Regional Systems Analysis', in Carol A. Smith, ed., *Regional Analysis*, Vol. 1, *Economic Systems* (New York: Academic Press, 1976) and also his 'Urban and Rural in Chinese Society', in G. William Skinner, ed., *The City in Late Imperial China* (Stanford: Stanford University Press, 1977).

30 In contrast to some of its neighbours (notably Japan and Korea), China did not develop rigid caste divisions. See Philip Kuhn's argument in Chapter 2 and also G. DeVos and H. Wagatsuma, eds., *Japan's Invisible Race* (Berkeley: University of California Press, 1966). For another approach see H. Passin, 'Untouchability in the Far East', *Monumenta Nipponica*, 11, 3 (1955), pp. 27–47.

31 On this topic see Ezra F. Vogel, 'Preserving Order in the Cities', John P. Emerson, 'Manpower Training and Utilization of Specialized Cadres, 1949–68', and Janet Salaff, 'Urban Residential Communities in the Wake of the Cultural Revolution', all in John W. Lewis, ed., *The City in Communist China* (Stanford: Stanford University Press, 1971). It is clear from these essays that the measures taken to check rural-to-urban migration did not always work, especially in the aftermath of intense political campaigns. Nonetheless, the post-revolution pattern of migration is very different from that which prevailed during the late imperial era.

2. KUHN: CHINESE VIEWS OF SOCIAL CLASSIFICATION

1 *Sanguozhi, Wushu*, in *Ershisi shi jiaotianben* (The twenty-four dynastic histories), Beijing, p. 1230. See also the excellent treatment of classical ideas on stratification by Ch'ü T'ung-tsu, 'Chinese Class Structure and

Its Ideology', in John K. Fairbank, ed., *Chinese Thought and Institutions* (Chicago: University of Chicago Press, 1957), pp. 235–50.

2 Zhou Fagao, ed., *Yenshi jiaxun huizhu* (The household instructions of Yen Zhitui with collected commentaries) (Taipei, 1960), p. 33. The passage is referring derisively to high official-literati families who abandon scholarly ambition as soon as they achieve a slight advancement in rank.

3 Liang Qichao, 'Lun qiangquan' (On power), in *Yinbingshi quanji, zawen*, p. 32.

4 Raymond Williams, *Keywords: A Vocabulary of Culture and Society* (New York: Oxford University Press, 1976), p. 52.

5 Tazoe Tetsuji, in a 1955 Tokyo edition, ed. Kishimoto Eitarō, *Katayama Sen, Tazoe Tetsuji shū*, p. 214. An earlier work that may have used the term similarly is Fukui Junzō, *Kinsei no shakaishugi* (1909), translated into Chinese in 1903. I have not been able to find a copy of this work. See Martin Bernal, *Chinese Socialism to 1907* (Ithaca: Cornell University Press, 1976), pp. 94–5. It may have been through Fukui's work that the Marxist use of 'class' first became available to Chinese readers.

6 Takeuchi Minoru, ed., *Mō Takutō shū* (Collected Writings of Mao Zedong) (Tokyo, 1972), 1, pp. 57–69.

7 Takeuchi Minoru, *Mō Takutō shū*, 1, p. 83. Later in the piece the term 'proletariat' or 'propertyless class' occurs once, but it is in quotes (exotic foreign term) and in context simply means poor people.

8 For example, see the memorial of Ge'ertai to the Yongzheng Emperor (1723), concerning a certain pariah group in Zhejiang: 'They cannot occupy professions proper to ordinary subjects (*simin*); they cannot register in the same registers in which ordinary subjects are inscribed.' *Yongzheng zhupi yuzhi*, Ge'ertai, 1b.

9 Niida Noboru, *Chūgoku hōsei shi* (Tokyo, 1963), pp. 123–42.

10 *Daqing lichao shilu*, Yongzheng, 56:27–28b. The memorial which started all this was apparently by the censor Nianxi dated Yongzheng 1:3 (1723). *Yongzheng zhupi yuzhi*.

11 Nevertheless, the agnatic descendants of indentured servants who had redeemed their freedom would still be held to observe 'the distinction between masters and servants' if they had been born in the master's household. The Jiangnan gentry were not about to put up with the loss of their servants quite so easily.

12 Hong Mai, *Rongchai suibi, xia*, 864 (Shanghai, 1978 reprint).

13 Qian Yong (1759–1844), *Meixi Tsonghua* (Shanghai, 1936), *shang*, p. 111.

14 Qian Yong, *Meixi Tsonghua*, p. 114.

15 Qian Yong, *Meixi Tsonghua*, p. 109.

16 Liang Shaoren, *Qiuyu'an suibi* (Shanghai, n.d., Jinbushuju ed.), 1:26b.

17 'Eight cyclical characters' (*bazi*) refer to the notations of the year, month,

day, and hour of birth. Those sharing the eight characters are supposed
to be linked by fortune in some way, presumably astrologically.

18 *Xiandai Hanyu Cidian* (Beijing, 1973), pp. 122, 141.

3. SCHRAM: CLASSES, OLD AND NEW, IN MAO ZEDONG'S THOUGHT,
1949–1976

1 Stuart Schram, 'To Utopia and Back: A Cycle in the History of the
Chinese Communist Party', *China Quarterly*, 87 (September 1981),
especially pp. 414–15.

2 *Mao Zedong ji*, 2, p. 95.

3 *Ibid.*, pp. 90, 100.

4 H. Carrère d'Encausse and S. Schram, *Marxism and Asia* (London:
Allen Lane, 1969), p. 246. (In this work, we followed the dating of the
Comintern directive given in the standard Russian source, i.e., 26 August
1931. It turns out that in fact the correct date is July; see A. M. Grigor'ev,
Revolyutsionnoe Dvizhenie v Kitae 1927–1931 gg. (The Revolutionary
Movement in China, 1927–1931) (Moscow: 'Nauka', 1980), pp. 246–54
passim.)

5 The second of these is, of course, in revised form, the first item included
in the canon of the *Selected Works*. For extracts from both articles in the
original version, see Stuart Schram, *The Political Thought of Mao Tse-tung*,
revised edn (New York: Praeger, 1969), pp. 241–6, 210–14, 247.

6 *Selected Works*, 4, p. 363.

7 *Eighth National Congress of the Communist Party of China* (Peking: Foreign
Languages Press, 1956), 2, pp. 213–14.

8 Stuart Schram (ed.), *Mao Tse-tung Unrehearsed, Talks and Letters: 1956–71*
(Harmondsworth: Penguin, 1974), p. 269.

9 Su Shaozhi, *Tentative Views on the Class Situation and Class Struggle in China
at the Present Stage* (Beijing: Institute of Marxism–Leninism Mao Zedong
Thought, Chinese Academy of Social Sciences, 'Selected Writings on
Studies of Marxism', no. 6, February 1981, p. 35). Chinese text: 'Shi lun
woguo xian jieduan de jieji zhuangkuang he jieji douzheng', in *Xueshu yanjiu jikan* (Zhengzhou), 1 (October 1979). The conclusions which Richard
Kraus has drawn regarding the probable contents of the original version
of this speech are thus quite correct. See his *Class Conflict in Chinese Socialism*
(New York: Columbia University Press, 1982), pp. 43–8.

10 Su Shaozhi, *op. cit.*, pp. 22–6; Liao Gailong, *Shehuizhuyi shehui zhong
de jieji douzheng he renmin neibu maodun wenti* (Class struggle and contradictions among the people in socialist society), pp. 9–12. (Report delivered
on 19 December 1981 at a national forum on research and teaching
regarding Party history convened by the Central Party School.)

11 *Selected Works*, 5, p. 393.

12 'Wei shimo yao zhengfeng?' ('Why do we want to carry out rectification?'),

Renmin ribao, 2 May 1957. For the judgment quoted above regarding Mao's approval for the editorial, see Liao Gailong, 'Guanyu xuexi "jueyi" zhong tichu de yixie wenti de jieda' ('Answers and explanations regarding some questions which have been posed in connection with the study of the "Resolution"'), *Yunnan shehui kexue*, 2 (March 1982), pp. 104–5. (Given at a meeting of Party and state cadres in Yunnan on 8 October 1981.)

13 'Things are Beginning to Change', 15 May 1957, *Selected Works*, 5, p. 440.
14 *Ibid.*, p. 395.
15 'The Situation in the Summer of 1957', July 1957, *Selected Works*, 5, pp. 479–80.
16 'Beat Back the Attacks of the Bourgeois Rightists', 9 July 1957, *Selected Works*, 5, pp. 469–70.
17 *Ibid.*, p. 444.
18 Schram, *Mao Unrehearsed*, pp. 112–13.
19 *Miscellany of Mao Tse-tung Thought*, pp. 85–6; *Wan-sui* (1969), pp. 180–1.
20 *Selected Works*, 5, p. 357.
21 Liao Gailong, 'Lishi de jingyan he women de fazhan daolu' ('The experience of history and the path of our development'), in *Zhonggong yanjiu* (Taibei), September 1981, p. 123. (This report, delivered on 25 October 1980 at a meeting for the academic discussion of the history of the Chinese Communist Party called by the Central Party School, has not been officially published in China, but there is every reason to believe that the text reproduced in Taibei is authentic. It was on this occasion that Liao put forward proposals for what he then called a 'Gengshen gaige', or 'Gengshen reforms', after the cyclical characters for the year 1980.)
22 *Wan-sui* (1969), pp. 228, 235–6, 239–40 (speeches of 5 and 8 September 1958).
23 *Renmin ribao*, 13 October 1958.
24 Speech of 11 September 1959 to the Military Affairs Committee, Schram, *Mao Unrehearsed*, pp. 147–8.
25 'The Origin of Machine Guns and Mortars', 15 August 1959, *Chinese Law and Government*, 1, 4 (1968–9), p. 73.
26 *Wan-sui* (1967), p. 192. For an earlier reference to 'putting on airs like overlords', see Mao's speech of November 1958 on Stalin's *Economic Problems of Socialism in the USSR* in *Wan-sui* (1967), pp. 117–18.
27 Schram, *Mao Unrehearsed*, p. 168.
28 *Wan-sui* (1969), p. 424.
29 *Ibid.* (1967), pp. 206, 210.
30 Schram, *Mao Unrehearsed*, p. 217.
31 *Wan-sui* (1969), pp. 498–9.
32 *Ibid.*, p. 587.
33 Schram, *Mao Unrehearsed*, p. 198. (Remarks at the Spring Festival Forum on Education.)

34 *Wan-sui* (1969), pp. 582–8.
35 *Ibid.*, pp. 597–8.
36 Schram, *Mao Unrehearsed*, pp. 169–70.
37 *Wan-sui* (1969), p. 426.
38 *Ziliao xuanbian* (Beijing), January 1967, p. 277.
39 *Miscellany of Mao Tse-tung Thought*, p. 351; *Wan-sui* (1969), pp. 494–5.
40 *Miscellany of Mao Tse-tung Thought*, p. 433; *Wan-sui* (1969), pp. 602–3.
   For the dating of this text, see the discussion in the index to Mao's post-1949 writings published in 1981 by the Institute of Humanistic Studies, Kyoto University, p. 47.
41 Su Shaozhi, *op. cit.*, pp. 18–19.
42 Joseph W. Esherick, 'On the "Restoration of Capitalism": Mao and Marxist Theory', *Modern China*, 5 (January 1979), pp. 60–1.
43 *Ibid.*, pp. 57–8, 71–2.
44 *Wan-sui* (1969), p. 351.
45 Esherick, *op. cit.*, pp. 66–7.
46 *Ibid.*, pp. 67–8.
47 *Ibid.*, pp. 68–71.
48 This statement regarding Mao's position during his last years corresponds to the view commonly expressed by responsible theoretical workers, at the Chinese Academy of Social Sciences and elsewhere, in conversations conducted in April and May 1982.
49 Kraus, *op. cit.*, especially Chapter 7, but also Chapters 2–6 *passim*.
50 Yao Wenyuan, *On the Social Basis of the Lin Piao Anti-Party Clique* (Peking, 1975), pp. 7–8.
51 *Peking Review*, 21 (1976), p. 9.
52 See, in addition to Kraus, *op. cit.*, the essay by Jean-François Billeter, 'The Class Status System', in S. Schram (ed.), *The State in China*, 1 (Forthcoming).
53 *Peking Review*, 52 (1968), pp. 6–7.
54 *Mao Zhuxi guanyu guonei minzu wenti de lunshu xuanbian* (Selections from Chairman Mao's expositions regarding problems of nationalities within the country), ([Beijing]: Guojia minzu shiwu weiyuanhui disan si [Third Department of the State Commission on Minority Affairs], October 1978), p. 8.
55 *Ibid.*, pp. 6–7. (This quote is from the official Chinese record of the talks; to my knowledge, Snow never made use of this passage in his own writings.)

4. SHIRK: THE DECLINE OF VIRTUOCRACY IN CHINA

1 On the distinction between transformative and accommodative political philosophies in China see Thomas P. Metzger, *Escape from Predicament, Neo-Confucianism and China's Evolving Political Culture* (New York: Columbia University Press, 1977).

2 Personal interview, Chongqing, March 1980.
3 *Jiefang ribao*, 12 January 1980, BBC/FE, BII/1–3, 17 January 1980.
4 *Renmin ribao* (hereafter *RMRB*), 19 January 1980, and *Gongren ribao*, 31 January 1980.
5 On Iran's decision to admit students to institutions of higher learning according to their political-religious beliefs see *Le Monde*, 2 May 1980, p. 3.
6 '... revolutionaries do seize state power and use it against their opponents and also against those passive, withdrawn or simply fearful people whom the Puritans called "neuters". They use the state, or try to use it, to short-cut those long and difficult processes by which men are brought to pledge themselves to collective repression; they use it to reinforce the new and generally underdeveloped mechanisms of mutual surveillance. But when revolutionaries do this, they "freeze" the revolution, as St. Just realized too late. They themselves deny the possibilities of genuine self-government; they reestablish an older pattern of public conformity and private vice, and then the committed conscience of the saint and the virtuous will of the citizen become once again the "neutral and inwardly divided mind" of the subject.' Michael Walzer, 'The Revolutionary Uses of Repression', in Marvin Richter, ed., *Essays in Theory and History, An Approach to the Social Sciences* (Cambridge: Harvard University Press, 1970), p. 129.
7 Other approaches to understanding the decline of post-revolutionary systems are the decay of 'movement regimes' (Robert C. Tucker, 'Toward a Comparative Politics of Movement Regimes', *American Political Science Review*, 55 (June 1961), pp. 281–9) and policy cycles impelled by popular response to normative, coercive, and remunerative policies; see G. William Skinner and Edwin A. Winckler, 'Compliance Successions in Rural Communist China: A Cyclical Theory', in A. Etzioni, ed., *Complex Organizations, A Sociological Reader*, 2nd edn (New York: Holt, Rinehart and Winston, 1969). Also see the essays in Chalmers Johnson, ed., *Change in Communist Systems* (Stanford: Stanford University Press, 1970).
8 A complete list of distribution rules would have to include lottery, election, need, age, physical strength, first-come-first-served, as well as rotation of the market. It is also important to distinguish between merit tests based on educational achievement or aptitude, and those based on actual work accomplishments (such as piecework). For a proposal on the use of educational lotteries (in combination with merit tests) see Ronald Dore, *The Diploma Disease: Education, Qualification and Development* (Berkeley: University of California Press, 1976), p. 161.
9 Max Weber, 'The Types of Authority and Imperative Co-ordination', in Parsons, ed., *The Theory of Social and Economic Organization* (New York: Free Press, 1964), pp. 324–423. I have coined the term 'virtuocracy'

because there is no existing word for a society in which individuals are selected for occupational roles according to some definition of moral excellence. The term 'aristocracy' originally meant rule by the 'best', but it implies intellectual (or even artistic) abilities more than moral rectitude, and by now it has come to mean rule by individuals of high birth. The term 'feodocracy' has been adopted for lack of a more satisfactory word to describe societies in which roles are assigned according to individuals' ascriptive status.

10 The political advantages and disadvantages of different distribution rules are vividly illustrated in *Fanshen*, the study of the land reform process in Long Bow village; see William Hinton, *Fanshen* (New York: Random House, 1966). At that early stage of social transformation the cadres shifted from distribution of 'fruits' according to economic status or need, to distribution according to degree of political participation (a form of virtue) in order to provide incentives for people to speak out against the landlords. The consequence of that decision is that today when people speak out in meetings, other people assume that they are motivated by a desire for the 'fruits' of activism.

11 The influence of meritocratic principles was, however, still strong even among those who knew they would benefit from virtuocratic redistribution. An autobiographical novel about land reform has a poor peasant saying, 'You say I can get the land without paying for it and I don't believe it … I always tell my children not to take anything they haven't worked for. I don't want them to be led astray.' Chen Yuan-tsung, *The Dragon's Village* (New York: Pantheon Books, 1980), pp. 88–9.

12 For a clear statement of the Maoist model see Thomas E. Weisskopf, 'The Relevance of the Chinese Experience for Third World Economic Development', *Theory and Society*, 9 (March 1980), pp. 283–318.

13 Max Weber, 'The Routinization of Charisma', in Talcott Parsons, ed., *The Theory of Social and Economic Organization*, p. 364.

14 A notion proposed by John R. Logan, 'Growth, Politics, and Stratification of Places', *American Journal of Sociology*, 84 (1978), pp. 404–16, and applied to the Soviet Union by Victor Zaslavsky, 'Socioeconomic Inequality and Changes in Soviet Ideology', *Theory and Society*, 9 (March 1980), p. 391.

15 The fact that 'the concept of looking upon service work as something inferior can be found in every corner of society', is blamed on the influence of 'feudal ideology'. *Beijing Review*, 6 (11 February 1980), p. 19. Contempt for service and agricultural roles, however, does not seem to be withering away under socialism. Campaigns to change status values seem to have strengthened rather than weakened them. For example the resettlement of urban youth in the countryside reinforced the urbanites' disdain for peasants; the only change in status attitudes which resulted was an elevation of the status of urban industrial labour. See Thomas P.

Bernstein, *Up to the Mountains and Down to the Villages: The Transfer of Youth from Urban to Rural China* (New Haven: Yale University Press, 1977), p. 103. Moreover, the restrictions on mobility instituted by the socialist state also have had a strong effect on the status value of occupational roles: when people are asked why they would prefer a job in a state-owned factory to one in a collective factory, they answer, 'You can transfer from a state factory to a collective one, but you can't move up from a collective factory to a state one'; and they explain the higher status of urban over rural work by saying, 'You can move from the city to the countryside but not from the countryside to the city.'

16 The complexity of political evaluations is illustrated by the 'Guiding Principles for Inter-Party Political Life' adopted at the Fifth Plenary Session of the 11th Communist Party Central Committee in early 1980. The document explains that there are not just two types of political mistakes (those representing non-antagonistic and antagonistic contradictions), but *four* types of political mistakes which must be clearly distinguished: 'One must not describe an ordinary mistake in work or a mistake in understanding as a political mistake; nor must one describe an ordinary political mistake as a mistake in political line; or mix up a mistake in political line which is still in the nature of inter-Party struggle with a question of a counter-revolutionary nature involving attempts to subvert the Party and the socialist state.' *Beijing Review*, 14 (7 April 1980), p. 17. The document offers no clues to help Party members categorize the mistakes of their comrades.

17 'Lin Piao and the Gang of Four first accused the person whom they wanted to destroy and then tried to find the proof from that person's work, which means they found out the author's motive and then tried to create some effect to prove it. Thus they could sentence anyone to political death or academic death at will ... Sometimes the objective effect doesn't reflect the motive at all. Social life is so complicated that a good motive can sometimes bring the opposite result.' 'Eliminate the Obstacles to Academic Democracy', *Guangming ribao*, 10 March 1979, in *Xinhua yuehbao*, 4 (1979), p. 15.

18 According to interviews with coaches at two prominent athletic schools in China, during the Cultural Revolution when the use of the back-door (favouritism for the children of officials and other people with personal influence) became rampant at regular schools and universities, it was much less common at sports schools. The coaches said that because athletes had to prove their skill in public contests, it was impossible for an official to pass off an untalented son or daughter as deserving of admission.

19 This is a problem for Party and Youth League members who have to determine whom to admit into their organizations. Student League members I interviewed said that in order to cull out the phoney activists

from the genuine ones they looked at family class background and *how long* the person had behaved actively. There is a widespread assumption that phonies will not be able to keep up their act for long, and therefore that someone who behaves like an activist for a long period must be genuinely committed (see 'The Revolutionary Road Must be Taken by Yourself', *Gongren ribao*, 18 February 1980).

20 As one articulate expression of post-Cultural Revolution dissent, the 'Li I-che Poster', put it, 'It is not always easy to distinguish between fragrant flowers and poisonous weeds, between the correct and the erroneous, and between the revolutionary and the counter-revolutionary.' And under a democratic dictatorship, if you demand democracy, they will label you a reactionary; and if you are a reactionary you must be deprived of democracy. Therefore they say the fixing of political labels cannot be left to leaders: 'There must be a process; and the distinction must be tested by time.' Li I-che, 'Concerning Socialist Democracy and Legal System', quoted in Susan L. Shirk, 'Going Against the Tide: Political Dissent in China', *Survey*, 24 (106) (Winter 1979), pp. 91–7.

21 Max Weber, 'The Protestant Sects and the Spirit of Capitalism', in H. H. Gerth and C. W. Mills, eds., *From Max Weber: Essays in Sociology* (Oxford: Oxford University Press, 1946), pp. 302–22.

22 James S. Coleman, *The Adolescent Society* (New York: The Free Press, 1961), p. 319. This is the main reason for the widespread preference for piecework wages among workers.

23 In some fields peer review may be seen by participants as preferable to operating under the edicts of outside authorities, despite the social strains inevitably created by the internal process.

24 Walzer, *op. cit.*, p. 127.

25 Reinhard Bendix points out that the Soviets view mutual criticism as the true test of activist's loyalty to the Party. It is 'the touchstone of socialist consciousness in our people, because it is an indication of their capacity to put the interests of society above their own peace of mind'. M. A. Leonov, *Kritik und Slebstkritik* (Berlin: Verlag Kultur und Fortschritt, n.d.), p. 34, quoted in R. Bendix, *Work and Authority in Industry, Ideologies of Management in the Course of Industrialization* (Berkeley: University of California Press, 1956), p. 417.

26 Arthur L. Stinchcombe, in personal correspondence, helped me clarify this distinction between 'zero-sum-ness' and focusing on a single victim.

27 Jerome Ch'en, ed., *Mao Papers* (London: Oxford University Press, 1970), p. 57.

28 The traditional Confucian examinations for aspiring officials were an example of testing for virtue by examining intellectual merit. Although Weber describes the Confucian examination as a 'cultural examination for the literati', he points out that it had a 'magical-charismatic meaning'

in the eyes of the masses. Max Weber, 'The Chinese Literati', in Gerth and Mills, *op. cit.*, p. 433.

29 Weber views charisma as a 'personal gift' which cannot be taught or trained: 'Either it exists *in nuce*, or it is infiltrated through magical rebirth – otherwise it cannot be attained'. ('The Chinese Literati', p. 426.) The Chinese position on the possibility of attaining redness is more ambiguous. It asserts that people are malleable and that revolutionary values can be instilled in schools, but that differences in family environment make some people more inclined to accept these values than others.

30 The debate over the ascriptive and behavioural definitions of class is the subject of Richard Kraus' excellent book, *Class Conflict in Chinese Socialism* (New York: Columbia University Press, 1982). Also see Gordon White, *The Politics of Class and Class Origin: The Case of the Cultural Revolution* (Canberra: Australian National University, 1976), for an insightful analysis of the debate's impact on Red Guard factionalism.

31 This analysis is based on in-depth interviews with thirty-one student refugees and three teacher refugees in Hong Kong, which I conducted in 1971 and 1977–8. It also draws upon interviews I conducted with factory cadres, technicians, and workers in Hong Kong and Chongqing, December 1979–April 1980, and on the work of Michel Oksenberg, 'Getting Ahead and Along in Communist China: The Ladder of Success on the Eve of the Cultural Revolution', in John W. Lewis, ed., *Party Leadership and Revolutionary Power in China* (Cambridge: Cambridge University Press, 1970); Andrew G. Walder, 'Work and Authority in Chinese Industry: State Socialism and the Institutional Culture of Dependency', PhD dissertation, University of Michigan, 1981; and Martin King Whyte, *Small Groups and Political Rituals in China* (Berkeley: University of California Press, 1974). A detailed analysis of the impact of virtuocratic recruitment on student social relations can be found in my book, *Competitive Comrades: Career Incentives and Student Strategies in China* (Berkeley: University of California Press, 1982).

32 The impact of opportunity structure on behaviour is vividly illustrated by comparing social patterns in specialized senior high schools (which guaranteed students city jobs) and in private (*minban*) schools (which offered no chance for university or good city jobs) with social patterns in general high schools (which confronted students with risk). Students with a 'sure-thing' future were more political but less competitive than those in general high schools. Those with hopeless futures were much less political but more competitive for friends than those in general high schools. See Shirk, *Competitive Comrades*, Chapter 2.

33 Walder, *op. cit.*

34 Oksenberg, *op. cit.*, pp. 323–4.

35 The expressions used to describe good activists came directly from the traditional Confucian lexicon: 'sincere' (*zhencheng*), 'sincere in belief

and intention' (*zhenxin chengyi*), 'honest' (*laoshi*), and 'genuine' (*zhenzheng*). The term frequently used to differentiate the activists worthy of respect was *yigi*, a traditional moral category translated as 'a sense of honour'. The term combines the notions of loyalty and righteousness. An individual should combine balanced personal loyalties (to friends, family, the village or work group) with more transcendant commitments (to the Party, nation, revolution) while maintaining personal integrity. The expression used to describe bad activists was *xiangyuan*, translated as 'hypocritical' but with the connotation of moral betrayal. In personal communication, Thomas P. Metzger helped me clarify the themes of sincerity and hypocrisy which emerged from the interviews. The notion of *xiangyuan* is discussed in Metzger's book, *Escape from Predicament* (see n. 1).

36 Mutual help became more competitive than cooperative especially during 1964–5 when there was a campaign to put Mao Zedong Thought into practice and to emulate the self-sacrifice of the political model, Lei Feng. According to student informants, aspiring activists, by washing everyone's clothes and giving away all their shoes and other possessions, monopolized the opportunities for helpfulness so aggressively that there was no way for others to demonstrate their own altruism.

37 For example, a poignant short story in a Red Guard newspaper described how Youth League activists called a youth a 'selfish hypocrite' merely because he inadvertently spooned out for himself the only piece of meat in the soup; this label destroyed his chances of entering the Youth League. 'A Piece of Meat', *Tiaozhan* (Challenge) (Canton), 1 (March 1968), p. 4.

38 The obsequiousness of activists has drawn the criticism of dissidents for many years in China. The 1957 Hundred Flowers period dissidents lambasted activists 'who will praise and please their superiors obsequiously, who know how to read their superiors' minds from their faces, and who attack others'. Quoted in Dennis J. Doolin, *Communist China, the Politics of Student Opposition* (Stanford: The Hoover Institution, 1964), pp. 46–7. Ten years later the Red Guards echoed this refrain, denouncing activists who 'bluff and curry favour ... and struggle for their individual "future" and "prominence"'. 'A Piece of Meat', p. 4.

39 Walder, *op. cit.*

40 Activists also have an interest in keeping their distance from non-activists. Because people are judged by the company they keep, there is a risk involved in appearing too socially comfortable with political unreliables. As one respondent observed, 'It was almost impossible for activists and non-activists to hang around together as friends. The latter feared being reported and the former feared bad connections.'

41 On friendship as a 'protective environment' from the political pressures of virtuocracy in China see Shirk, *Competitive Comrades*, Chapter 5.

42 Albert O. Hirschman, in *Shifting Involvements, Private Interest and Public Action* (Princeton: Princeton University Press, 1982), pp. 127–9, describes important asymmetry between public and private action which creates the likelihood of privatization. Whereas people will not tolerate any suggestion of private, self-serving objectives in public action, in private action it is considered acceptable that someone 'do good by doing well'. Because public action is always susceptible to the accusation of hypocrisy, 'the charge, that is, that public action is essentially self-serving', the turn to public life can be viewed 'as a move toward reality, sincerity, and even humility'.

43 Nevertheless, Mao never advocated the complete abolition of class background labels for recruitment and promotion. He never decided which was the most serious threat to Chinese socialism, the old middle class (sustained by the persistence of meritocracy) or the new official elite (aided by both virtuocracy and feodocracy), and never resolved the ambiguous combination of inherited and behavioural definitions of class. See Kraus, *op. cit.*

44 There was, of course, an element of career motivation involved as well. Students worried that under the new virtuocratic rules, failure to participate in the Cultural Revolution would be interpreted as a sign of political apathy or timidity.

45 *Kiren ribao*, 7 March 1972; *Union Research Service*, 67 (15), p. 211.

46 The destruction of staff management, an ostensibly 'anti-bureaucratic' reform, also had the effect of concentrating power in the hands of factory and workshop leaders. See A. Walder, 'Some Ironies of the Maoist Legacy in Industry', *The Australian Journal of Chinese Affairs*, 5 (January 1981), p. 32.

47 In addition to posts in political and administrative offices, places in the work unit's Mao Zedong Thought Propaganda Team, an employees' song and dance troupe which performed at all local occasions, were used by leaders to reward their favourite followers. Members of the team rehearsed and performed on a full-time basis and were relieved of other more tedious responsibilities; they also had many opportunities to travel. According to informants, youth, physical attractiveness, and loyalty to the leader were the only criteria for selection; talent was not required. In many factories the propaganda team became the backbone of the leading faction. Some factory leaders took advantage of the vagueness and subjectivity of promotion criteria to extort gifts from employees (for an egregious example see *Gongren jibao*, 24 January 1980).

48 On the important function of character assassination in the politics of the Roman Catholic Church, see Andrew M. Greeley, *The Making of the Popes 1978, The Politics of Intrigue in the Vatican* (Kansas City: Andrews and McMeel, 1979).

49 Li I-che, Shirk, 'Going Against the Tide' (see n. 20), p. 94.

50 For a provocative analysis of the economic costs of authoritarian rule see Wlodzimierz Brus, *Socialist Ownership and Political Systems* (London: Routledge and Kegan Paul, 1975).

51 A pattern noted in other socialist systems by W. Weslowski: 'It appears that the objective contradiction of interests implied in the unequal distribution of goods following from the application of the principle "to each according to his work", does not arouse such strong tendencies towards the creation of conflicts as the defects in its application.' See 'The Notions of Strata and Class in Socialist Society', in Andre Beteille, ed., *Social Inequality* (Harmondsworth: Penguin, 1969), p. 136.

52 See Hu Yaobang's speech at the Second National Congress of the Chinese Scientific and Technical Association, *Beijing Review*, 15 (14 April 1980), pp. 13–16.

53 *RMRB*, 9 March 1981, *Foreign Broadcast Information Service Daily Report China* (hereafter *FBIS*), 9 March 1981, pp. L22–31; 'Deng Xiaoping's 18 August 1980 Speech to the Politburo', *Chan wang* (Hong Kong), 16 April 1981, *FBIS*, 22 April 1981, pp. W1–14.

54 Anhwei Provincial Service, 5 June 1978, *FBIS*, 12 June 1978, p. G2. Another article explains that under the old recommendation system 'appraisal by the masses often turned out to be a mere formality' and, in actuality, the door was closed to the children of ordinary people. 'This situation became a source of general dissatisfaction. The new enrolment system provides children of workers and peasants with wide opportunity to take part in examinations for entering college, so they support this way of doing things.' See 'Enrolment System: A Meaningful Discussion', *Beijing Review*, 30 (28 July 1978), p. 19.

55 The distrust of local authorities is also reflected in current procedures for university entrance examinations. Examination scores are publicly posted as a protection against favouritism by local officials. And whereas in the past academic promise was measured by a combination of school grades and examination scores, today admissions officers look only at examinations because they no longer trust the validity of school grades.

56 As one newspaper article said, the advantages of the point system are that it has 'clear standards', a 'concrete method', and uses 'less time for evaluation'. *RMRB*, 17 September 1979.

57 This was a difficult and time-consuming task of central planning. The national leadership probably would like to establish uniform piecework quotas rather than allowing them to be determined by individual factories but this is so difficult that so far the only industry to have nationwide quotas is the construction industry, which set its quotas in the early 1960s.

58 The egalitarian pressures operating in small, face-to-face work groups are extremely strong. For example, when workers receive high bonuses they sometimes use the money to give a banquet for their co-workers

or to buy them such things as candy or socks in order to avert their envious criticism (*Gongren ribao*, 11 December 1978).

59 Meritocratic competition is conflictual as long as the number of winners is fixed (a zero-sum game). There have been some preliminary efforts in industrial management reforms to tie individual and group incentives so that, for example, more bonuses are allocated to work groups with more total output. But by and large, competition remains zero-sum. Although piecework overfulfilment wages are not fixed and theoretically everyone could make more if they produced more, the setting of the quota is a zero-sum process: the advanced worker who doubles the quota every month and causes the authorities to raise the quota, creates costs for all fellow-workers. (See 'Why are Advanced Comrades the Object of Satire and Irony?', letter to the editor, *Gongren jibao*, 22 February 1980.) People, moreover, may disagree about the proper definition of merit. For example, many old workers object to the use of written technical tests as a basis for raises. Because many of them are illiterate or barely literate they argue that actual work accomplished rather than theoretical knowledge should be the sole criterion. The difficulty in defining merit is one reason why the first wage increases after the Cultural Revolution were based primarily on work seniority. Like age, seniority is a distribution rule highly conducive to group solidarity: it appears fair, objective, and everyone will eventually benefit from it. As Adam Smith said when comparing age to the 'invisible qualities' of wisdom and virtue: 'Age is a plain and palpable quality which admits of no dispute.' *An Inquiry into the Nature and Causes of the Wealth of Nations*, excerpted in Stanislav Andreski, ed., *Reflection on Inequality* (London: Croom Helm, 1975), p. 54. The Chinese leaders have now replaced seniority with merit as the basis for wage increases because they believe that seniority was conducive to unity but not to productivity.

60 On the need for political leaders to wear convincing masks see F. G. Bailey, 'The Management of Reputations and the Process of Change', in F. G. Bailey, ed., *Gifts and Poison, the Politics of Reputation* (Oxford: Basil Blackwell, 1971), p. 293.

61 Alec Nove, 'The Soviet Economy: Problems and Prospects', *New Left Review*, 119 (January–February 1980), pp. 3–13.

62 'On Economic "Retreat"', *RMRB*, 29 January 1981, *FBIS*, 17 February 1981, p. L9. Also see Deng Xiaoping's speech at the 25 December 1980 Central Work Conference, *Ming Bao* (Hong Kong), 1 May 1981, *FBIS*, 1 May 1981, p. W1. Newspaper articles have also tried to calm readers' fears by reminding them that the Soviet Union also changed economic course very often, and that flexibility in policy-making should be praised rather than condemned. For example, *RMRB*, 29 January 1981, *FBIS*, 9 February 1981, pp. L10–12.

63 For a report on a CCP Central Committee Propaganda Department

meeting on conducting education on the economic situation see *Xinhua*, 14 April 1982, *FBIS*, 16 April 1982, p. K2 and Hunan Provincial Service, 13 April 1982, *FBIS*, 15 April 1982, p. P5.

64 *Hongqi*, 7 (1 April 1981), *FBIS*, 7 May 1981, p. K8.

65 'Ren Zhongyi Speaks at Zhongshan University', *Wenwei bao* (Hong Kong), 22 September 1981, *FBIS*, 2 October 1981, p. W2. Rumour has it that some of the high-ranking government officials who have travelled abroad in recent years were shocked at the contrast between China's backwardness and the modern living conditions in Japan and the West, and are themselves having serious doubts about the superiority of socialism.

66 *Ibid.*

67 Speech by Zhang Guangdou, vice president of Qinghua University, quoted by Fox Butterfield, *The New York Times*, 11 May 1980. These arguments are similar to those used by the Soviet leadership to defend the superiority of the Soviet Union (see Zaslavsky, 'Socioeconomic Inequality and Changes in Soviet Ideology', pp. 383–407).

68 'Ren Zhongyi Speaks at Zhongshan University', p. W2. *RMRB* commentator, 'Education in Patriotism is our Constant Subject', *RMRB*, 10 February 1982, *FBIS*, 12 February 1982, p. K1.

69 'In selecting cadres ... we must first take note of the political performance of cadres and see whether they are politically reliable.' *RMRB*, 21 April 1982, *FBIS*, 21 April 1982, p. K3, Also see *Xinhua ribao* (Nanjing), 22 January 1982, *FBIS*, 2 February 1982, p. O2.

70 *Shaanxi ribao*, 11 February 1981, *FBIS*, 12 February 1981, p. T3; *Xinhua*, 9 February 1981, *FBIS*, 10 February 1981, p. L21. There is an obvious political struggle being waged between the Party leaders who want to reverse the reforms of 1978–80 and return to virtuocracy and those who want to defend the meritocratic reforms. The latter group argues, 'Some hold: the reason we stress publicizing the implementation of the four basic principles is that we [maintain?] such an idea is erroneous.' *Hebei jibao*, 19 January 1981, *FBIS*, 12 February 1981, p. R5.

71 *Xinhua*, 5 February 1982, *FBIS*, 9 February 1982, p. K8.

72 *Hubei ribao*, 27 December 1981, *FBIS*, 19 January 1981, p. P5.

73 *Nanfang ribao*, 29 March 1982, *FBIS*, 14 April 1982, p. P1.

74 *Sichuan ribao*, 14 May 1981, *FBIS*, 29 May 1981, p. Q1.

75 Anhui Provincial Service, 3 February 1981, *FBIS*, 4 February 1981, p. O2. One sign of the spiritual and moral inferiority of foreign societies is their high crime rate, which is often discussed in school textbooks and political speeches. For example, 'Speech by Zhang Youyu on February 23 1981', *Inside China Mainland* (Taipei), November 1981, pp. 2–3.

76 As Hua Guofeng argued in 1980, since China has a large population and is still poor, 'political and ideological work is therefore all the more important ... Work must be done to raise people's consciousness ... to

encourage them to build the country in the revolutionary spirit of diligence and thrift.' *Beijing Review*, 20 (19 May 1980), p. 8. Political education is also substituted for material rewards at the macroeconomic level. One article pointed out, for example, that because some sectors took heavy losses during the period of economic readjustment, it was particularly necessary to 'do ideological work' to help them 'subordinate their individual interests to collective interests and take the whole situation into consideration'. *RMRB*, 9 March 1981, *FBIS* 11 March 1981, p. L16. The political rehabilitation of the Daqing oilfields as a model of industrial management signals the renewed emphasis on moral incentives. (*Gongren ribao*, 7 January 1982, *FBIS*, 2 February 1982, p. K14.)

77 Zygmunt Bauman, 'Officialdom and Class: Bases of Inequality in Socialist Society', in Frank Parkin, ed., *The Social Analysis of Class Structure* (London: Tavistock Publications, 1974), pp. 129–48. This virtuocratic resurgence is remarkable for the almost total absence of a populist rationale. Why doesn't the Party disguise its own vested interest in virtuocracy by stressing the ways in which it helps the 'have-nots' such as the peasants?

78 One article argued that meritocracy ('economic methods') and economic modernization were compatible with virtuocracy: 'When economic methods are effectively applied and the economy is well developed, we can advocate the revolutionary spirit more forcefully and do ideological and political work more easily ... while implementing the principle "to each according to his work" and, enacting reward systems with economic methods, we should encourage the attitude of labour without considering the payment, understand the difficulties of the state, help our neighbours and develop the communist style.' *Dazhong ribao*, 14 February 1981, *FBIS*, 17 February 1981, p. O3.

79 *Shaanxi ribao*, 11 February 1981, *FBIS*, 12 February 1981, p. T4.

80 Guangdong Provincial Service, 1 February 1981, *FBIS*, 4 February 1981, p. P2.

81 The anti-foreign theme has become increasingly prevalent in the official press. For example, 'the corrosion of bourgeois ideology from abroad ... [has made Chinese youths] unable to tell right from wrong'. *Hongqi*, 23 (1 December 1981), *FBIS*, 30 December 1981, p. K17.

82 'Guiding Principles for Inner-Party Life', adopted at the Fifth Plenary Session of the Eleventh Communist Party Central Committee, *Beijing Review*, 14 (7 April 1980), p. 16.

83 *RMRB*, 11 May 1981, *FBIS*, 13 May 1981, pp. K–K6; *Hongqi*, 23 (1 December 1981), *FBIS*, 24 December 1981, p. K9. Tang Tsou has argued that at least in the realm of literature and art, Party leaders are trying to find a new form of ideological control which is based on 'an improvement of the style of Party leadership, a political and economic

program attuned to the immediate interests of the people, and a reinterpretation of Marxism–Leninism–Mao Tsetung Thought'. 'Paradoxes in Political Reform in Post-Mao China', paper presented at the conference on 'China: The 1980s Era', University of Chicago, November 1981, p. 19.

84 For example, in one unit a dispute between two leaders over a minor issue about the allocation of workers' housing turned into a serious political battle because one reported the other to the upper level for 'egalitarianism' and the other one reported him for 'paternalism'. (*Beijing ribao*, 3 March 1981, *FBIS*, 12 March 1981, p. L1.)

85 *RMRB*, 28 December 1981, *FBIS*, 15 January 1982, pp. K8–10; *RMRB*, 4 January 1982, *FBIS*, 19 January 1982, pp. K15–17.

86 As Mao Zedong himself recognized, 'Some people consider knowledge as their own possession and wait to get a good price in the market. When the price is not high enough, they will refuse to sell their knowledge.' 'Reading Notes on the Soviet Union's "Political Economics" (1961–62)', quoted in Gordon White, *Party and Professionals, The Political Role of Teachers in Contemporary China* (Armonk, New York: M. E. Sharpe, 1981), p. 90.

87 Party leaders recognize that public faith in government was a casualty of the Cultural Revolution. 'It is much more difficult to build socialist spiritual civilization today than it was in the 17 years before the "Great Cultural Revolution".' *Guangming ribao*, 20 February 1981, *FBIS*, 3 March 1981, p. L16.

88 Some people even believe that Lei Feng is a fictional invention of the Party propaganda organ and others say, 'He was a loser, who would want to be like him?' See Linda Matthews' story in *The Los Angeles Times*, 1 May 1980.

89 *Hongqi*, 24 (16 December 1981), *FBIS*, 13 January 1982, p. T3.

90 *Xinhua*, 5 February 1982, *FBIS*, 9 February 1982, pp. K1–3; *Xinhua*, 16 February 1982, *FBIS*, 17 February 1982, p. K2.

91 Chalmers Johnson, 'The Failure of Socialism in China', *Issues and Studies*, 15, no. 7 (July 1979), p. 29.

92 For example, one article said that although some Party cadres sought special privileges and engaged in bureaucratic behaviour, it was unfair to say that they were all bad or that there was a 'bureaucratic class' in China. Therefore, 'any words and actions which hurt the Party's prestige are impermissible'. *Hongqi*, 2 (16 January 1981), *FBIS*, 4 February 1981, p. L9. Also see 'Trust and Uphold Party Leadership', *Hubei ribao*, 16 January 1981, *FBIS*, 10 February 1981, p. P4. On this issue of the Party as a 'bureaucratic clsss', see *Zhongguo qingnian bao*, 7 February 1981, *FBIS*, 23 February 1981, pp. L27–30. See Hirschman, *op. cit.* (n. 42), p. 124, for an insightful discussion of the interactive effects of political disaffection and corruption.

5. PARISH: DESTRATIFICATION IN CHINA

An earlier version of this paper was part of the proceedings of the Research Project on 'Political Leadership and Social Change at the Local Level in China from 1850 to the Present', University of Chicago, which was funded by the National Endowment of the Humanities. Acknowledgment is made to the Center for Far Eastern Studies for permission to reproduce material which appeared in its 'Select Papers' (for private circulation), no. 4, 1979–80.

1 For sources of these statistics and for additional comparisons, see Martin K. Whyte and William L. Parish, *Urban Life in Contemporary China* (Chicago: University of Chicago Press, 1983).

2 Note throughout that the generalizations in this paper apply to the urban sector alone. The rural–urban average income gap has been a tremendous three to one and gaps among different villages are large as well. See William L. Parish and Martin K. Whyte, *Village and Family in Contemporary China* (Chicago: University of Chicago Press, 1978), p. 376.

3 US Department of Commerce, Bureau of the Census, Consumer Income, *Current Population Reports*, Series P-16, no. 105 (Washington, DC: US Government Printing Office, 1977), p. 19. The Chinese distribution is more similar to the Polish distribution – see Walter D. Connor, *Socialism, Politics, and Equality* (New York: Columbia University Press, 1979), p. 235.

4 On these sorts of privileges for national level officials in Peking, see Fox Butterfield, *China: Alive in the Bitter Sea* (New York: Times Books, 1982), Chapter 3.

5 Erik Allardt and Wlodzimierz Wesolowski, eds., *Social Structure and Change: Finland and Poland* (Warsaw, Poland: Polish Scientific Publishers, 1978), p. 131.

6 The administrative level is scored 2 to 6, with 2 being for commune seats and 6 for national municipalities like Peking and Shanghai. The room differential is the actual number of rooms in a dwelling minus the Chinese architectural ideal of a separate room for each married couple plus a separate room by sex for children age thirteen and over. A grandmother should live with teenage children of either sex.

7 We have made no allowance for the rent subsidy implicit in public and official unit owned housing – a subsidy which works to the advantage of professionals and officials.

8 Figure 6 combines negative labels such as counter-revolutionary and landlord under the capitalist label, intermediate labels such as middle peasant under the staff label, and so on.

9 Throughout, occupations are ranked into thirty-two groups on the basis of the average monthly income of each group, giving a scale which runs from 22 to 103, thereby approximating the standard occupational prestige score which covers a similar range.

10 Though given the small cadre sample sizes – seven before 1966 and eighteen afterwards – one should not make too much of this trend, even if it does coincide with occasional press reports and impressions of some emigres.

11 The tension between growth and equality is not unique to Chinese ideological thinking. For an account of the long history of tension between these two ideals in socialist thinking see Benjamin Schwartz, 'China and the West in the "Thought of Mao Tse-tung"', in Ho Ping-ti and Tang Tsou, eds., *China in Crisis* (Chicago: University of Chicago Press, 1968), pp. 365–79.

12 A long line of research and commentary on this theme followed publication of Kingsley Davis and Wilbert E. Moore's 'Some Principles of Stratification', *American Sociological Review*, 10 (1945), pp. 242–9.

13 See Carl Riskin, 'Maoism and Motivation: Work Incentives in China', in Victor Nee and James Peck, eds., *China's Uninterrupted Revolution* (New York: Pantheon, 1975).

6. UNGER: THE CLASS SYSTEM IN RURAL CHINA: A CASE STUDY

1 These interviews were conducted by Anita Chan, Richard Madsen, and myself for the book *Chen Village: The Recent History of a Peasant Community in Mao's China* (Berkeley: University of California Press, 1982). Drs Chan and Madsen have kindly permitted me to use our collective interview data for this paper. However, the views and interpretations presented here do not necessarily coincide with those of my colleagues.

2 For more complete discussions of the class distinctions and labels deriving from land reform (for north China, 1948) see William Hinton, *Fanshen* (New York: Random House, 1966), pp. 623–6, 400–10; and C. K. Yang, *A Chinese Village in Early Communist Transition* (Cambridge, Mass.: MIT Press, 1959), p. 141 (for Guangdong, 1950).

3 Families whose heads had served in the revolutionary wars as Party officials or military officers ('revolutionary cadres') or whose heads had died in the revolution ('revolutionary martyrs') were considered the 'reddest' of the rural families. But there were no such households in Chen Village.

4 The upper-middle peasant households were those whose incomes before land reform had derived largely from their own labour, but which had also hired a labourer or rented out modest amounts of land beyond what family members themselves could till.

5 William L. Parish and Martin K. Whyte, in a survey of sixty-three Guangdong villages, estimated that 73 per cent of the peasantry had been classified as poor-and-lower-middle peasants, 13 per cent as middle peasants, another 3 per cent as upper-middle peasants, 4 per cent as rich peasants and 2 per cent as landlords (*Village and Family in*

Contemporary China (Chicago: University of Chicago Press, 1978), p. 99. By these figures, Chen Village has a slightly higher proportion of poor-and-lower-middle peasants and, perhaps, a slightly lower proportion of bad-class households than the average village.

6 Not all of Chen Village's four-bad elements came under attack during campaigns. For example, two rich-peasant brothers from Chen Village were among the men most knowledgeable about agriculture, and they regularly had made this knowledge available to their team's leaders. Moreover, they were industrious workers and went out of their way never to give offence to any of their better-class neighbours. As a result, they were the only members of the four-bad categories whose legal 'hats' had been removed by the village and commune cadres (though they continued to be counted as bad class). In comparison, their mother and the wife of one were quarrelsome. Their 'hats' remained in place, and they were among those 'struggled' against and jailed in the Cleansing of the Class Ranks campaign.

7 The son of the old guerrilla who had been labelled a rotten element was luckier than the descendants of landlords and rich peasants, since he could legally claim a 'poor peasant' origin – even though an officially tainted one.

8 For example in 'The Political Report of the Party Central Committee' (September 1956) it states: 'Except in a few localities, the feudal landlords have ... been eliminated as a class. The rich peasants are also being eliminated as a class. Landlords and rich peasants who used to exploit the peasants are being reformed; they are making a fresh start in life and becoming people who live by their own work.' (See *Eighth National Congress of the Communist Party of China* (Beijing: Foreign Languages Press, 1956), 1, p. 15.

9 Whereas in Chen Village in the 1950s, the phrase 'class enemy' reflected genuine sentiments, there were communities where the peasants had thought no one warranted a 'class enemy' label and where 'class struggle' sessions became an artificial performance acted out to satisfy higher authorities. For example, in the mountain hamlet of one interviewee, 'The only really respected person was a man in his fifties who'd been branded a historical counter-revolutionary, because in the old days he'd negotiated with bandits in the hamlet's behalf and somehow later became connected with them. There was no other four-bad element in our hamlet – the old landlord had lived elsewhere – so during campaigns he'd be dragged down to the commune headquarters for struggle meetings. I remember him being marched away one day, accompanied by representatives from the hamlet to struggle against him and with the hamlet militia to keep him under armed guard. But when he came back later that day everyone slapped him on the back in a friendly way.'

10 E.g., Ho Ping-ti, *The Ladder of Success in Imperial China* (New York:

Columbia University Press, 1962), pp. 18–19, 55–6; Mark Elvin, *The Pattern of the Chinese Past* (Stanford: Stanford University Press, 1973), p. 248; Ch'ü T'ung-tsu, 'Chinese Class Structure and Its Ideology', in John K. Fairbank, ed., *Chinese Thought and Institutions* (Chicago: University of Chicago Press, 1957), pp. 249, 387; Eugene Anderson, 'The Boat People of South China', *Anthropos*, 65, 1–2 (January 1970), p. 253.

11 Mark Elvin (*op. cit.*, p. 258) shares that perception: 'Chinese rural society in the nineteenth and the early twentieth century was ... one of the most fluid in the world, lacking any of the status and caste restraints which typified late pre-modern Japan or India.'

12 James L. Watson, 'Chattel Slavery in Chinese Peasant Society: A Comparative Analysis', *Ethnology*, 5, 4 (October 1976) and his 'Transactions in People: The Chinese Market in Slaves, Servants and Heirs', in J. L. Watson, ed., *Asian and African Systems of Slavery* (Oxford: Basil Blackwell; and Berkeley: University of California Press, 1980).

13 In some villages (though not Chen Village), the internal segmentation of the lineages had an important impact upon 'class struggle'; and this warrants some comments. Prior to the revolution Chen Village's five lineage branches had possessed less land than the central ancestral hall and were relatively weak. Thus lineage ceremonies had centred on the central hall which honoured the most important ancestors. In some Guangdong villages, lineage branches were not only stronger but their members had competed among themselves for power within the lineage. An interviewee from Taishan County, Guangdong, came from a village where each lineage branch occupied a different hamlet (and thus had become a different production team). As part of the continuing rivalry between branches, the good-class peasants of each branch/production team were happy to attack the bad-class members of *other* branches/teams. The interviewee mentioned how the political authorities consciously took over this practice for their own purposes: 'During the fighting of the Cultural Revolution the lineage-branch struggles developed into something fierce. The authorities later stepped in and squashed the conflicts by pulling out and struggling against some former landlords. They were only attacked as an excuse, since it was more difficult to punish the poor and lower-middle peasants in all the various lineage branches. You know the saying: "Kill a chicken to alarm the monkeys".'

In most of the countryside, however, even in south China, the production teams did not coincide with lineage branch memberships. New loyalties based on the profit-sharing teams replaced old branch identities; and 'class struggle' was not constrained or distorted by any residual branch feelings. In Chen Village, many young men by the early 1970s did not even know to which lineage branch their families had belonged.

14 H. H. Gerth and C. Wright Mills, eds., *From Max Weber: Essays in Sociology* (Oxford: Oxford University Press, 1946), pp. 190, 276.

15 Tantamount to a racist slur, interviewees sometimes referred to these households as 'black'.

16 Gerth and Mills, *op. cit.*, p. 190; W. G. Runciman, ed., *Max Weber: Selections in Translation* (Cambridge: Cambridge University Press, 1978), p. 60; Max Weber, *Economy and Society* (Berkeley: University of California Press, 1978), p. 306.

17 There was an important exception here: In Chen Village the class line did *not* extend to wages. The landlord sons earned nearly as much as good-class men of equivalent labour power. In many other villages, however, there was economic discrimination against the bad-class peasantry. A letter to the editor from a Guangdong peasant (*Renmin ribao* (hereafter *RMRB*), 11 December 1978) complained: 'I am a young man born into a landlord family. Both my parents died when I was very young and I was brought up by my brother who is a teacher. When the payments for labour were worked out, we people from an exploiting class background received only 70 per cent of what other commune members were getting. What is the reason for this? The cadre ... said: "Although the upper levels have instructed that you will get the same treatment as others, it must be in a manner suitable to local conditions ... You must receive less, because most of you are good at labour and have savings. If you are paid like the rest of the commune members, this will have a bad effect."'

18 See W. R. Geddes, *Peasant Life in Communist China*, Society for Applied Anthropology, Monograph No. 6, 1963; and Elisabeth Croll, 'Chiang Village: A Household Survey', *China Quarterly*, 72 (December 1977), pp. 7, 9. Croll's demographic survey of a village in the Pearl River delta contains evidence that neglect of female infants persisted into the 1970s. The village population included twenty-five males under the age of nine, but only fourteen females. It is, of course, dangerous to draw conclusions based on such small samples but the evidence is suggestive.

19 This was especially true for those who had political aspirations. An interviewee observes of one Chen Villager: 'He was a Party member and a cadre. If he married a wife with an unreliable class background, he would have a hard time taking responsibility for any important work. He wouldn't be considered trustworthy, because a wife can change a person.'

20 The groom's family would be wary, however, of a marriage that linked them to a bad-class family from their own or a nearby community. On their side, a bad-class woman's family knew that if she married near home, the stigma of her origin might continue to haunt her. Thus, whereas good- and middle-peasant brides usually married into households nearby, the bad-class brides from Chen Village tended to marry into families from other counties.

21 Edwin E. Moise, 'Downward Social Mobility in Pre-Revolutionary

China', *Modern China*, 3, 1 (January 1977), pp. 3–30.

22 Other interesting examples of how bad-class peasants found marriage partners can be found in Janet Salaff, 'The Emerging Conjugal Relationship in the People's Republic of China', *Journal of Marriage and the Family*, 35 (1973), pp. 712–13.

23 Anita Chan, Stanley Rosen and Jonathan Unger, 'Students and Class Warfare: The Social Roots of the Red Guard Conflict in Guangzhou (Canton)', *China Quarterly*, 83 (Autumn 1980).

24 *RMRB*, 30 January 1979, in *Foreign Broadcast Information Service Daily Report China*, 1 February 1979, pp. E17–20. The former landlords and rich peasants who still wore legal 'hats' now numbered only 50,000. Only months earlier, at the end of 1978, there had been more than 4 million such people in the Chinese countryside. See 'Class Status in the Countryside: Changes Over Three Decades', *Beijing Review*, 3 (21 January 1980), p. 14; and Party Central Committee Document, No. 4, 1979, in *Issues and Studies*, September 1979, p. 111.

7. WHITE: BOURGEOIS RADICALISM IN THE 'NEW CLASS' OF
SHANGHAI, 1949–1969

1 On the proletarians, see Lynn White, 'Worker Politics in Shanghai', *Journal of Asian Studies*, 36 (November 1976), pp. 99–116. The present essay is partly intended as a sequel on middle classes.

2 See Weber's essay, 'Class, Status, Party', in R. Bendix and S. M. Lipset, *Class, Status, and Power* (Glencoe: Free Press, 1953), pp. 63–75.

3 The best concise treatments may still be Ezra Vogel's chapter on 'Central Control: The Legacy of Land Reform, 1951–1953', in his *Canton under Communism* (Cambridge, Mass.: Harvard University Press, 1969), pp. 91–124; and John Gardner, 'The *Wu-fan* and Campaign in Shanghai: A Study of the Consolidation of Urban Control', in A. Doak Barnett, ed., *Chinese Communist Politics in Action* (Seattle: University of Washington Press, 1969), pp. 477–539.

4 The classic is Mao Tse-tung, *Analysis of the Classes in Chinese Society* (Peking: Foreign Languages Press, 1968).

5 *Zhanwang* (Prospects) (Shanghai), July 7, 1965.

6 Gordon White, *The Politics of Class and Class Origin: The Case of the Cultural Revolution* (Canberra: Australian National University, Contemporary China Centre, 1976), pp. 2ff, has a similar description, which differs from the text above in minor ways because it takes account of popular usages of terms throughout the country, which differ from the legalisms applied in Shanghai.

7 *Zhanwang*, loc. cit.

8 See Milovan Djilas, *The New Class: An Analysis of the Communist System* (New York: Praeger, 1957), and 'Yugoslavia and the Expansionism

of the Soviet State', *Foreign Affairs*, 58, 4 (Spring 1980), esp. pp. 852–4.
9 François Bourricauld, *Power and Society in Contemporary Peru* (New York: Praeger, 1970), *passim*, esp. pages such as 81 or 93.
10 See Joan Nelson, *Migrants, Urban Poverty, and Instability in Developing Nations* (Cambridge, Mass.: Harvard University Center for International Affairs, 1969); and Wayne Cornelius, *Politics and the Migrant Poor in Mexico City* (Stanford: Stanford University Press, 1975).
11 Albert O. Hirschman, 'The Changing Tolerance for Income Inequality in the Course of Economic Development', *World Development*, 1, 12 (1973), pp. 24–36. This is Hirschman's 'tunnel effect': a stalled lane may not envy accelerated movement in a parallel lane, at least for a while, because of hopes that the whole jam is clearing. Certain Latin American countries, such as Brazil, have exemplified this effect; and it may be relevant to some Asian places such as Taiwan and Hong Kong.
12 For careful information on these subjects, in rural contexts especially, see the path-breaking articles by Martin King Whyte, 'Inequality and Stratification in China', *China Quarterly*, 64 (December 1975), pp. 684–711; and Richard Curt Kraus, 'Class Conflict and the Vocabulary of Social Analysis in China', *China Quarterly*, 69 (March 1977), pp. 54–74.
13 The clearest debate, concerning such conflicts in China, concerns diverse explanations for the rise of Communist power. The first major salvo was Chalmers A. Johnson, *Peasant Nationalism and Communist Power: The Emergence of Revolutionary China, 1937–1945* (Stanford: Stanford University Press, 1962), which deals mainly with the precipitating causes of the conflict that became a civil war and revolution. The importance of leadership skills, nurtured in urban areas, is suggested in works by Roy Hofheinz, 'The Ecology of Chinese Communist Success: Rural Influence Patterns, 1923–45', in Barnett, *Chinese Communist Politics in Action*, pp. 3–77; and by Kau Ying-mao, 'Urban and Rural Strategies in the Chinese Communist Revolution', in John W. Lewis, ed., *Peasant Rebellion and Communist Revolution in Asia* (Stanford: Stanford University Press, 1974), pp. 253–70. However, Lucien Bianco, *The Origins of the Chinese Revolution, 1915–1949* (Stanford: Stanford University Press, 1971), practically asserts the importance of non-precipitating factors by emphasizing the peasant masses' 'loss of sympathy' for the KMT government under wartime conditions. The underlying causes of this giant conflict have been at once evident to see and difficult to link with its specific events. Just as classes are most clear-cut when they conflict, so also the reasons for their strife may be more amenable to research than other underlying reasons for their existence.
14 Mark Elvin, 'The Gentry Democracy in Shanghai, 1905–1914', PhD thesis, University of Cambridge, 1967.
15 Mary Backus Rankin, *Early Chinese Revolutionaries: Radical Intellectuals*

in Shanghai and Chekiang, 1902–1911 (Cambridge, Mass.: Harvard University Press, 1971).

16 Kau Ying-mao, 'Urban and Rural Strategies' (see n. 13).

17 Derek J. Waller, 'The Evolution of the Chinese Communist Political Elite, 1931–56', in Robert A. Scalapino, ed., *Elites in the People's Republic of China* (Seattle: University of Washington Press, 1972), pp. 41–66.

18 O. Edmund Clubb, *Communism in China, as Reported from Hangkow in 1932* (New York: Columbia University Press, 1968), p. 96.

19 *Qunchong* (Masses), Shanghai (hereafter *QC*), 11, 5 (June 3, 1946), p. 6.

20 Suzanne Pepper's *Civil War in China: The Political Struggle, 1945–1949* (Berkeley: University of California Press, 1978) will for many years be the main work on this topic.

21 *Guancha* (Observer), Shanghai (hereafter *GC*), 2, 14 (May 31, 1947), p. 5.

22 'Students Raise a Revolutionary Banner', by Chu Anping (later a leader of the liberal-lining Democratic League, suppressed in 1957), *GC*, 2, 14 (May 31, 1947), p. 3.

23 *QC*, 31 (August 28, 1947), p. 14; *QC*, 32 (September 4, 1947), p. 14; and *QC*, 36 (October 2, 1947), p. 18. A similar report on shopkeeper and student resistance to the KMT and to American activities in Japan may be found in *Zhanwang*, 2, 5 (May 29, 1948), p. 8.

24 Sima Lu, *Douzheng shiba nian* (Eighteen years of struggle) (Hong Kong: Ziyou chuban she, 1967), pp. 181–3.

25 The executive of Shanghai Guangdahua Life was Lu Xucheng, who later became head of the Trade Department of the new Communist military administration; and *ibid.*

26 *Laodong bao* (Labour News), Shanghai (hereafter *LDB*), May 13, 1950, p. 1.

27 Lyman van Slyke, *Enemies and Friends: The United Front in Chinese Communist History* (Stanford: Stanford University Press, 1967), pp. 229–31.

28 Interview in Hong Kong of an ex-Party member with experience in this campaign.

29 On this officiousness, see the critique of neighbourhood cadres exceeding their authority in *Jiefang ribao* (Liberation Daily), Shanghai (hereafter *JFRB*), September 13, 1951. On a change from street substations to residence committees, see for example *Dagong bao* (L'Impartial), Hong Kong (hereafter *DGB*), November 5, 1951.

30 See Gardner 'The *Wu-fan* Campaign'.

31 Calculated from Robert Michael Field, Nicholas R. Lardy, and John Philip Emerson, *A Reconstruction of the Gross Value of Industrial Output by Province in the People's Republic of China: 1949–73* (Washington:

US Commerce Department, July 1975), p. 21. It can also be estimated from figures on p. 9 that the annual 1949–52 rate was 25 per cent (also in 1952 prices), but this was largely a matter of using capacity that wars has idled. The 1956–7 rate was only 5 per cent.

32 Examples are reported in *Shanghai News* (hereafter *SN*), September 3 and 6, and December 7 and 13, 1952.

33 New China News Agency, Shanghai (hereafter *NCNA*), July 13, 1955.

34 In fact, in the first stage, before the Party took over administration of this campaign from the Federation of Industry and Commerce, it was called the 'Four Anti' movement.

35 *NCNA*, July 13, 1955 and Lynn White, 'Low Power: Small Enterprises in Shanghai', *China Quarterly*, 73 (March 1978), pp. 45–76.

36 *JFRB*, April 8, 1953.

37 Data from several schools in factory districts are offered in *DGB*, Shanghai, July 17, 1952; and *NCNA*, October 14, 1952.

38 *Yi bao* (Further News), October 4, 1952.

39 *LDB*, October 4, 1952.

40 Quoted in Donald W. Klein and Anne B. Clark, *Biographic Dictionary of Chinese Communism, 1921–1965* (Cambridge, Mass.: Harvard University Press, 1971), p. 434.

41 Pan had been Mao Zedong's representative in secret negotiations with the Fujian Provincial Government and the Nationalist 19th Route Army before their rebellion against the KMT in late 1933. See Warren Kugo, *Analytical History of the Chinese Communist Party* (Taipei: Institute for International Relations, 1968), Book 2, p. 554. See also Sima Lu, *Douzheng shiba nian*. This section is partially based on an interview in Hong Kong with Mr Sima, an independent publisher who knew Pan personally at Kangda (Resist-Japan University) in Yanan during the war.

42 Quoted from a mainland source in *1967 feiqing nianbao* (1967 Yearbook of Chinese Communist Affairs) (Taipei: Feiqing Yenjiu Cazhi She, 1967), p. 583. Hu Feng was mentioned in the same accusation; and the text's interpretation would allow a connection between their cases, although the nature of the link (except in time of purge) is not clear.

43 *Caimao zhanbao* (Finance and Trade War Bulletin), August 14, 1968.

44 Interview with an ex-cadre in Hong Kong, 1969.

45 Robert Loh, *Escape from Red China* (New York: Coward McCann, 1962), pp. 149–50. Pan dined with a prominent capitalist (his friend and bridge partner) on the night before his flight and arrest. Chen Yi did indeed move to Peking later. It is conceivable that the Central Government found evidence against Pan in the process of an investigation before approving his promotion to become Mayor. A Hong Kong interviewee stated that during the *sufan* movement, evidence was collected against a man who had been Pan Hannian's close friend before Liberation, and who was jailed in the special prison (*kanshou*

suo) of the Public Security Bureau that Yang headed. Pan used his influence to free this suspect, who thereupon fled to Hong Kong, taking information about pre-1949 activities in Shanghai that might have incriminated Pan. Because Pan had broken state laws, on the presumption that he had suppressed evidence against him in this way, he was tried in an ordinary court. Cultural Revolution accounts of the Pan–Yang case add baroque frills, which are less credible: *Zhongnan diqu hongqi* (Red Flag of the South Central District), No. 3 (Canton, March 1968) claims that Luo Ruiqing was the real villain behind Pan and Yang, that Pan was a secret KMT member since pre-Liberation times, and that the Centre had decided to purge Pan and Yang along with Gao and Rao – although the 1950s' evidence from Shanghai suggests otherwise. *Guangdong wenyi zhanbao* (Kwangtung Arts War Bulletin) (Canton, n.d., probably August 1967) tells us that Pan and Yang gave information that allowed the KMT Air Force to carry out its surprisingly accurate bombing of the Shanghai Yangshupu Power Plant on February 6, 1950. Some of these reports go so far as to cast doubt on the usefulness of some Cultural Revolution materials for supplying information on the events of the 1950s.

46 Shen Ximeng, *et al.*, *On Guard Beneath the Neon Lights* (Peking: Foreign Languages Press, 1966).

47 *JFRB*, January 19, 1955.

48 For three such articles, see *Xinwen ribao* (News Daily), Shanghai (hereafter *XWRB*), July 12, 1955, p. 4.

49 *XWRB*, September 11, 1955, p. 6. Another Shanghai case was decried nationally in Peking's *Zhongguo qingnian bao* (China Youth News), November 15, 1955.

50 Robert Loh, *Escape*, pp. 136–9. Loh was the capitalist who caved in to these demands. He reports with some glee that the four arbitrators, having failed to make the class enemy be exploitative in proper style, were transferred by the Party to less important posts outside of Shanghai.

51 *XWRB*, April 14, 1955, p. 4. The name of this 'Revolutionary Committee of the KMT' (*Zhongguo guomindang geming weiyuanhui*) brings to mind the title of a kind of organization that the Communist Party also begat more than a decade later.

52 It established a 'Shanghai Study Committee for Families of Industry and Commerce Circles', whose members advised their husbands to be patriotic and activist in social transformation. *NCNA*, Shanghai, December 11, 1955.

53 *NCNA*, January 21, 1956.

54 *NCNA*, July 12, 1956.

55 *NCNA*, January 20, 1956, and *ZW*, January 28, 1956.

56 *NCNA*, November 24, 1956.

57 *XWRB*, November 6, 1956. A 'large' firm is apparently one that uses

mechanical power and has more than fifteen employees, or uses no power and has more than thirty employees.

58 *LDB*, June 12, 1956, and *XWRB*, March 2, 1957.

59 *Qingnian bao* (Youth News), Shanghai (hereafter *QNB*), March 22, 1957.

60 Interview. Xu Jianguo was identified as being in charge of military recruitment in Shanghai for 1957.

61 Franz Schurmann, *Ideology and Organization in Communist China* (Berkeley: University of California Press, 1966), p. 132.

62 Interview, in Hong Kong, with an ex-student of capitalist background who had lived in Shanghai during the mid-1950s.

63 *NCNA*, July 13, 1956.

64 *NCNA*, July 22, 1956.

65 *NCNA*, April 13 and 17, 1957. A photograph, which shows Mao at a banquet with Shanghai bourgeois people in July and which can be interpreted interestingly, is reprinted in Richard H. Solomon, *Mao's Revolution and the Chinese Political Culture* (Berkeley: University of California Press, 1971), p. 321.

66 *XWRB*, April 30, 1957.

67 *XWRB*, May 4, 1957.

68 *NCNA*, April 17, 1957.

69 *XWRB*, November 28, 1957.

70 *XWRB*, May 15 and 19; and *ZW*, August 7, 1957.

71 More can be found in Lynn White, 'Leadership in Shanghai, 1956–1969,' in Scalapino, *Elites in the People's Republic of China*, pp. 317–27.

72 *XWRB*, September 23, 1957.

73 *NCNA*, August 21, 1957.

74 *Wenhui bao* (Wenhui News), Shanghai (hereafter *WHB*), October 8, 1957.

75 *Renmin ribao* (People's Daily), Peking (hereafter *RMRB*), January 25, 1958.

76 See *WHB*, editorial, December 5, 1957. On a visit by Zhou to sent-down personnel from Shanghai's Academia Sinica to the suburbs, see *XWRB*, December 23, 1957.

77 *NCNA*, March 21, 1958.

78 Basic on campaigns in China include Gordon Bennett, *Yundong: Mass Campaigns in Chinese Communist Leadership* (Berkeley: University of California, Center for Chinese Studies, 1976), and Charles P. Cell, *Revolution at Work: Mobilization Campaigns in China* (New York: Academic Press, 1977).

79 See *NCNA*, Peking, April 6, 1958; 'Shanghai Newsletter' (hereafter SHNL) in *South China Morning Post* (Hong Kong), February 4, 1960; *Tianfeng* (Heavenly Wind), Shanghai, March 31, 1958, p. 3, and June 16, 1958, p. 12, and July 28, 1958, p. 15.

80 *NCNA*, February 3 and 7, 1959. When studying Shanghai politics, it is as useful to read the advertisements as the editorials, and to look at periods between campaigns as well as the famous movements.

81 *XWRB*, January 1, 1959. The 3.6 figure in the text is based on calculations.

82 *WHB*, October 12, 1958.

83 *XWRB*, October 18 and 21, 1958.

84 *QNB*, December 8, 1959.

85 *NCNA*, November 2, 1959.

86 *Guangming ribao* (Bright Daily), Peking (hereafter *GMRB*), March 10, 1961.

87 For example, see *Jingji yanjiu* (Economic Research), Peking, No. 9 (September 7, 1962), pp. 61–5. Also *GMRG*, March 14, 1961.

88 See *Current Scene*, 1, 6 (July 10, 1961), pp. 4–7.

89 *South China Morning Post*, July 14, 1962.

90 *Hong Kong Standard*, February 6, 1963.

91 Kraus, 'Class Conflict and the Vocabulary' (see n. 12), is excellent on this subject in general.

92 Throughout this essay, the term 'middle class' is used synonymously with 'managerial class', without any attempt to distinguish an 'upper class' from it.

93 It is not always realized that, on a national basis, the post-Leap depression affected industry notably after it affected agriculture, because of the origin of the crisis in rural areas, urban inventories, and time lags in the economy. CIA estimates suggest that real agricultural production decreased in 1959 and 1960 from the 1958 peak, and then resumed its earlier increase – but real industrial production rose quickly in those years, declining only (and precipitously) in 1961, before a revival from 1962–3 to re-attain the reported 1960 peak level only in 1965. The industrial effects were sharper than the agricultural ones, and were delayed behind them by somewhat more than a year. See *China: A Statistical Compendium* (Washington: CIA National Foreign Assessment Center, July 1979), p. 3.

94 *Xinmin wanbao* (New People's Evening News), Shanghai (hereafter *XMWB*), December 13, 1962.

95 SHNL, April 30, 1962.

96 *Xingdao ribao* (Sing Tao Daily), Hong Kong, December 29, 1968.

97 Huang Zhenxia, ed., *Zhonggong junren zhi* (Mao's Generals) (Hong Kong: Research Institute of Contemporary History, 1968), p. 394. On Yao Wenyuan and Wang Hongwen, see below. The fourth member of the 'Gang', Jiang Qing, has the strongest claim to proletarian origin. She grew up in mostly impoverished circumstances, with separated parents. On the other hand, after marriage, she developed tastes that can be called 'bourgeois' with no difficulty at all. Rich documentation

on all of this is in Roxane Witke, *Comrade Chiang Ch'ing* (Boston: Little, Brown, 1977).

98 The definitive intellectual analysis is Lars Ragvald, *Yao Wenyuan as a Literary Critic and Theorist: The Emergence of Chinese Zhdanovism* (Stockholm: University of Stockholm, Department of Oriental Languages, 1978). On biographical details, see also Liu Cunshi, *Yao Wenyuan wenji* (Hong Kong: Lishi Ziliao Chubanshe, 1971), preface. I am indebted in this section to the research of Mr Stephen O. Huff.

99 *Mengya* (Sprouts), Shanghai (hereafter *MY*), February 16, 1957.

100 *MY*, May 16, 1957.

101 *MY*, June 1, 1957.

102 *MY*, May 16, 1957.

103 This was He Qifang's statement. See Merle Goldman, *Literary Dissent in Communist China* (New York: Atheneum, 1971), p. 266.

104 Hans Granqvist, *The Red Guard: A Report on Mao's Revolution* (New York: Praeger, 1967), p. 124, says that 90,000 of the 100,000 officially classified 'capitalists' in all China lived in Shanghai by the mid-1960s. This seems excessive and may reflect a somewhat revolutionary attitude toward statistics, although the present author has found no specific data to disprove it.

105 See Barry M. Richman, *Industrial Society in Communist China* (New York: Random House, 1969), pp. 269 and 579–80; and *NCNA*, April 26, 1966.

106 Interview with an ex-cadre in education, long resident in Shanghai.

107 Branko Bogunovic, 'Too Good to Last', *Far Eastern Economic Review*, 59, 5 (February 1, 1968), pp. 195–6; and *China News Service*, Shanghai, January 9, 1963.

108 Robert Guillain, *When China Wakes* (New York: Walker, 1966), p. 107.

109 A local example of such a meeting, in Huangpu District, is reported in *XMWB*, September 20, 1964.

110 See *NCNA*, April 29, 1965, which says that 13,600 workers held such posts in Shanghai plants. On the political power such functionaries can wield in industrial contexts, see Michel Crozier, *The Bureaucratic Phenomenon* (Chicago: University of Chicago Press, 1964).

111 See Lynn White, 'Worker Politics in Shanghai' (see n. 1).

112 See Hirschman, 'Changing Tolerance for Income Inequality' (see n. 11).

113 Peking *DGB*, August 17, 1963.

114 *NCNA*, July 18, 1963.

115 *XMWB*, August 4, 1964; and *NCNA*, August 6, 1964.

116 Reprinted in *WHB*, July 6, 1964.

117 *XMWB*, November 24, 1964.

118 *XMWB*, April 4 and December 15, 1964, and January 26, 1965.

119 *XMWB*, August 1, 1964.

120 *XMWB*, September 7 and 16, 1964.

121 *XMWB*, September 5, 1964.

122 *XMWB*, January 29, 1954.

123 *Zhongguo qingnian* (China Youth), Peking (hereafter *ZGQN*), 21 (November 1, 1964), pp. 24–6.

124 *XMWB*, December 28, 1964.

125 *XMWB*, December 16, 1964.

126 *XMWB*, January 10 and 15, 1965; and *JFRB*, November 17, 1964.

127 *XMWB*, December 15, 1964.

128 Interview in Hong Kong. This team was later criticized during the Cultural Revolution for 'attacking the majority' in the factory.

129 Interview with an ex-employee of the Public Utilities Bureau, a unit under a good deal of central control.

130 Confirming evidence from Canton is suggested in Ronald N. Montaperto, 'From Revolutionary Successors to Revolutionaries: Chinese Students in the Early Stages of the Cultural Revolution', in Scalapino, *Elites in the People's Republic of China*, pp. 596–7. See also Marc J. Blecher and Gordon White, *Micropolitics in Contemporary China* (White Plains: M. E. Sharpe, 1979), esp. pp. 77–81. The next paragraph in the text presents the gist of many articles from March 1965. For example, the *GMRB* of March 1 reports a forum that lasted for four hours and ninety-one speeches, and the same newspaper of March 29 contains an analytic article by an apparently pseudonymic author, Hu Shui, on the same topics.

131 See the important research of Gordon White, *The Politics of Class and Class Origin* (see n. 6), pp. 30–1.

132 Some biographical information on radicals is available in the appendix of Parris H. Chang, *Radicals and Radical Ideology in China's Cultural Revolution* (New York: Columbia University Research Institute on Communist Affairs, 1973). Reference to the biographies in Klein and Clark, *Biographic Dictionary*, is also useful.

133 The job has been most recently done in an excellent and controversial monograph by Andrew G. Walder, *Chang Ch'un Ch'iao and Shanghai's January Revolution* (Ann Arbor: University of Michigan Center for Chinese Studies, 1978), whose bibliography cites previous interpretations.

134 *Decision of the Central Committee of the Chinese Communist Party Concerning the Great Proletarian Cultural Revolution* (Peking: Foreign Languages Press, 1966).

135 *XMWB*, August 14, 1966.

136 *Shanghai wanbao* (Shanghai Evening News) (hereafter *SHWB*), August 28, 1966.

137 Lynn White, *Careers in Shanghai* (Berkeley: University of California Press, 1978).

138 *JFRB*, February 20, 1966; and *WHB*, May 5, 1966.
139 *NCNA*, August 28, 1966.
140 *China News Summary*, September 21, 1967.
141 *Pravda* (Truth), Moscow, September 16, 1966, quoted in personal communication from an office of a NATO government that does not wish to be cited, October 25, 1966.
142 A tabloid from Peking, *Beijing hongqi* (Peking Red Flag), December 26, 1966, indicates that most Scarlet Guard leaders in that city were Party members.
143 See Lynn White, 'Shanghai's Polity in Cultural Revolution', in Lewis, *The City in Communist China*, pp. 325–70.
144 *Ibid.*; Walder, *Chang Ch'un-ch'iao*; and Lynn White, 'Local Autonomy in China during the Cultural Revolution', *American Political Science Review*, 70 (June 1976), pp. 479–91.
145 *WHB*, January 6, 1967.
146 *Honggong zhanbao* (Red Worker War Report), Shanghai, February 6, 1967.
147 *WHB*, February 28, 1967.
148 See *ibid.*, another article.
149 *Jidian zhanbao* (Machine and Electricity War Report), Shanghai, February 19, 1967. Official translations may be found in the *Hanying shishi yongyu cidian: gailiang zhuyi, zhezhong zhuyi, xiao tuanti zhuyi, zongpai zhuyi.*
150 *Bayisan hongweibing* (August 13 Red Guard), Shanghai, February 8, 1967.
151 *WHB*, February 17, 1967.
152 *Jidan zhanbao, loc. cit.* See also Neale Hunter, *Shanghai Journal* (New York: Praeger, 1969), pp. 253–8; p. 307 refers to the April 5 issue of *Jidian zhanbao.*
153 This is the theme emphasized in Walder, *Chang Ch'un-ch'iao*, Chapter 5, 'The Central Dilemma: Revolution and Production', pp. 27–37.
154 *WHB*, February 21, 1967.
155 *WHB*, March 7, 1967.
156 *NCNA*, April 13, 1967.
157 *XDRB*, May 20, 1968. This accusation of 'betrayal to the proletariat' suggests that many were unaware of Zhang's own background then.
158 *WHB*, March 1, 1967.
159 *WHB*, August 9, 1967. The incident under discussion here, not just the words of the report, seems in fact to have been violent.
160 *WHB*, August 11, 1967.
161 Quoted in *China News Summary*, 202, January 24, 1968, p. 5.
162 *RMRB*, December 1, 1967, in an article about Shanghai factories.
163 *NCNA*, Shanghai, June 3, 1969.
164 This purports to quote a notice from the CCP Central Committee, in

Guangtie zongsi (Guangdong Railways General Headquarters), No. 28, early February 1968, tr. *Survey of the China Mainland Press*, No. 4129, p. 1.

165 But see Walder (n. 133) where the interpretation suggests a steadier policy of Zhang toward political constituencies.
166 Rambling talk by Zhang, quoted in *Wenge tongxun* (Cultural Revolution communique), Canton, No. 13, 1968.
167 *JFRB*, February 2, 1968.
168 *JFRB*, January 10, 1968.
169 *JFRB*, June 22, 1968.
170 *XDRB*, December 19, 1968.
171 A possible exception may be found in the flexibility of Yao Wenyuan's social criticism, despite the sureness of its polemic tone. See Lynn White, 'Leadership in Shanghai' (see n. 71), pp. 339–40.
172 'Huairen gan huaishi tong haoren gan huaishi yao qubie kailai.' This whole section is based on *Gongren zaofan bao* (Workers' Rebel News), Shanghai, August 17, 1968.
173 'Zichan jieji youpai tong yiban zichan jieji fenzi yao qubie kailai.'
174 Computed from Field, Lardy, and Emerson, *Reconstruction* (see n. 31), p. 9.
175 *WHB*, October 19, 1968.

8. CROLL: MARRIAGE CHOICE AND STATUS GROUPS IN CONTEMPORARY CHINA

1 B. Barber, *Social Stratification* (New York: Harcourt Brace and World, 1957), p. 123.
2 Jack Goody, 'Class and Marriage in Africa and Eurasia', *American Journal of Sociology*, 76 (1971), p. 588.
3 G. A. Marshall, 'Marriage: Comparative Analysis', in *Encyclopaedia of Social Sciences* (Chicago: Free Press, 1968), p. 11.
4 A. B. Hollingshead, 'Cultural Factors in the Selection of Marriage Mates', *American Sociological Review*, 15 (1950), pp. 619–27; A. C. Kerckhoff, 'Patterns of Homogamy and the Field of Eligibles', *Social Forces*, 42 (1963–4), pp. 289–97.
5 W. J. Goode, 'The Theoretical Importance of Love', *American Sociological Review*, 24 (1959), p. 475; Goody, *op. cit.*, p. 599.
6 In traditional China, the number of kin prohibitions had been so large that surname exogamy was a general rule in many parts of China.
7 Most lineage rules and village studies suggest that families negotiating a marriage were guided by the old maxim that 'wooden doors should match wooden doors and bamboo doors with bamboo doors'.
8 In the early 1950s a number of social reforms such as the modification of the education system, the introduction of an egalitarian incomes structure, the redistribution of land and capital and the gradual reduction

of the private ownership of the means of production were all intended to alter substantially the former balance of class advantages. It was anticipated that these structural changes would soon be reflected in patterns of marriage.

9 A field of eligible mates can be defined by the operation of two principles, that of incest avoidance and ethnocentric preference. It is the balance of each which determines the composition and breadth of an individual's range of potential spouses.

10 The Marriage Law reduced the exogamous group to lineal blood relatives and exempted affines and collateral relatives by marriage from this list of prohibitions. As to prohibiting marriage between collateral relatives by blood beyond that of brother and sister born of one or both parents, but within the fifth degree of relationship, the law of 1950 allowed the question to be determined by custom. The 1981 Marriage Law simply prohibits marriage between partners who are lineal relatives by blood or collateral relatives by blood (up to the third degree of relationship).

11 Wu Zhangzhen, 'The Principles of Freedom of Marriage Should not be Abused', *Guangming ribao*, 27 (February 1957). See also Elisabeth Croll, *The Politics of Marriage in Contemporary China* (Cambridge: Cambridge University Press, 1981).

12 Henan All-China Democratic Women's Federation, *On Marriage, Love and Family Problems* (Zhongzhou, 1955), pp. 29–36; Song Tingzhang, *A Correct Perspective in Matters of Love* (Shenyang, 1957), pp. 9–16.

13 'Letters on Courtship', *Zhongguo qingnian* (hereafter *ZQ*), 16 June 1983.

14 Lu Yang, *The Correct Handling of Love, Marriage and Family Problems* (Jinan, 1964), p. 115.

15 'What Attitude Should a Husband Take towards his Wife?', *Zhongguo funu* (hereafter *ZF*), 1 Oct. 1964.

16 *ZQ*, 16 June, 1963.

17 Liu Luochun, 'Why Our Marital Relationship Became Strained', *ZF*, 1 November 1955.

18 'The Correct Approach to Marriage', *ZQ*, 22 Feb. 1962.

19 Lo Pinchi, 'Father and Daughter', *China Reconstructs* (hereafter *CR*), 1 May 1957.

20 *ZQ*, 22 Feb. 1962.

21 Lin Hua, 'It's Right that This Affair of Blind Love Should Be Considered as Closed', *ZQ*, 4 Jan. 1955.

22 *Renmin ribao* (hereafter *RMRB*), 26 June 1980; *Women of China*, 1 April 1981. This is also the theme of a popular play entitled *Love*. See *Survey of World Broadcasts* (hereafter *SWB*), 26 July 1979 (FE/6177/B11/18).

23 *New China News Analysis* (hereafter *NCNA*), 2 July 1957.

24 Shu Ping, 'A Talk with Young Comrades on Love and Marriage', *Shaanxi ribao*, 8 March 1958 (see *Survey of China Mainland Press* (hereafter *SCMP*), no. 1769, p. 29).

25 'Demobbed Militiaman Poses as Party Member', *Xinwen huabao*, 28 April 1957 (see *SCMP*, no. 1556, p. 26).

26 *SWB*, 25 Aug. 1979 (FE/6203/B11/17).

27 In 1949, or thereabouts, members of each household were categorised according to their class position either on the eve of land reform in rural areas or the public ownership of industry in urban areas. For instance, the rural population was divided into landlords, rich, middle, lower middle and poor peasants according to the amount of land they owned and worked with their own hands and the number of implements in their possession. Those who hired labour to work their land or employed workers were said to belong to the former 'exploiting' classes.

28 'Marriage Problems during Land Reform', *Nanfang ribao*, 13 Feb. 1952.

29 'Does One Lose One's Class Stand by Marrying a Person Born of a Family of Exploiting Class?', *Gongren ribao*, 6 May 1965.

30 'What Is the Criterion in Choosing a Husband?', *ZF*, 1 May 1964.

31 'How to Help those of Bad Class Origin Make Progress', *Nanfang ribao*, 8 March 1965; 'A Selection of Letters on Problems of Family Class Background', *Gongren ribao*, 7 Nov. 1965; 'Problems in Marriage for those of Exploiting Class Origins', *ZQ*, 16 Oct. 1965.

32 Jack Chen, *A Year in Upper Felicity* (London: Harrap, 1973), pp. 74, 104.

33 *SWB*, 25 May 1979 (FE/6125/B11/13); *SWB*, 25 June 1980 (FE/6454/B11/7).

34 'How Can Problems of Love and Marriage be Correctly Treated by those of Exploiting-Class Origins?', *ZQ*, 1 May 1965.

35 *Gongren ribao*, 6 May 1965.

36 'Letters of Criteria for Choice of Spouse', *ZF*, 1 Feb. 1963.

37 Janet Salaff, 'The Urban Communes and Anti-City Experiment in Communist China', in J. W. Lewis, ed., *The City in Communist China* (Stanford: Stanford University Press, 1971), p. 322.

38 Chen, *op. cit.*, p. 81.

39 *Huadong zhengfu xuebao*, 15 Dec. 1951 (*Survey of China Mainland Magazines*, 65:5); Lu Yang, *op. cit.*, p. 13.

40 'Who Is to Blame for the Breakdown in Marriage', *ZF*, 16 April 1959; Wang Jing, 'How He Invites Further Trouble', *ZF*, 1 May 1959.

41 'What Is the Criterion in Choosing a Husband?', *ZF*, 1 Sept. 1964.

42 'What Do Women Live For?', *ZF*, 1 Sept. 1963.

43 *Ibid.*

44 *SWB*, 5 August 1978 (FE/5883/B11/14–15); *Beijing Review*, 12 Feb, 1979, 9 March 1979; *SWB*, 25 August 1979 (FE/6203/B11/13); *RMRB*, 16 Sept. 1980; *CR*, 1 March 1981; *Women of China*, 1 April 1981; *SWB*, 4 Feb. 1982 (FE/6945/B11/13).

45 *SWB*, 18 July 1979 (FE/6170/B11/10).

46 *CR*, 1 March 1981.

47 *SWB*, 18 Oct. 1979 (FE/6248/B11/16); *NCNA*, 25 Sept. 1980.

48 Tso Sungfen, 'New Marriage, New Families', *People's China*, 16 Nov. 1957; Liu Guihua, 'Marriage by Purchase Really Harms People', *ZF*, 1 Feb. 1966; *CR*, 1 March 1981.
49 Chen, *op. cit.*, pp. 80–1.
50 'Change of Marriage Customs Encouraged in China', *NCNA*, 29 Dec. 1978; *Beijing Review*, 30 Nov. 1979; *RMRB*, 16 Sept. 1980.
51 *ZF*, 1 Sept. 1964.
52 *Ibid.*
53 Lu Yang, *op. cit.*, pp. 12–17.
54 'Give Correct Guidance to the Problems of Rural Youth in Love and Marriage', *ZQ*, 1 Nov. 1956.
55 'A Word to the Judicial Personnel Who Deal with Marriage Disputes', *Guangming ribao*, 14 Jan. 1957; 'How to Tackle the Problem of Love', *NCNA*, 1 July 1957.
56 'Marriage by Party Members Need not be Approved by Party', *RMRB*, 12 Jan. 1957.
57 Editorial on Marriage, *ZF*, 14 Nov. 1959.
58 Letters on Choosing a Spouse, *ZF*, 14 Jan. 1960.
59 Letters on Choosing a Spouse, *ZF*, 14 Dec. 1959.
60 *Ibid.*
61 'What is the Criterion in Choosing a Spouse', *ZF*, 1 July 1964.
62 *Ibid.*, *ZF*, 1 Sept. 1964.
63 Yang Xiu, 'Correctly Deal With the Ideological Influences of Families and Relatives', *ZQ*, 16 Sept. 1963.
64 *ZF*, 1 August 1964.
65 One report cites current sayings which illustrated this trend: 'I shall marry a man whose hair is groomed, who wears leather shoes, and carries a watch; I shall not marry one whose head is clean shaven, who handles a hoe and works with a pick', and 'My prospective husband is to be either a worker, a cadre or a schoolmaster, I'd rather die than marry one who works on a farm' (*Huadong zhengfu xuebao*, 15 Dec. 1951).
66 *NCNA*, 2 July 1957.
67 Lu Yang, *op. cit.*, p. 12.
68 *Gongren ribao*, 29 Dec. 1957.
69 'Is it Possible to Compromise with Parents Who Refuse to Give Consent to a Marriage?', *ZQ*, 27 Nov. 1962.
70 'What Is the Criterion for Choosing a Husband?', *ZF*, 1 May 1964.
71 *SWB*, 14 Feb. 1974 (FE/4526/B11/1).
72 *Ibid.*
73 *Women of China*, 1 April 1980.
74 *Gongren ribao*, 29 Dec. 1957.
75 J. Lelyweld, 'The Great Leap Forward', *New York Times Magazine*, 28 July 1974. It was much more difficult for an inexperienced *xiaxiang* boy to earn as much as a peasant boy long experienced in agriculture

and he had not the resources of a peasant household behind him. See Gordon White, 'The Politics of Hsia-Hsiang Youths', *China Quarterly*, 59 (1974), p. 504.

76 *Women of China*, 1 Jan. 1966.

77 Lucy Jen Huang, 'Attitudes Towards Inter-Class Marriage', *China Quarterly*, 12 (1962), p. 189.

78 For accounts of the operation of Marriage Bureaux see *CR*, 1 March 1981, 'Finding a Husband/Wife in Shanghai' by You Yuwen; *Women of China*, 1 April 1981, 'A Matchmaking Service'.

79 These findings are also duplicated in a recent poll taken by an academic society in Beijing University in which at least 50 per cent of the women students admitted openly that they wanted a partner of equal or superior qualifications. See *Women of China*, 1 April 1981, p. 40.

80 *Guardian*, 26 Nov. 1981.

81 Impression derived from formal interviews and informal conversations in Beijing and Shanghai in August 1980.

9. KING WHYTE: SEXUAL INEQUALITY UNDER SOCIALISM: THE CHINESE CASE IN PERSPECTIVE

The author was assisted in preparation of this paper by Jessica Musoke, and aided by an earlier, related, paper by William Parish.

1 For a more detailed assessment, see Sharon Wolchik, 'Politics, Ideology, and Equality: The Status of Women in Eastern Europe', unpublished PhD dissertation, University of Michigan, 1978. See also Hilda Scott, *Does Socialism Liberate Women?* (Boston: Beacon Press, 1974); and Barbara W. Jancar, *Women Under Communism* (Baltimore: Johns Hopkins University Press, 1978).

2 See William L. Parish and Martin King Whyte, *Village and Family in Contemporary China* (Chicago: University of Chicago Press, 1978), especially Chapter 12.

3 For a positive view, see William J. Goode, *World Revolution and Family Patterns* (New York: The Free Press, 1963). More pessimistic views are presented in Ester Boserup, *Women's Role in Economic Development* (London: Allen and Unwin, 1970); and in Irene Tinker, 'The Adverse Impact of Development on Women', in I. Tinker, M. Bramsen, and M. Buvinic, eds., *Women and World Development* (New York: Praeger, 1975).

4 One investigation of Western countries found that the degree of occupational segregation by sex tended to be higher in the more developed countries, but also seemed paradoxically to decrease within each country with further development. See Katherine A. Gaskin, 'Occupational Differentiation by Sex: An International Comparison', unpublished PhD dissertation, University of Michigan, 1979.

5 In fact, in the United States the ratio of female to male wages moved

downward from the mid-1950s to the mid-1960s, as women's labour force participation was increasing. See Abbott L. Ferriss, *Indicators of Trends in the Status of American Women* (New York: Russell Sage Foundation, 1971), p. 141. It should be noted that wage comparisons are one of the most difficult aspects of inequality to be conclusive about. Depending upon which types of employed persons and what types of payments are included or excluded, figures on the female/male earnings ratio can vary substantially. For example, recent figures provided by the International Labour Organization (in its *1977 Yearbook of Labour Statistics* (Geneva: ILO, 1977), pp. 632–9) show this ratio ranging to above 80 per cent in some capitalist countries, higher than the figures displayed in Table 1.

6 It will be apparent from the figures in Table 1 that the index of occupational segregation is generally higher in the more developed countries, as was noted in n. 4.

7 See, for example, R. Bibb and W. Form, 'The Effects of Industrial, Occupational, and Sex Stratification on Wages in Blue-Collar Markets', *Social Forces*, 55 (1977), pp. 974–96; M. Blaxall and B. Reagan, *Women and the Workplace* (Chicago: University of Chicago Press, 1976); Valerie K. Oppenheimer, 'The Sex Labelling of Jobs', *Industrial Relations*, 7 (1968), pp. 219–34; and William Bridges, 'Industry Marginality and Female Employment', *American Sociological Review*, 45 (1980), pp. 58–75.

8 Figures from Maurice Duverger, *The Political Role of Women* (Paris: UNESCO, 1955), p. 104.

9 Figures from Center for the American Woman and Politics, *Women in Public Office*, 2nd edn (Metuchen: Scarecrow Press, 1978).

10 Changes in sex-role attitudes are reviewed in K. Mason, J. Czajka, and S. Arber, 'Change in U.S. Women's Sex-Role Attitudes 1964–1974', *American Sociological Review*, 41 (1976), pp. 573–96. On the issue of husbands helping around the house, see Joseph Pleck, 'Married Men: Work and Family', in National Institute of Mental Health, *Families Today*, vol. 1 (Rockville: NIMH, 1980). However, it should be noted that women who work outside the home do reduce the time they spend on domestic chores somewhat.

11 See Jessie Bernard, *The Future of Marriage* (New York: Bantam Books, 1972); Walter Gove, 'Sex, Marital Status, and Mortality', *American Journal of Sociology*, 79 (1973), pp. 45–67.

12 See International Labour Office, *Yearbook of Labour Statistics*, Geneva, various years.

13 Computed from figures in Tsentral'noe Statisticheskoe Upravlenie, *Itogi Vsesoyuznoi Perepisi Naselenia 1970 goda* (Results of the All-Union Census of Population of 1970), vol. 6 (Moscow, 1973), Tables 2 and 18.

14 Michael Sacks, *Women's Work in Soviet Russia* (New York: Praeger, 1976), pp. 80–7.

15 *Ibid.*, pp. 88–9.

16 See the discussion and data in Wolchik, *op. cit.*, Chapter 3; and Jancar, *op. cit.*

17 Walter Conor computes figures ranging from $r = -.44$ to $r = -.98$ for the correlation between the average wage in a sector of the economy and the percentage of women in that sector in 1973 for Bulgaria, Czechoslovakia, Hungary, Poland, Rumania, and the USSR (using 4–12 economic sectors). Walter Connor, *Socialism, Politics and Equality* (New York: Columbia University Press, 1979), p. 239.

18 Cited in Sacks, *op. cit.*, p. 91.

19 Michael Swafford, 'Sex Differences in Soviet Earnings', *American Sociological Review*, 43 (1978), pp. 657–73.

20 Data for Eastern Europe on this point are analysed in detail in Wolchik, *op. cit.*, Chapter 4.

21 Sacks, *op. cit.*, Chapter 5.

22 These data come from a collaborative research project entitled 'Urban Life in Contemporary China' being carried out with William L. Parish and supported by a grant from the National Science Foundation.

23 Much of our analysis involves looking at variations within our sample, rather than stating averages for the whole sample. For a general discussion of how we deal with problems of bias and selectivity in Hong Kong interview data, see the methodological appendix in an earlier rural study – Parish and Whyte, *op. cit.* In much of the analysis reported here we will use not the full household census sample, but what we call our weighted Lingnan household sample (referred to as our weighted sample for short). This sample is designed to correct at least in part for selectivity problems. Informants from cities in Guangdong and Guangxi provinces (roughly what G. William Skinner refers to as the Lingnan region) were overrepresented in our ordinary sample, and among informants from those provinces those from large cities, and particularly from Canton, were overrepresented. In our Lingnan weighted sample we have excluded cases supplied by informants from outside the Lingnan region, and we have then weighted our household cases in accord with the distribution of cities of various sizes within that region, in order to correct for the overrepresentation of cases from large cities. The resulting weighted sample is our effort to approximate what a representative sample of urban households in cities of all sizes in the Lingnan region would look like, and we place most confidence in conclusions drawn from this weighted sample.

24 Figures cited in *Beijing Review*, 1 (7 Jan. 1980), p. 18.

25 Official Chinese statistics from Gao Yi, *et al.*, eds., *Zhongguo Gaodeng Xuexiao Jianjie* (Brief Introduction to Chinese Universities) (Peking: Education and Science Publishers, 1982), p. 9.

26 We wish to caution the reader, however, that the nature of our data may exaggerate the trend somewhat. Our data refer to members of

current urban populations of various ages, and not to the urban populations that existed at earlier points in time. A goodly share of the older
members of the current urban population originated in rural areas
and moved into the cities as adults in the 1950s, when such migration
was still relatively easy. Assuming that the underrepresentation of
females in schools was and is more marked in rural areas than in cities,
the margin shown between males and females in the earliest cohorts in
the figure is probably larger than it would actually have been for the
urban population at the time.

27 See E. M. Beck, P. Horan, and C. Tolbert, 'Stratification in a Dual
Economy', *American Sociological Review*, 43 (1978), pp. 704–20; R.
Edwards, M. Reich, and D. Gordon, *Labor Market Segmentation*
(Lexington, Mass.: D. C. Health, 1975).

28 See Swafford, *op. cit.* However, part of the difference may be due to the
fact that the Soviet study Swafford used employed very crude category
breakdowns for industrial sector (8) and occupational level (5). If he
had been able to use finer categories in his regression analysis, more
of the wage differences might have been attributed to women's segregated
job situation, rather than simply to their gender.

29 See Jancar, *op. cit.*, p. 27; Larry Suter and Herman Miller, 'Income
Difference between Men and Career Women', *American Journal of
Sociology*, 78 (1973), pp. 657–73.

30 Figures from *Peking Review*, 35 (26 Aug. 1977), pp. 7, 14–17. The 9th
Congress of the CCP in 1969 chose a Central Committee that was 8.2 per
cent female, and the 10th Congress in 1973 chose a Central Committee
that was 12.8 per cent female. Figures cited in James Seymour, *China:
The Politics of Revolutionary Reintegration* (New York: Thomas Crowell,
1976), p. 233.

31 Figures from *Peking Review*, 10 (10 Mar. 1978), pp. 41–2; and from
Beijing Review, 11 (16 Mar. 1981), p. 6; and *ibid.*, 12 (23 Mar. 1981),
p. 5.

32 A vivid account of the duties of these lowly offices is presented in M.
Bernard Frolic, 'My Neighborhood', in his book, *Mao's People*
(Cambridge, Mass.: Harvard University Press, 1980). We should note
that having women serving as formal neighbourhood leaders is an
innovation, one initially difficult for some urbanites to accept. See
Franz Schurmann, *Ideology and Organization in Communist China*, 2nd edn
(Berkeley: University of California Press, 1968), p. 377.

33 After we completed this article a new Chinese study appeared which
attempted to replicate the international time budget study whose figures
we used in Tables 1 and 2. Data were collected from 2293 individuals in
the two largest cities in Heilongjiang Province, Harbin and Qiqihar.
These data yielded figures of 5.2 hours spent on domestic chores daily

by the average woman and 3.9 hours by the average man, or 1.3 hours extra by women. The study also reported an average of 2.5 hours of free time daily for men and 1.7 hours of free time for women, or a female 'deficit' in leisure time of 0.8 hours. See Wang Yalin and Li Jinrong, 'Chengshi zhigong jiawu laodong yanjiu' (Research on the Domestic Chores of Urban Workers and Employees), *Zhongguo shehui kexue*, no. 1 (1982), pp. 177–90.

34 See Robert Blood, Jr, and Donald Wolfe, *Husbands and Wives* (New York: The Free Press, 1960), Chapter 3; Beverly Duncan and O. D. Duncan, *Sex Typing and Social Role* (New York: Academic Press, 1978), Chapter 8. We might note that Sacks found little variation by socioeconomic background in his time budget analysis of Soviet household chore data. See Sacks, *op. cit.*

35 The Soviet, Swedish, and Finnish data were presented in only three-step scales, rather than five-step ones – husband, shared, and wife. We have assumed, for comparison purposes, that 'husband' was comparable to combining 'husband alone' and 'usually husband' alternatives in the Blood and Wolfe-type studies. So in these cases we used conversions of 3.5, 2 and .5 for male scores and .5, 2 and 3.5 for female scores, and proceeded as indicated in the text.

36 Data showing that housewives have not cut down the time spent on housework in the US in the last fifty years are presented in Joann Vanek, 'Time Spent in Housework', *Scientific American*, 231 (1974), pp. 116–20.

37 The recent time budget study conducted in Heilongjiang (Wang Yalin and Li Jinrong, *op. cit.*) makes it appear that men help out more with chores than our own data imply and than is common in other societies, from the evidence given in Tables 1 and 2 and Figure 5. Since no detailed sampling and interviewing procedure information is provided for the Chinese study, it is not possible to say whether this disparity is an artifact of different methods or not. But the main argument that the authors of the Chinese study advance is that the burden of household chores for both men and women is significantly heavier than in any of the other societies included in the earlier international time budget study, and that as a consequence both sexes have less free time and more burdens coping with their daily routines than is the case in other societies.

38 For the details on rural China, see Parish and Whyte, *op. cit.*, Chapter 12.

39 One distinctive feature of some urban divorces complicates the rural–urban comparison. Divorces brought about by a political error – usually of the husband – are fairly common in our urban study, but were quite rare in our earlier rural study, and it is particularly in such politically inspired divorces that the female's claims will be most heavily weighted. On the continued importance of patrilineal orientations in rural China today, see Martin King Whyte, 'Revolutionary Change and Patrilocal

Notes to pp. 236–8

Residence in China', *Ethnology*, 18 (1979), pp. 211–27.
40 For our ten-category occupational breakdown, the ID of occupational segregation by sex was computed as 30. Broken down by age cohorts, the index was computed as 20 for the cohort aged 20–9, 34 for those 30–9, 43 for those 40–9, 35 for those 50–9, and 55 for those 60–94. In other words, the lowest degree of sex segregation in jobs is in our youngest cohort, with generally higher levels in older cohorts.

CONTRIBUTORS

ELISABETH CROLL

Fellow, Queen Elizabeth House, Oxford, and Consultant to the International Labour Office and the United Nations Research Institute for Social Development in Geneva. She is author of *Feminism and Socialism in China* (Routledge, Kegan Paul, 1978), *Women and Rural Development in the People's Republic of China* (ILO, 1980), and *The Politics of Marriage in Contemporary China* (Cambridge University Press for the CCI, 1981).

PHILIP A. KUHN

Professor of Chinese History at Harvard University and Director of the John King Fairbank Center for East Asian Research. He is author of *Rebellion and its Enemies in Late Imperial China: Militarization and Social Structure, 1796–1864* (Harvard University Press, 1970 and 1980) and other works on modern Chinese history.

WILLIAM L. PARISH

Professor of Sociology and Director, Center for Far Eastern Studies, at the University of Chicago. He is co-author (with Martin K. Whyte) of *Village and Family in Contemporary China* (University of Chicago Press, 1978) and *Urban Life in Contemporary China* (University of Chicago Press, 1983).

STUART R. SCHRAM

Professor of Politics with reference to China at the School of Oriental and African Studies, University of London, and founding Head of the Contemporary China Institute. He is author of *The Political Thought of Mao Tse-tung* (Praeger, 1963 and 1969), *Mao Tse-tung Unrehearsed, Talks and Letters: 1956–71* (Penguin, 1974), and editor of *Authority, Participation and Cultural Change in China* (Cambridge University Press for the CCI, 1973).

SUSAN L. SHIRK

Associate Professor of Political Science at the University of California, San Diego. She is author of *Competitive Comrades: Career Incentives and Student*

283

Strategies in China (University of California Press, 1982) and articles on Chinese education, dissent, and industry.

JONATHAN UNGER

Assistant Professor of East Asian Cultures and Sociology at the University of Kansas, Lawrence. He is author of *Education Under Mao: Class and Competition in Canton Schools, 1960–1980* (New York, 1982) and co-author of *Chen Village: The Recent History of a Peasant Community in Mao's China* (University of California Press, 1982).

JAMES L. WATSON

Professor of Anthropology at the University of Pittsburgh. From 1974 to 1983 he was lecturer in Asian Anthropology at the School of Oriental and African Studies, University of London, and Head (1978–81) of the Contemporary China Institute. He is author of *Emigration and the Chinese Lineage* (University of California Press, 1975) and editor of *Asian and African Systems of Slavery* (Basil Blackwell, University of California Press, 1980).

LYNN T. WHITE III

Associate Professor of Politics and Director, Undergraduate Program of the Woodrow Wilson School, at Princeton University. He is author of *Careers in Shanghai* (University of California Press, 1978) and other works on Chinese politics and urban sociology.

MARTIN KING WHYTE

Professor of Sociology and Associate of the Center for Chinese Studies at the University of Michigan, Ann Arbor. He is author of *Small Groups and Political Rituals in China* (University of California Press, 1974) and co-author (with William L. Parish) of *Village and Family in Contemporary China* (University of Chicago Press, 1978) and *Urban Life in Contemporary China* (University of Chicago Press, 1983).

INDEX

Index